Nomos Universitätsschriften

Politik

Volume 201

Victor-David Cruz-Aceves

The Diffusion of Morality Policies

State-Level Comparative Analyses
in the United States of America

Institut für Sicherheitspolitik
an der Christian-Albrechts-
Universität zu Kiel

The Deutsche Nationalbibliothek lists this publication in the
Deutsche Nationalbibliografie; detailed bibliographic data
are available on the Internet at http://dnb.d-nb.de

a.t.: Kiel, Univ., Diss., 2018

ISBN   978-3-8487-8420-2 (Print)
         978-3-7489-2796-9 (ePDF)

British Library Cataloguing-in-Publication Data
A catalogue record for this book is available from the British Library.

ISBN   978-3-8487-8420-2 (Print)
         978-3-7489-2796-9 (ePDF)

Library of Congress Cataloging-in-Publication Data
Cruz-Aceves, Victor-David
The Diffusion of Morality Policies
State-Level Comparative Analyses in the United States of America
Victor-David Cruz-Aceves
206 pp.
Includes bibliographic references.

ISBN   978-3-8487-8420-2 (Print)
         978-3-7489-2796-9 (ePDF)

Onlineversion
Nomos eLibrary

1st Edition 2021
© Nomos Verlagsgesellschaft, Baden-Baden, Germany 2021. Overall responsibility
for manufacturing (printing and production) lies with Nomos Verlagsgesellschaft mbH
& Co. KG.

Mamá, Papá, Abuelitos, Hermanos y Tíos,

eterna y profundamentemente
agradecido, endeudado con
y orgulloso de Uds.

Acknowledgements

This book would not have been possible without the time and support from the following people.

I highly appreciate the kind and generous support from the Institut für Sicherheitspolitik (ISPK)—especially from Prof. Dr. Joachim Krause and Dr. Stefan Hansen—for the publication of this manuscript.

I owe a huge debt to Prof. Dr. Christian Martin, who not only guided me through this phase—in person, by phone, video chat, you name it—and always showed openness, care and enormous patience, but also listened to and supported all my projects. I thank Prof. Dr. Wilhelm Knelangen and colleagues of the CPIG research group at the CAU for their helpful comments.

I also thank Dr. Marcel Dirsus, Dr. Sebastian Bruns and Victor Luna for their support, but most important, for their friendship. A special thanks is awed to Claudia Härterich, who provided endless motivation, unlimited patience, and never hesitated neither to comment nor to discuss my drafts.

Table of Contents

List of Figures

List of Tables

Abstract

The field of morality policy lacks comparative analyses across laws that vary in the degree to which they reflect characteristics of morality policy. This study takes state-level Same Sex Marriage Bans, Medical Marijuana Laws and Anti-Obesity legislation in the USA as cases with varying levels of morality policy's characteristics and investigates the way their diffusion differs. I explain differences in the magnitude of learning-driven diffusion, controlling for theoretically relevant domestic factors, through Event History Analysis and Seemingly Unrelated Estimations. I find that the magnitude of diffusion increases as policies reflect less characteristics of morality policy. Moreover, based on the results I infer that policies with high moral content diffuse preceded by a bounded-learning process, information about which is heavily drawn from polities with similar moral attributes; learning about legislation with moderate and minimal characteristics of morality policy not only occurs selectively, but rather, information is retrieved from ideologically dissimilar polities, too.

1. Introduction

After the 2016 US presidential election, commentators argued that moral values had become a crucial criterion on which candidates were assessed by voters: "candidates who understand that... voters reward candidates who are effective preachers for a set of moral concerns... realize that electoral campaigns are not won just by articulating the most effective policy responses" (Ekins and Haidt 2016). Behind this journalistic account lies a phenomenon that academics have been exploring more systematically for over two decades, namely, that basic moral values have a relevant impact on political behavior (Haider-Markel and Meier 1996; Mooney and Schuldt 2008; Tatalovich and Daynes 1988).

Scholarly attention on morality policy has been devoted for the most part to the test of whether these policies exist and constitute a different policy type (Lowi 1988). From these—mostly single-policy, quantitative—studies we have learned that policies on abortion (Dennis and Medoff 2011; Mooney and Lee 1995), death penalty (Lee 1996; Mooney and Lee 1999a), gay rights (Haider-Markel and Meier 1996; Klawitter and Hammer 1999), and drug-related legislation (Ferraiolo 2004; Meier 1994) are more intractable, technically simple, salient and elicit passionate moral conflict, compared to legislation that does not address moral issues. However, this research program lacks analyses that compare theoretically relevant factors across legislation that varies in the degree to which they reflect characteristics of morality policy (Mooney and Schuldt 2008, 212).

This dissertation will refine our understanding of morality policymaking by comparing legislation[1] with varying moral[2] content[3], specifically focusing on one understudied dimension, their diffusion. In other words, I

---

1 The following terms are used interchangeably throughout the dissertation: (state-level/subnational) policy, law, legislation.
2 The following terms are used interchangeably throughout the dissertation: moral content, moral questions, fundamental beliefs, first principles, questions of right or wrong, principled moral commitments, morally principled arguments.
3 The following terms are used interchangeably throughout the dissertation: varying moral content, differences in the degree to which legislation may be considered morality policy, differences in the degree to which legislation feature the theoretical characteristics of morality policy, variation in policies' emphasis on morality, differences in the presence of morality politics, varying degrees of morality policy,

investigate whether variation in the degree to which legislation reflects the theoretical characteristics of morality policy has implications for their diffusion process. Analyzing the diffusion of morality policies comparatively allows us to explore how characteristics of the policies influence their acceptance and dissemination. This is a relevant contribution, as these features are some of the most manipulable aspects of the determinants of policies' spread across jurisdictions[4], i.e., it is easier to alter a law's salience than, for instance, to change the levels of state wealth (Mallinson 2016). Moreover, morality policies matter, especially to electorally-minded lawmakers. Policy makers care about this type of legislation because the simplicity, salience and the perception of morality legislation as threat to non-negotiable core values (Mooney and Lee 1999b, 768) makes it more likely that larger numbers of citizens express their demands to their representatives (Hollander and Patapan 2016, 16–17; Pierce 2009, 6–7).

In general, I argue that a) morality policies diffuse as a result of a process where policy makers[5] learn about past experiences from other polities, b) that such learning occurs through cognitive heuristics[6], and c) that the level of moral content will affect these learning and diffusion patterns. Let me elaborate.

I mentioned above that legislators care about morality policy, however, how do they react when they are confronted with the existence of a novel morality policy in other polities? When legislators have to decide whether to enact a given morality policy, they face uncertainty about the substantive and electoral consequences of adopting[7] it. In this situation, policy makers react by searching for information—i.e., learning—about costs and benefits of previous morality policy enactments in other jurisdictions. I

---

number of appeals to morality and moral principles, policies' level of moral content.

4 The following terms are used interchangeably throughout the dissertation: (subnational) unit, subject, polity, state, state-year, entity and jurisdiction.

5 The following terms are used interchangeably throughout the dissertation: policy makers, legislators, law makers, (public) officials, to refer to elected officials legal authority to influence policy adoption, although there are other political actors involved in state legislative policymaking in the USA, e.g., governors, judges, high-level bureaucrats, and citizens (in the case of referenda/initiatives), as elsewhere done (Mooney and Lee 2000, 224)

6 The following terms are used interchangeably throughout the dissertation: inferential-, cognitive shortcuts and heuristics, as has been done elsewhere Weyland (2006)

7 The following terms are used interchangeably throughout the dissertation: adoption, (bill) enactment, passage, event occurrence.

claim that such a learning process proceeds through cognitive shortcuts, where information retrieved from a biased sample of sources is overestimated (Weyland 2009, 400). Given that morality policies deal for the most part with values and culture (Doan 2014; Mooney and Schuldt 2008), I believe that information from jurisdictions with similar values, cultural and ideological characteristics that have (not) adopted a given morality law become valuable sources of information in this respect (Butz, Fix, and Mitchell 2015; Grossback 2004; Hays and Glick 1997; Hollander and Patapan 2016, 18).

In other words, I suggest that policy makers from unit i are interested in the consequences that morally-similar units j experienced as a result of enacting morality policy Y, because if the public from unit j responded to a given morality policy not all to negatively, the policymaker from i could infer (in a bounded fashion) that her constituency might react similarly—alternatively, the policy effectiveness of a policy with fewer "morality" characteristics Z enacted in j could play out similarly in i—given the similar moral and demographic profiles of these states. If we find evidence supporting this, we could say that morality policy decisions exhibit interdependence, i.e., morality-policy Y enacted at time t-1 in state j diffuses to state i in time t as a consequence of legislator from i learning (in a bounded fashion) from j.

Regarding the third part of the argument, I argue that we can refine the proposition that variations in the degree of morality should affect the "politics" of this type of legislation (Mooney and Schuldt 2008; Pierce and Miller 2000) by focusing on one dimension in particular, their diffusion. Given the lack of previous studies in this regard, I draw on the body of works that focuses on policies' attributes to study for the first time effects of variation of morality-policy characteristics on their diffusion.

For this purpose, I analyze the diffusion of three policies distinctly situated in a "morality continuum"—Same-Sex Marriage bans (SSM), Medical Marijuana Laws (MML), and Anti-Obesity Legislation (AO)—enacted in the USA at the state level between 1995 – 2011. The analysis proceeds in two steps. First, I analyze these policies individually through Event History Analysis. Next, to increase comparability, I drop the policy-specific variables and use Seemingly Unrelated Estimations (SUE), in order to compare the magnitude of the diffusion effect across these laws.

1. Introduction

1.1. Contribution and Research Questions

This dissertation will contribute to the literature in two respects. First, the literature on morality policy has concentrated for the most part on the effect of domestic factors on the likelihood of morality policy enactment. In this project, I theorize on the nature of interdependence that this type of legislation might exhibit and explore the testable implications of a morality-policy diffusion theory. Second, the field of morality policy lacks comparative analyses across laws that vary in the degree to which they reflect characteristics of morality policy (Mooney and Schuldt 2008, 212). I contribute to the literature with a comparison of the diffusion of three policies with varying degrees of morality-policy characteristics.

The guiding research questions read:

> What is the role of bounded learning in the diffusion of morality policies?
> How does the diffusion of policies vary in function with the degree to which they reflect the characteristics of morality policy?
> More specifically, how does the learning-driven diffusion of policies vary as their degree of "morality" differs?

1.2. Structure of the Dissertation

In the **Literature Review**, I point to the gap in the literature that this project contributes to. In that section I show that the diffusion of morality policy is an area that has remained understudied, and that there is a lack of cross-morality-policy comparative analyses. I fill these gaps based on insights from the literature on policy attributes. Hence, I provide an overview of the most relevant academic works on morality policy, policy diffusion and policy attributes. In the **Theory** chapter, I will put forward the theories that I will test in this work. I open this section with the main argument of the dissertation. Next, I elaborate on the components of the argument and ground them with theoretical and empirical evidence. Afterwards, I formulate a comparative- and a diffusion theory and derive testable hypotheses. I conclude that section with hypotheses regarding theoretically relevant domestic factors.

In the **Research Design** section, I will first comment on the case selection process and provide a brief overview of the selected policies. Next, I operationalize the concepts. Then, I describe the strategy for the individual and the cross-policy analyses. I end that section with a description of the model building procedure. The section called **Analysis** contains the empirical analyses and is divided in four sections. The first three parts analyze the selected policies individually. In these sections, I first provide a description of the dependent variable, followed by descriptive statistics. Then, I guide the reader through the model selection procedure, select the best fitting model and describe and discuss the results. The final models will be accompanied by reduced models containing theoretically relevant different sets of domestic factors. In the last section of this chapter, I estimate cross-policy models and make inferences about how the diffusion of policies varies as a function of differences in their level of moral content. In the last chapter called **Conclusions**, I provide a summary of my results, discuss their generalizability, elaborate on limitations of the project and point towards avenues of further research.

1.3. Findings

The findings of this project support my initial argument, i.e., the diffusion of policies does vary in function with the degree to which they exhibit attributes of morality policy. Specifically, the incentive to learn about the consequences of previous enactments of morality policies in jurisdictions that share similar values and culture grows as laws show less characteristics of morality policy. Therefore, the magnitude of the diffusion effect on the likelihood of policy passage increases as the policy in question turns less salient and less technically simple. However, as the level of morality-policy characteristics decreases, policies diffuse not only driven by learning from similar polities, in addition to that, information about—less salient, more technically complex—morality policies is also retrieved from ideologically dissimilar units. Moreover, I found that unified Republican governments and rates of adherence to fundamentalist religions were significantly associated with adoptions of medical marijuana policy and same-sex marriage bans (negatively for the former, positively for the latter); electoral competition is positively and substantially associated with legislation with high and moderate levels of morality-policy characteristics; and last, as the degree of morality decreases, the effect of unified Republican government decreases, too.

Looking at the individual analyses, I provide evidence that these three policies diffused in the period of analysis as a consequence of a process where lawmakers reacted to the uncertainty—about what political and policy consequences the enactment of these policies would bring about—

by searching for information, i.e., by learning. Learning about same-sex marriage bans was exclusively bounded to the experiences of polities with similar culture and values, and the information drawn from these sources decreased the likelihood of future adoptions. Learning about medical marijuana laws and anti-obesity legislation was bounded to similar states, too, but in addition—and presumably due to the lower levels of technical simplicity and salience—these policies also diffused following a process of learning from ideologically contrasting units. Moreover, enactments of medical marijuana laws and anti-obesity legislation increased the odds of future enactments thereof. Additionally, I find a) the same associations between the domestic factors and the probability of enacting same-sex marriage bans and medical marijuana laws identified in the comparative analyses (unified Republican governments, electoral competition and fundamentalist religious adherents significantly associated with their adoptions), b) that neither political nor morality-related explanations predict anti-obesity legislation, and c) that interest groups exerted significant effects only on the odds of enactment of medical marijuana laws.

2. Literature Review

The goal of this section is to point towards the gap in the literature that this project will fill. In general, I show that the diffusion of morality policy is an area that has remained understudied, and that there is a lack of cross-morality-policy comparative analyses, and as such, we do not know how diffusion varies with the characteristics of morality policy. Moreover, these gaps in the literature can be filled with insights from the literature on policy attributes. For these reasons, I will provide an overview of the most relevant academic works on morality policy and policy diffusion. It categorizes the former in three sections, namely, works whose main goal is to define this type of policy, contributions that analyze the determinants of morality policy enactment and morality policy types. The review of policy diffusion literature is divided in three sections; on the one hand, a review on the literature on the causal mechanisms that have been attributed to policy diffusion, followed by a review of the literature on policy innovation and diffusion in the USA. I finish this section with a review of the literature on policy attributes.

2.1 Morality Policy Characteristics

Although scholars have not come up with a uniform definition of morality policy (Doan and McFarlane 2012, 616; Kreitzer 2015b; Mooney and Schuldt 2008, 201; Smith 2002), in this project morality legislation will be defined as technically-simple and intractable policies that give rise to highly polarized disputes that revolve around values, belief systems and culture, with high citizen participation rates, whose debate is strongly polarized, and whose main aim is to regulate social behavior that is rooted in core moral values (Doan and McFarlane 2012, 616; Meier 1993; 1993; Mooney and Lee 1995, 609; Tatalovich and Daynes 1988). Below, I review the literature that elaborates on these characteristics.

Conflict over Belief Systems

At its core, morality legislation questions individuals' "belief systems" by asking what is morally acceptable in a society. Belief systems stem from primary forms of individual identity, such as race, gender, sexual identity, nationality, ethnicity, but especially from religious beliefs (Doan 2014). Basic moral principles by definition do not have universal support (Mooney and Lee 1995, 606). One undisputed characteristic of morality policies is that they generate passionate conflicts amongst society, given that this legislation basically aims to determine what is just and which moral conventions will be protected by justice and law (Hollander and Patapan 2016, 15), i.e., this type of policies are efforts to impose basic moral principles (Gardner and Rossi 2010, 1398; Mooney and Lee 1995, 606). People's opinion on morality issues are strongly based on these core moral values (Doan 2014; Klawitter and Hammer 1999, 24; Mooney and Schuldt 2008).

> "Among its scholars, the most frequently discussed feature of morality policy is that the conflict underlying at least some of its debate is based on fundamental first principles and basic moral values rather than, for example, economic interests... the conflict of such values [is] especially unique and interesting. People do not chain themselves to cars or commit murder over a change in telephone regulation, but they have done these things—and more—in the debate over abortion regulation" (Mooney and Schuldt 2008, 201)

Intractability

Actors involved in morality policy advocate for their causes using moral arguments (Haider-Markel and Meier 1996), presented as self-evident and morally compelling, and as such, morality policy gives rise to clashes of first values that cannot or can hardly be resolved by argument (Mooney 1999). Hence, conflicts over morality in the political sphere are inherently inflexible, in that the cornerstones of policymaking process, e.g., compromise, negotiation, diversified coalition building, are hard to exercise (Doan and McFarlane 2012; Meier 1994; Mooney 2001a; Mooney and Lee 1995; 1999b). The disputes arising from morality policy is rigid, in such a way that proponents and opponents perceive political compromise as an aggravating undervaluation of the basic moral values that are at stake (Doan 2014, 763; Mooney 2001b). Namely, "compromise may be especially difficult on morality policy because it is harder to split the difference between

core moral values than, say, permissible levels of industrial benzene emis-
sions" (Mooney and Schuldt 2008, 201). In this vein, constituencies are
more likely to perceive the conflict arising from this type of legislation as
one where there is one side that wins and another side that loses. (Mooney
and Lee 1999b, 768–69). The little room for compromise and the conflict
over basic moral values have implications for the impetus and type of
citizen involvement. Involved actors have deep-rooted personal reasons
to defend their moral views; when it comes to giving up deeply held
traditions, people is more likely to incur in greater efforts to defend their
causes (Hollander and Patapan 2016, 16–17).

> "Either a state holds that human life is sacred or it does not; either
> a state holds homosexuality to be an unacceptable perversion or it
> does not. Morality policy therefore cannot be redefined as distributive
> policy in the same way that economic redistributive policy often is."
> (Mooney and Lee 1999b, 769–70)

Other types of legislation, e.g., economic redistribution, can indeed be
enacted as a result of political compromise, where one group buys off
its opponents by reducing costs or making side payments; in the case of
morality policy this is hardly the case, since the values involved are not
so easily divisible, simply because when values of fundamental right and
wrong are at stake, compromise is unthinkable (Mooney and Lee 1999b,
769–70).

Simplicity and Salience

Conflict over basic conceptions of right versus wrong can lead to debates
that are less technically complex and that engage a broader range of people
(Mooney and Schuldt 2008, 201). Even though the issues that morality
policies tackle are more often than not complex issues or are connected
with broader socio-economic structures, legislators, advocates and/or opponents resort to "simplistic rhetoric" to discuss the conflict (Tatalovich
and Daynes 2011). Such rhetorical strategy moderates participation costs
for the electorate because knowledge-based prerequisites do not exist or
are minimal; instead, the possession of a belief system suffices, making
these conflicts "easy issues" for the people (Lindaman and Haider-Markel
2002). Hence, morality issues are accessible for general debate because
the majority of citizens ascribe to a given set of values (Doan 2014, 763–
64; Mooney and Schuldt 2008). The audience that is alert of this type

of policy is less likely to get confused by technicalities of a given policy (Meier 1994); instead, the general public feels qualified to cast informed opinions and make political evaluations about morality legislation (Meier 1994; Mooney and Lee 1995; 1999b; 2000). In this vein, common sense and values—instead of expertise—characterize the policy making process of morality politics (Doan 2014; Klawitter and Hammer 1999, 24; Mooney and Schuldt 2008).

All this makes it more likely that people feel knowledgeable about morality policy disputes. To give some perspective on this, an average citizen might not comprehend the details of, e.g., a progressive income tax; that person, however, may believe that she has an informed opinion on a morality issue, e.g., the appropriateness of the death penalty. People have clear positions on these matters, since the main issue at stake is not about whether a given law will have a given effect, but rather whether the values that morality policies "threat" are validated (Mooney and Lee 1999b, 768–69):

> "When… moral values are threatened, people care. And it may well excite deeper passion in certain people when the government bans abortion or executes a criminal, for example, than when it enacts a new social welfare program. The link to one's economic values in the latter case may be tenuous, but for many people the threats to their basic moral values in the former cases are palpable and a stimulus for political action." (Mooney and Lee 1999b, 768)

These characteristics—little technical complexity, conflict over moral principles and high participation rates—have another implication for the political process of this policy type. Citizens more often than not have both the incentive and the ability to make their views known to their representatives (Hollander and Patapan 2016, 16–17; Meier 1994; Pierce 2009, 6–7), i.e., it is more likely that constituents demand their representatives to take action regarding such controversial issues. For these reasons, the likelihood that policy makers ignore morality policies is low. Instead, elected officials usually have a special interest to react to citizens petitions when it comes to morality policy (Mooney and Lee 2000, 223–24).

The only empirical evidence up to date on what constitutes morality policy concluded, based on results from surveys of morality policy scholars and of Illinois residents (N~700), that there exists indeed a class of public policies with attributes that distinguish them from other policies (Mooney and Schuldt 2008, 199–200). A central contribution of these authors is their suggestion that there should exist variation within this policy type regarding the attributes that make morality policies different. They proposed that there existed a continuum along which morality policies' characteristics vary, which should have empirical implications for the political process of morality policies.

2.2 Morality Policy Enactment

Scholarship on morality policy mainly deals with the role that values, identity and culture have over the determination of policy disputes (Tatalovich and Daynes 1988). Most of the scientific production on morality policies has focused on how the policy-making process of this policy type plays out in the USA, particularly at the state level (Tatalovich and Daynes 2011). In fact, most of what we know about these policies is based on these findings (Engeli, Green-Pedersen, and Larsen 2012). The general goal of this research program, however, has evolved minimally (Engeli, Green-Pedersen, and Larsen 2012; Mooney and Schuldt 2008; Tatalovich and Daynes 2011). Since the beginning of this research program the goal was to explore whether the politics of morality policy differed from those of nonmorality policy in systematic, explainable ways, i.e., whether this type of legislation were truly different to other policy types (Doan 2014; Engeli, Green-Pedersen, and Larsen 2012; Mooney and Schuldt 2008, 200). These early works usually built upon the seminal work of Lowi (1964) that asked whether the policy "area" determined the "politics" or the political process of such area, with the purpose of identifying "policy types", based on theoretically relevant characteristics. Researchers noted that Lowi's policy typology—that at the time consisted of distributive, regulative, and redistributive policies (1964, 689)—was not able to explain the politics a particular set of policies, and as such, suggested that a fourth policy type might exist.

Most of the scholarship on morality policy focuses on the factors that are relevant to one dimension of the policy-making process in particular, namely, policy enactment. Most of these works, however, have emphasized for the most part the role of domestic factors, while potential interdependence effects have been neglected. Moreover, most scholarship on morality policy focuses on one single policy (Berry and Berry 2014; Karch 2007a; Nicholson-Crotty 2009), e.g., abortion (Dennis and Medoff 2011; Kreitzer 2015b; Mooney and Lee 1995), death penalty (Mooney and Lee 1999b; 2000), same-sex related legislation (Haider-Markel 2001a; Lewis 2011; Lewis and Oh 2008; Roh and Haider-Markel 2003; Taylor et al. 2012—for an exception, see Beer and Cruz-Aceves 2018), lotteries (Berry and Berry 1990; Jensen 2003), marijuana laws (Ferraiolo 2014; Meier 1994), living will laws (Hays and Glick 1997). There is no doubt that these works have indeed contributed to our knowledge about specific policy areas, however, it has been pointed out that the literature on comparative public policy in general and on morality policy in particular would benefit from comparing theoretically relevant factors across policies (Engeli, Green-Pedersen, and Larsen 2012; Mallinson 2016, 100; McNeal et al. 2003, 67), and above all legislation that varies in the degree to which they reflect characteristics of morality policy:

> "A very basic problem with much morality policy research [is] the lack of variation on the central independent variable.... Many morality policy studies have described the politics of only a single policy—a morality policy—and then compared those politics to some assumed or implied politics of nonmorality policy. A better test would be to observe a given political process for policies that generate various levels of conflict on basic values and compare these politics directly." (Mooney and Schuldt 2008, 212).

We can categorize the scientific production on the field according to the explanations that they usually attribute to the enactment of morality policies. On the one hand, scholarship that has emphasized explanations related to political representation, such as partisanship or electoral competition. On the other hand, a group of works has highlighted the role of moral-related explanations, e.g., ideology, religious groups. I turn to review these works.

2.2.1 Political Representation

Observers of the morality policy process recognize that popularly elected branches are constrained by electoral pressures, hence, these scholars assume that political actors are, on the one hand, "risk-averse", who in turn prefer to avoid moral conflicts. The literature also assumes that policy-makers are also "electorally-minded". I mentioned above that the characteristics of this policy type make it more likely that constituents vehemently communicate their demands to their representatives. Hence, policy makers usually have to address those concerns (Mooney and Lee 2000, 223–24; Tatalovich and Daynes 2011, 35). In this line, electorally-minded lawmakers have an incentive to side with policies that are favored by sizeable numbers of people, given that supporting popular legislation would improve their chances of reelection. However, gauging what most people favor is not an easy task. Public opinion, hence, is a major concern for policy makers, given that these figures can provide information regarding what constituencies want (Lewis and Oh 2008; Medoff, Dennis, and Stephens 2011; Mooney and Lee 2000). In this vein, the level of electoral competition may also affect the way elected officials react on citizen demands regarding morality issues (Holbrook and van Dunk 1993; Lewis 2011). Electorally-minded officials' interest in taking electorally-risky stances on morality issues might be higher when they serve in jurisdictions where electoral competition is high, given that in those polities, politicians' reelection chances are more uncertain compared to electorally uncompetitive jurisdictions.

Policies involving a moral component tend to invoke high levels of partisan conflict (Meier 1994; Mooney and Lee 1995). Parties have distinct policy platforms, especially regarding issues that involve moral questions. Moreover, legislators tend to support policies that aligns with their party platform. The nature of morality policies allows Republicans and Democrats to benefit from this type of laws in that morality issues allows the former to mobilize conservative and liberal constituents, correspondingly, in different ways. Tatalovich describes that the preferred strategy of the Democratic party is to say as little as possible regarding controversial issues, as a way a) not to offend public opinion b) nor alienate the liberal wing of the party, whereas Republicans are usually more outspoken regarding morality issues (2011, xxxv). By the same token, the literature has shown that Republicans tend to be more ideologically conservative and are supported by the conservative Christian community, and that Democratic governments tend to support to a larger extent liberal policies (Lewis 2011, 374). It has been documented too, that the Republican Party has been in general less supportive towards legislation with strong liberal morality content than the Democratic Party (Kreitzer 2015b; Lewis 2011).

2.2.2 Morality Policy

The literature has documented that morality policies are usually accompanied by two types of organized interest, grass-root movements and official interest groups (Meier 1994, 13; Mintrom 1997; Mooney and Lee 2000, 229; Stream 1999; Sylvester and Haider-Markel 2016). They have in common that they are typically single-issue groups, that vehemently promote resolute, non-negotiable positions, and as such, generate more polarized debates and might increase the salience of the issue (Tatalovich and Daynes 2011). In general, these groups contrast sharply from organized interests that mobilize over other types of policies, whose goal is to advocate, for instance, for economic interests.

Interest groups are said to have disproportionate influence on the policy-making process generally (Mooney and Lee 2000), and they are not absent from state-level politics (Nice 1994). These organizations basically articulate demands and present alternatives to policy-makers, and as such, these groups have the ability to influence policy making in several ways, for instance, they can influence the alternatives that policy makers consider. Regarding morality issues, these groups sometimes align with one party, contingent on parties' disposition to support the cause advanced by these groups. In this vein, positions regarding morality issues can have the power to mobilize partisan voting (Engeli, Green-Pedersen, and Larsen 2012, 166).

Some authors argue that the influence of registered interest groups, however, are more likely to be stronger on non-morality policies, given that their low salience and technical complexity lowers the likelihood of high public involvement, hence, allowing interest groups to exert higher influence. In this vein, the literature suggests that when it comes to morality policy, where salience is high and technical complexity is low, neither government ideology nor interest groups should exert significant effects on the odds of enactment of these policies (Ferraiolo 2004; Mooney and Lee 2000).

Given that core moral values are at stake, the policy making process of morality policy is also sometimes accompanied by grass-roots advocacy groups that mobilize as a result of their interest to defend their principled causes; this type of advocacy is expected to exert significant influence on the process of morality policies (Tatalovich and Daynes 2011, xxxiv). A consistent finding in the literature if the role of religious-based advocacy groups. As above mentioned, the issues that morality policy addresses are at their core conflict about the appropriateness of values and morality. The source of individuals' attitudes towards several morality policies is more often than not religion, given that they have explicit moral codes (Meier 1994, 98). Religious-based advocates have been frequently found as significant players in studies on morality politics (Berry and Berry 1990; Chamberlain and Haider-Markel 2005; Haider-Markel 2001a; Haider-Markel and Kaufman 2006; Mooney 2001a; Mooney and Lee 1995; Pierce and Miller 2000; Pierce and Miller 2004). The high rates of religious adherence in a country where political figures express their religious beliefs openly

(Engeli, Green-Pedersen, and Larsen 2012, 166–67), provide religious-based organized groups with substantial political influence in the US. Religious groups may influence public policy either indirectly through public opinion or directly by attempting to influence policy trough lobbying.

2.2.3 Morality Policy Types

A small body of literature has suggested that not all morality policies elicit identical political processes, rather, certain issues give rise to "more complex symbolic politics" (Pierce and Miller 2000, 702), and as such, important distinctions can be made among morality policies (Knill 2013; Meier 1999; Mooney and Lee 1999b; 2000; Pierce 2009; Pierce and Miller 2004). These works suggest that morality legislation can be differentiated analytically into two types[8], namely, consensus or contentious-, based on public opinion about morality policies (Mooney and Lee 2000), and manifest or latent issues, based on morality policies' underlying interest constellations (Knill 2013). At their core, these authors reach common ground in that they suggest that domestic politics of morality policies should be affected by the level of legislation's moral content. Unfortunately, whether these variations have consequences for the diffusion of morality policies has not been explored yet.

Contentious morality policies are characterized by a lack of a clear majority that either supports of opposes a given law, i.e., public opinion regarding these salient issues is usually split. Under such circumstances, the message that legislators receive from the public is mixed (Mooney and Lee 2000, 224):

---

8 A third category is proposed in the literature, which differentiates morality policies based on the existence of legitimate opposition to a given morality issue (Meier 1994, 143): sin and redistributive morality issues. Redistributive morality policies are those where there exists legitimate citizen advocacy and opposition regarding a given morality law. They are "redistributive" because both sides are interested in the redistribution of specific core values or first principles (as opposed to material or financial resources). Sin morality policies are "one-sided" issues, where no legitimate opposition exists, e.g., drunk driving, it would be hard to come up with legitimate arguments to oppose this regulation (Meier 1994, 143; Mooney and Lee 1999b; Pierce and Miller 2000). This differentiation, however, does not suggest differential effects for the politics of policies with varying degrees of morality, for this reason, I do not discuss it at length.

"policy makers' responses... may vary between contentious and consensus morality policy... Electorally responsive policy makers will likely use the best information they have about what the public wants, and [regarding morality policies] the public will have the ability and the incentive to make its opinions known... when public opinion is split [i.e.,] when most citizens [do not] favor a certain policy... policy makers need to monitor it more closely, and fine nuances may have a greater effect than when majorities are sizable. For example, variations in public sentiment between 45 % and 55 % in favor of a policy undoubtedly concern an electorally motivated policy maker far more than variations between 60 % and 70 %." (Mooney and Lee 2000, 230)

The concept of contentious morality policies keeps a close resemblance to what another author calls "latent morality policies". The latter depicts policies in which value conflicts might break out under certain conditions, i.e., debates about latent morality issues need not be entirely moral-laden, but they contain elements that are highly susceptible to be reframed in moral terms. In this type of issues, we might observe competing actors try to shift the political debate in order to achieve their economic or political objectives, either from an instrumental, less or non-moral debate towards one with more value conflicts, or vice versa (de-moralization of political debates), for instance, by emphasizing health issues or economic matters. In other words, these issues can be instrumentally "morally exploited" (Knill 2013, 313).

The fine line between the concepts of latent and contentious morality policies lies in that the former pays closer attention to advocates or opponents' instrumental interests, recognizes that involved actors can strategically use frames to de- or moralize latent morality policies and is more explicit about the idea that these issues are contingent to change across time (Knill 2013, 313–14).

2.3 Policy Diffusion

The section will start with the definition of policy diffusion that will be adopted throughout this work and a short overview on the causal mechanisms that have been attributed to policy diffusion. Next, a review of the literature on policy innovation and diffusion in the USA will be offered. In general, I show that just as the literature on morality policy, the study of policy diffusion across the US states consists of single-policy studies, that we know little as to whether morality policies diffuse and more important-ly, whether variations in morality policy characteristics affect the diffusion of this type of policy. I then draw on the literature on policy attributes and argue that insights from this literature can help fill the gap in the literature that this dissertation will fill.

Throughout this project, I will use the term policy diffusion to refer to the process that materializes when the policy choices of a given subject are substantially affected by policy choices of another subject, due to the fact that these subjects exhibit interdependence. The theory of policy diffusion argues that explanations for why legislation Y is adopted in unit i is a function not only of factors internal to that unit, but also that factors from other units, say j, could exert a relevant effect on the outcome of interest. If the former is true, unit j and i might be interdependent. Find-ing evidence—and more importantly, identifying the nature thereof—is the goal of policy diffusion scholars. In other words, scholarship on poli-cy diffusion focuses on interdependence amongst units, and claims that explanations of policy choices that fail to consider the role of factors that are external to the units of analysis portray an incomplete picture; as such, explanations of whether and why legislation diffuse across polities is central to the understanding of the larger policy process (Grossback 2004; Haider-Markel 2014).

2.3.1 Policy Diffusion Mechanisms

Once we have defined that diffusion is a product of interdependence, we need to further specify what kind of interdependence is theoretically relevant for the issue at hand. The literature more often than not refers to different types of interdependence as diffusion mechanisms (Maggetti and Gilardi 2015, 4). In this vein, the literature categorizes different types of diffusion according to what is hypothesized as its plausible cause, i.e., what type of interdependence or mechanism could have triggered the phenomenon (Martin 2010).

Diffusion mechanisms can be better understood following Goertz' con-cept's structure (2006), as elsewhere suggested (Maggetti and Gilardi 2015, 5). This approach describes concepts as theories that indicate "what some-thing is" and argues that concepts have a structure that consists of three levels: basic, secondary and indicator. Diffusion, our concept of interest, would be positioned in the basic level. In order to infer that the concept occurred, one has first to operationalize the concept with a variable (positioned in the "indicator" level), but most important, concept and indicator must be theoretically related through a "causal mechanism" (which would be positioned in Goertz' secondary level). Mechanisms are the theoretically grounded associations between a given phenomenon and a operationalization thereof. In other words, if one explores the phenomenon of diffusion, one needs first to define what the phenomenon is, with a "concept", and if one wishes to test empirically whether the phenomenon took place, one needs first operationalize the concept with a given variable. Most important, the latter two must be theoretically associated. This theoretical association between concept and variable is called "causal mechanism" (Goertz 2006). In our context, in order to infer that policy diffusion occurred as a consequence of units' interdependence, one needs to provide theoretical— and empirical, if available—evidence that the concept is associated with the empirical measurement (Martin 2010).

For one, policy diffusion can be driven by "competition". A classic example of this is the adoption of a state lottery, which can represent a drain of funds for a non-lottery state, if residents of the latter go to lottery states to buy lottery tickets. In such scenario "competition" is the plausible cause as of why certain jurisdictions are encouraged to enact the same policy (Berry and Berry 1990; Jensen 2003). The motivation to enact a policy existing in another jurisdiction needs not be of a competitive nature, it can be triggered by normative pressures, in that a given policy is adopted because, inter alia, it has reached a taken-for-granted recognition that justifies its adoption on symbolic grounds, in which case, the literature talks about "emulation" or "imitation" mechanisms (Maggetti and Gilardi 2015). Last, legislators can observe the consequences of the passage of a given policy in another jurisdiction, and such pieces of information can be used in a less symbolic, more or less rational decision process of whether to adopt the policy. The latter process is assigned to the "learning" mechanism (Butz, Fix, and Mitchell 2015; Weyland 2009).

2.3.2 Subnational Policy Diffusion in the USA

In this section, I argue that, similar to the literature on morality policy in the USA, scholarship of diffusion across subnational units in the USA also has a strong emphasis on single-policy studies (Berry and Berry 2014; Grossback 2004; Haider-Markel 2014). An exception are the recent works that focus on policy attributes. Second, we still know little regarding whether morality policies diffuse, why, and whether variations in morality policy characteristics affect the diffusion of these policies.

Scholarship on policy diffusion has studied a wide range of phenomena, such as the diffusion of revolutions (Weyland 2009), same-sex civil unions (Fernandez and Lutter 2013), regulatory agencies (Jordana, Levi-Faur, and i Marin, X. F. 2011), etc. Contrary to the scholarship on morality policy, political scientists have studied the process of diffusion across a wider variety of settings, e.g., OECD countries (Füglister, Gilardi, and Luyet 2009), Europe (Martin, Genovese, and Kern 2017), Latin America (Weyland 2006). A substantial proportion of attention in the scholarly literature on this subject, however, has been devoted to the study of diffusion of public policies amongst the 50 US-American states.

The interest on policy diffusion across subnational units in the USA, however, grew out of a more general interest in understanding why states "innovated" in the first place. Early works on the policy process were interested in explaining why jurisdictions adopted innovative programs in the first place, and used to resort to intra-state factors (Gray 1973). However, Walker (1969) explored whether conditions outside of the states could broaden our understanding of government innovativeness. Walker was concerned with potential information externalities amongst US jurisdictions and basically argues that governments were interested in minimizing information costs, and to do so, when introducing new policy measures, governments resorted to the experiences of other states (Martin 2010, 8). Walker not only complemented the literature on government innovativeness, his findings gave rise instead to a new interest in those "external determinants of government innovation". As time went by, scholars shifted the attention from the determinants of government innovativeness in general, to the determinants of innovation of specific policies (Berry and Berry 2014; Mintrom 1997), particularly after Berry and Berry's seminal work on state lottery adoptions (Berry and Berry 1990), that not only introduced a method capable to simultaneously testing the effect of domestic and external determinants of policy adoptions, but also the so called "Unified Model of Government Innovation"[9], inspired in the

---

9 Basically, the unified model groups covariates according to their substantive area of concern. This conceptual framework is in turn built off two frameworks Henderson (2014, 34–36)), each consisting of sets of rival hypotheses with which to explain the diffusion of legislation. The first framework ("diffusion" or "external determinants") draws on the diffusion literature whereas the second ("internal determinants") is built upon hypotheses from different literatures. Whereas this tool was developed to provide a more comprehensive account of why states enact-

literature on innovations in organizations (McNeal et al. 2003, 57; Mohr 1969), which would serve as the basis to organize inquiry (Schlager 2007, 293)[10] of a myriad of works that would examine adoption patterns of a large number of issues, e.g., enterprise zones (Mossberger 2000), state tax incentives (Leiser 2015), charter schools (Wong and Langevin 2007), student-grant programs (Doyle 2006), cigarette taxation (Martin 2010), etc. For a comprehensive review, see Berry (2014).

The tradition of this research program of focusing on one single policy has allowed the accumulation of a sizable amount of evidence regarding policy-specific diffusion; this literature, however, just as the literature on morality policy, lacks cross-policy comparative analyses, without which, we cannot fully understand the process of diffusion (Berry and Berry 2014; Grossback 2004; Haider-Markel 2014). However, this literature has paid only marginal attention to morality policies (Hollander and Patapan 2016, 1–2), as I show in the next section.

2.3.3 Morality Policy Diffusion

In this section, I show that we know little about the diffusion of morality policies, and even less about how variations in morality-policy characteristics affect their diffusion pattern, based on the results of the—surprisingly small—number of works whose main theoretical interest was policy diffusion (and not merely controlled for it) reviewed below. This review also shows that these rather mixed results would greatly benefit from cross-morality-policy analyses, which is virtually inexistent (Mooney and Schuldt 2008).

The evidence regarding death-penalty reforms does support the argument of distinct diffusion patterns based on policy characteristics, and highlights the importance of testing these findings across different policies. Mooney and Lee confirm that variation in the characteristics attributed to morality policies had observable implications for their diffusion

---

ed policy innovations, the unified model reinvigorated the research program on policy diffusion across the US-American states.

10 In addition to allowing the accumulation of knowledge, "frameworks" bound inquiry and direct the attention of the analyst to critical features of the social and physical landscape, in that they provide a foundation for inquiry by specifying classes of variables and general relationships among them, i.e., they identify the universal elements that a particular theory would need to include Schlager (2007, 293).

(Mooney and Lee 1999a; 2000). Regarding capital-punishment abolitions and reestablishments—a policy with high levels of salience, simplicity and moral-based debate—authors argue there was little room so that policymakers learned from the experience of previous reformers, and hence, the policy did not diffuse. On the contrary, when death-penalty reforms had lower levels of morality characteristics in an earlier period—laws that made capital punishment discretionary for murder—i.e., lesser salience, lesser role of basic moral judgments and higher technical complexity, policymakers did indeed react in a bounded-rational social learning process:

> "because these issues are simple technically and involve basic moral judgment, citizens have both the interest and the ability to draw their own conclusions and make their views known strongly to policymakers. Therefore, policymakers are not forced to use their own routine decisionmaking strategies, nor are they given the political leeway to do so. Democracy supersedes learning, and reasoned analysis or even boundedly rational lesson-drawing becomes unnecessary and irrelevant" (Mooney and Lee 1999b, 778)

Moreover, mixed evidence about differential diffusion of laws from another policy-area also indicates the need for cross-policy comparisons. Kreitzer' findings show how slight variations in morality content has implications for diffusion, even for a law that features all the characteristics of morality policy. The author notes that post-1973 pro-abortion policies fit less cleanly with the definition of morality policy, given that they are technically more complex and are less framed in terms of core values, compared to post-1973 state anti-abortion reforms, which did feature more of the morality policy characteristics; however, the author finds that the latter did and the former did not diffuse (2015b, 17). Unfortunately, given that the key independent variable of the project was not diffusion (author merely controlled for it), she did not theorize about the reasons what might have caused this result. On the contrary, in an earlier project, Mooney and Lee concluded that even at an earlier time, when abortion reforms did reflect all the characteristics of morality policy, state-level permissive abortion laws did diffuse; the authors, although vaguely, do suggest what might have caused this morality policy to diffuse. i.e., they argue that abortion supporters could have pointed to the lack of negative effects experienced by jurisdictions with similar moral profiles—which in the USA happen to be geographic neighbors—(Mooney and Lee 1995, 616).

Evidence from another policy area, which reflects characteristics morality policy to a lesser extent, confirms that variation of morality-policy characteristics of lottery-related laws does affect their diffusion. Although only marginally interested in policy diffusion, Pierce and Miller (2000) found that general-fund state lotteries did diffuse across neighboring states, as elsewhere suggested (Berry and Berry 1990; Jensen 2003); however, when lottery's revenue was dedicated to education—for which one could assume that this policy has even less characteristics of morality policy—authors did not find discernible diffusion effects. The authors conclude that, whereas the politics of non- and morality policy differ in general, different morality policies involve different constellations of values and hence, distinct politics (as they showed regarding their diffusion), and that identifying those variations within morality policies would yield important insights into the nature of this type of policy.

Evidence from another area—same-sex legislation—is also mixed. Klawitter explained the geographical diffusion of local anti-discrimination policy for sexual orientation across counties in the USA as a reactionary maneuver by opponents, who might have reacted to enactments of these policies in neighboring counties by mobilizing against it, and justifies this claim with anecdotal evidence about the reaction of opponents from Portland and nearby Lewiston, who immediately after policies that protected gay rights in these cities were enacted, mobilized by organizing a state-wide referendum process (1999, 24). This counter-mobilization effect has been proposed to have happened in the national campaign organized by religious activists against same-sex marriage bans enacted before 2001, for which Haider-Markel finds top-down instead of horizontal diffusion effects (2001a).

A recent, notable exception to the single-case morality policy studies was carried out by Hollander and Patapan (2016). With a qualitative research design, where they analyze whether federalism supports innovation and diffusion of morality policies, for which they select two distinct policies enacted at the state-level in the USA. However, they find ambiguous results, in that they conclude that federalism does encourage innovation and diffusion of morality legislation but that it also offers instruments for inhibiting it, moreover, the authors remain silent about whether a policy's location in the morality continuum ultimately affect their diffusion pattern. Nonetheless, although not explicitly discussed in "interdependence" terms, this work suggests an interesting causal mechanism responsible for the diffusion of some morality policies. The authors argue that the characteristic strong responses that morality policies evoke in the citizenry make it more likely that more people get involved in the process, and as such, larger numbers of motivated advocates might follow. In turn, given the characteristic intractability of the core values that these laws address (to different degrees), these active actors are more likely to engage in inter-state advocacy campaigns:

> "To the extent that moral questions in general make universal claims, asserting the goodness, justice or piety of something not just for me, or only here, but for all and everywhere, both moral claims and their opposing positions are framed as general matters of principle and therefore demand that they be advocated (or repudiated) irrespective of their territorial constraints… questions concerning morality demand those advocating or opposing the initiative do so as a matter of principle, focusing not only on individual benefits, but showing care and concern for the welfare of others. Therefore, innovations and their counter movements in morality policy will tend to go beyond jurisdictions and borders to defend, promote and assail the principle itself. Morality policy is therefore inherently oblivious to the territorial demands of federalism" (Hollander and Patapan 2016, 16–17).

All these studies provide initial evidence that policies' variation in the characteristics attributed to morality policies should have implications for their diffusion (Mooney and Schuldt 2008). Let me turn to a more recent, less single-policy centered literature, that has indeed focused on implications of policies' characteristics for diffusion.

2.4 Policy Attributes

The literature on "policy attributes" has been more explicit about differential effects of policies' characteristics and their diffusion patterns. Motivated by Gray's seminal work that suggested that the nature of the policy affected the legislation's temporal diffusion patterns (Gray 1973), this small body of work has recently begun to explore whether policies' characteristics affect learning patterns across certain policy types (Boushey 2010; 2012; Mallinson 2016; Nicholson-Crotty 2009) and within criminal justice (Boushey 2016; 2016; Makse and Volden 2011). These works, however, have not studied morality policy.

Gray's work (1973) challenged the findings of the field at that time by showing that the determinants of state policy innovation varied across policy areas (McNeal et al. 2003, 57). The article argued that the fact that the innovations that had been studied up until then in other disciplines—agricultural economics, communications, and sociology—diffused across time similarly—with slow rates of adoption and s-shaped cumulative adoption curves—could be attributable to their nature. In other words, those innovations were largely technical, which makes an argument of policy makers "learning" from experiences about the implementation of technologically complex or economic innovations more plausible. The s-shape of the curve is produced by a process that begins with a few initial units enacting a given policy, while the rest of the potential adopters wait to see (learn) the implications of enactment, before deciding whether to follow the example (Mallinson 2016, 100). There are three rationales to justify this interpretation. On the one hand, both formulation and implementation of these technically complex policies require extensive consultation with experts, which also increases the costs of decision-making (Boushey 2016, 200). On the other hand side, there exists simply more to be learned about policies with more technical details (Mooney and Lee 1999a). Third, legislators have a higher threshold of skepticism to overcome regarding these laws (Karch 2007a; Mallinson 2016). For these reasons, when a policy is adopted at such slow rates and produces such s-shaped curves and the researcher justifies theoretically the existence of interdependence, the literature assumes that these policies diffused as a result of legislators learning from past experiences (Boushey 2010; 2012; Mallinson 2016; Mooney and Lee 1999b; Nicholson-Crotty 2009). These works argue for the most part that lawmakers are risk-adverse actors that prefer to retrieve information about the potential costs and benefits of policies before they incur in the electoral risk of deviating from the status quo (Nicholson-Crotty 2009, 193).

More recently, researchers of policy attributes contributed to Grey's (1973) and Lowi's (1988) findings by highlight that another policy characteristic has substantial implications for the politics of certain policy types in general, and for their diffusion process in particular. Based on large data sets—comprising 57, 81 and 172 state policies that diffused between 1912 and 2009 (Boushey 2012; Mallinson 2016; Nicholson-Crotty 2009)—these authors coincide that the salience of a policy has implications for how law-makers react to policy innovations. In particular, these authors conclude that high salience of a policy has the opposite effect of policy complexity on the legislators' motivation to learn about new policies, in that their risk aversion is smoothed by the fact higher levels of policy salience translates into sizable number of people demanding action from their representatives regarding the highly publicized policy. In this scenario, lawmakers respond with less risk-aversion and more as electorally minded actors, in that they wait less time for policies to play out in other jurisdictions and learn from those consequences, and instead decide to take a stand regarding the popular policy with less information. These results were confirmed in two further studies that focused on state adoptions of 27 and 44 criminal justice policies between 1973 and 2008 (Boushey 2016; Makse and Volden 2011), and more importantly, in case studies that analyzed legislative deliberations about two policies with different levels of salience and complexity—three-strikes criminal sentencing and individual development accounts (Nicholson-Crotty 2009). In short, authors found that both of these policies characteristics have discernible impacts on the diffusion process of several policy types. Unfortunately, they do not include morality policies in their analyses, and although they justify their expectations theoretically, they focus on the implications of these characteristics on the shape of the cumulative curve of adoptions.

3 Theory

I open this section with the main argument of the dissertation. I then elaborate on its components and ground them with theoretical and empirical evidence from the literature. Next, I formulate a comparative- and a diffusion theory, outline their assumptions, and I derive testable hypotheses. In the final section, I formulate expectations regarding domestic factors.

3.1 Constituting Elements of the Argument

Concisely, I argue that a) morality policies diffuse as a result of a process where policy makers learn about past experiences from other polities, b) that such learning occurs through cognitive heuristics, and c) that the level of moral content will affect these learning and diffusion patterns. This argument generates a series of questions: why are legislators interested in learning about morality policies? What information do they look for? From where is such information retrieved? Last, why might morality-policy characteristics affect learning about morality policy and ultimately, their diffusion? In this section, I focus on the first two questions.

Regarding the first question, I argue that it is especially likely that citizens demand government responses regarding morality policies, which in turn makes it more likely that legislators cannot ignore, but rather respond to these demands. One plausible explanation is that support and opposition to these laws is less likely to remain local (Hollander and Patapan 2016). When it comes to support/opposition to legislation that addresses non-negotiable core values—whose passage (rejection) is frequently interpreted as a categorical denial of/affront towards the moral values of its advocates—people are more likely to organize and mobilize (Mooney and Lee 2000, 229), however not limited to their locality, but in every location where a policy that contradicts their first principles emerges, especially because the intractability of these issues shapes the advocacy efforts in a way that actors strive for conclusive resolutions to policies that cast doubt on their core values. Given that the latter are shared by sizable numbers of people grouped by, for instance, religion, involved actors have strong incentives to contact people that share their worldviews in other jurisdictions:

"Morality policy by definition is resistant to negotiation and compromise. Therefore, morality policy... will inevitably give rise to... a counter response seeking not only to contain [a given morality policy] innovation, but more ambitiously to eradicate it altogether wherever it appears. This 'moral dynamic' will generate such tensions that both those in favor and those opposed, rather than tolerating each other, will turn to any political or institutional means to assert their claims and resolve the tension in their favor."(Hollander and Patapan 2016, 2)

For these same reasons, it is likely that a sizable number of citizens organize and demand action from their representatives (Hollander and Patapan 2016, 16–17; Mooney and Lee 2000, 229; Pierce 2009, 6–7). As such, electorally-minded lawmakers cannot ignore this type of legislation (Mooney and Lee 2000, 229), given that a vote for (against) a given morality policy could have undesired electoral consequences (Butz, Fix, and Mitchell 2015; Meier 1994; Mooney and Lee 2000; Pierce 2009, 6–7).

"unlike general matters of innovation, where resistance is confined to the specific loss or disadvantage and in most cases there is no general attempt to undermine the innovation itself, questions concerning morality demand those advocating or opposing the initiative do so as a matter of principle, focusing not only on individual benefits, but showing care and concern for the welfare of others. Therefore, innovations and their counter movements in morality policy will tend to go beyond jurisdictions and borders to defend, promote and assail the principle itself. Morality policy is therefore inherently oblivious to the territorial demands of federalism... therefore innovations in morality policy in federalism generate powerful impulses that are not willing to abide with federalism's accommodation of diversity. Both sides to morality policy vehemently seek to assert and defend their principles, and are unwilling to give or take; they want to win it all. This means that innovation and policy diffusion regarding moral questions will seek to do away with the federal accommodation of diversity.... As a result both innovative and counter movements will seek a nonfederal solution to advocate (or reject) morality policy innovations." (Hollander and Patapan 2016, 16–17)

3.1.1 Morality Policy Learning

Such scenario—where legislators have to decide whether to support a given morality policy—generates uncertainty—such as regarding policy innovations in general. This leads to the question, how do policy makers react to this? I believe that before policy makers take a stand on a morality issue, they react to this uncertainty by searching for information—i.e., learning—about previous morality policy enactments.

However, I believe that learning about morality policies proceeds through cognitive shortcuts, in a process where information from a biased sample of sources is overestimated. Indeed, previous studies have relied on the literature on cognitive psychology and proven that policy makers react to uncertainty about new policy options by searching for information through cognitive heuristics; this literature refers to such process as "bounded learning" (Butz, Fix, and Mitchell 2015; Karch 2007a; Meseguer 2006; Weyland 2005a; 2005b). Such account argues that humans are constrained by time, by cognitive capabilities, and that information gathering is costly, hence, such conditions shape humans' comprehensiveness of information search and the criteria for information evaluation. Given these innate limitations and structural constraints, lawmakers gather and assess cues relying on cognitive shortcuts, particularly the "availability" and "representativeness" heuristics. The latter two shortcuts make humans believe that cues retrieved from an arbitrarily selected sample of sources are sufficient to reach informed conclusions (Weyland 2006).

An empirical implication of such information-search process is that not all information available is valued equally. In other words, this type of learning involves a selective cue-taking process, for which one criterion to define the group from which information is retrieved should exist (Gilardi 2004; Meseguer 2006)[11]. So how is this group defined in the context of morality policy making?

The literature on the diffusion of innovations (Rogers 2003) suggests that innovations diffuse as a product of information exchange between subjects, some of which have experimented with the innovation in question, and that such communication occurs predominantly amongst

---

11 A theory of rational learning would argue that decision makers scan all possible sources of information; however, I argue that such searches for information proceeds more in line with a theory of bounded learning, that predicts that individuals learn selectively, in that they draw information from a smaller, more manageable number of sources.

"homophilous" subjects. Indeed, the literature on comparative state public policy in the US and works from International Relations have grounded their expectations regarding bounded-learning accordingly (e.g., Hill and Klarner 2002, 1120; Seljan and Weller 2011; Weyland 2009, 400):

> "Homophily is the degree to which pairs of individuals who interact are similar in certain attributes, such as beliefs, education, social status, and the like. In a free-choice situation, when an individual can interact with any one of a number of other individuals, there is a strong tendency for him to select someone who is most like him- or herself... When they [the groups or individuals] share common meanings, a mutual subcultural language, and are alike in personal and social characteristics, the communication of ideas is likely to have greater effects in terms of knowledge gain, attitude formation and change, and overt behavior change." (Rogers 1983, 18–19)

Nevertheless, if decision makers weigh more heavily information retrieved from a purposeful sample of jurisdictions with which superficial similarities and stereotypical affinities exist (Weyland 2009, 400), how is this sample constituted when it comes to morality policy? The answer to this is related to the type of uncertainty that morality policies give rise to.

3.1.2 Morality-Policy Uncertainty

It has been documented that uncertainty derived from morality legislation differs from uncertainty related to non-morality policies, and that this is closely related with the nature of information that is sought after regarding morality policy. Given that morality policies are salient and technically simple, I believe that information about the electoral costs and benefits that followed policy enactment is particularly relevant for morality policy. Information about technical details might be retrieved in the learning process, too; however, the technical simplicity of morality policy makes it more likely that the searches for information focus on political consequences. In turn, morality policy should generate uncertainty about electoral consequences, e.g., how an electorate might react to a policy that addresses moral values (Grossback 2004, 540; Hollander and Patapan 2016, 18; Mooney 2001a, 105–6; Pierce and Miller 2004, Nicholson-Crotty 2009, 196). In this case, it is likely that information is retrieved in a bounded fashion from jurisdictions with similar culture, values and ideology.

3.2 Morality Policy Diffusion Theory and Hypotheses

From the arguments above presented, I argue that policy makers cope with morality-policy-derived uncertainty by observing the consequences of passing a given morality policy in other jurisdictions; learning, however, proceeds through cognitive shortcuts, where information retrieved from a biased sample of sources is overestimated. I claim that such learning is bounded to jurisdictions with morality-policy relevant attributes, namely values, culture and ideology (Butz, Fix, and Mitchell 2015; Doan 2014; Mooney and Schuldt 2008). Policy makers from unit i are interested in the consequences observed in morally-similar j as a result of enacting morality policy Y because, if the public from unit j responded to a given morality policy not all to negatively, the policymaker from i could infer (in a bounded fashion) that her constituency might react similarly, given the similar moral profiles of these states. In other words, the aftermath of enactments of morality policy in morally similar units can provide public officials with credible signals about whether a given law will be acceptable to their electorates (Grossback 2004, 540). If we find evidence supporting this, we could say that morality policy decisions exhibit interdependence[12], and that morality-policy Y enacted at time t-1 in state j diffuses to state i in time t as a result of legislator from i learning about consequences exhibited in morally similar j after experiencing Y.

I will investigate two potential sources from where legislators might have retrieved information, one based on a wide number of potentially similar moral attributes—a general diffusion effect—and another one based specifically on ideological similarity. When previous adopters of a given morality policy are ideologically dissimilar to a jurisdiction that has not adopted the policy in question, one might expect a negative effect on the likelihood that the latter enact this morality policy (Carley, Nicholson-Crotty, and Miller 2017, 438; Grossback 2004). The direction of the influence of the general source, however, needs not follow a determinate direction. If passage in units with—in general—similar moral profiles showed that the political risks of adoption are low, that law becomes a suitable candidate for adoption; alternatively, if political consequences were

---

12 Nonetheless, there is a second, citizen-centered, interdependence, where information about the existence of morality-policy Y, enacted at time t-1 in state j, diffuses to state i in time t as a result of citizens from i learning about occurrence of Y, which leads citizens from i to demand action to their legislators from i. In this dissertation, however, I do not explore this situation.

severe, those events might trigger a "backlash effect" (Ferraiolo 2014, 349; Mooney 2001a, 105–6; Pierce and Miller 2004), in which case, a negative diffusion effect can be observed. However, previous projects found a negative and a positive diffusion effect on the likelihood of enacting gay-related legislation (Klawitter and Hammer 1999; Lewis 2011, 375; Taylor et al. 2012, 84) and medical marijuana enactments (Bradford and Bradford 2016; Ferraiolo 2004, 200), correspondingly. Based on this empirical evidence, I expect to find a similar result in the SSM and MML cases. On the other hand, I did not find empirical evidence regarding diffusion effects and obesity-related legislation, for which I opt to allow the data to reveal the relations (Martin, Genovese, and Kern 2017, 7) between the general diffusion measure and the hazard of passing AO.

Based on the above-elaborated arguments, I derive the following testable implications:

> **General Diffusion Hypothesis:** Adoptions of SSM bans are negatively influenced by previous SSM bans enactments in morally similar jurisdictions; adoptions of MML are positively influenced by previous MML enactments morally similar jurisdictions.
> **Ideological Diffusion Hypothesis:** Adoptions of morality legislation in a state are negatively influenced by previous enactments of such policy in ideologically dissimilar jurisdictions.

3.3 Comparative Morality Diffusion Theory and Expectations

I posited earlier that, in line with scholars that have hypothesized that variations in the degree of morality should affect domestic politics (Mooney and Schuldt 2008; Pierce and Miller 2000), I argue that these variations should have a discernible effect for learning about morality policies and their diffusion. However, there exists virtually no empirical evidence on whether nor how variations in morality policies' characteristics might affect learning and diffusion patterns so as to formulate expectations. The literature on policy attributes above reviewed, however, has documented that salience and complexity of certain policy types affect their diffusion patterns (Boushey 2012; 2016; Makse and Volden 2011; Mallinson 2016; Nicholson-Crotty 2009, 196). This literature found out that as the levels of technical simplicity and salience of a policy decrease, the uncertainty about a) whether a policy will achieve the desired goals, and about b) the electoral consequences that policy enactment will bring about rises, which makes it more likely that that risk-averse and electorally-minded legislators opt to learn more from previous adopters about the implications of enactment, which in turn affects the diffusion of policies.

This proposition, however, has not been tested on morality policies. Nonetheless, given that, a) technical simplicity and salience are two of the main attributes of morality policies, and that b) the literature proposes that varying scores on these characteristics should have implications for the "politics" of morality policies (Mooney and Schuldt 2008), I use the findings from the literature on policy attributes to formulate my comparative theoretical expectation. Based on this, I would expect that, if learning is the mechanism driving morality policy diffusion, the higher the levels of salience and of technical simplicity of a morality policy, the smaller the motivation to learn from past experiences, i.e., the lesser the degree to which adoption of a morality policy will be influenced by—having learned from—past enactments. An implication thereof is that as the level of morality-policy characteristics rises, the magnitude of the diffusion effect will be smaller. Hence:

> **Comparative Diffusion Hypothesis:** The magnitude of diffusion will increase as policies reflect less characteristics of morality policy.

The following figure represents graphically the argument. Variation in morality policy characteristics (left rectangle) affects the uncertainty about the consequences of enacting a given policy (center rectangle)—which is also affected by domestic determinants (bottom rectangle)—which in turn affects the incentives for learning about past consequences of enacting morality policies, which ultimately shapes the magnitude of the diffusion effect (right rectangle) as follows: I expect that higher levels of morality policy characteristics—technical simplicity and salience (bottom arrow)— decrease the motivation to learn about consequences of previous enactments of morality policies; hence, the magnitude of diffusion will decrease (upper arrow):

Figure 1. Theoretical Argument

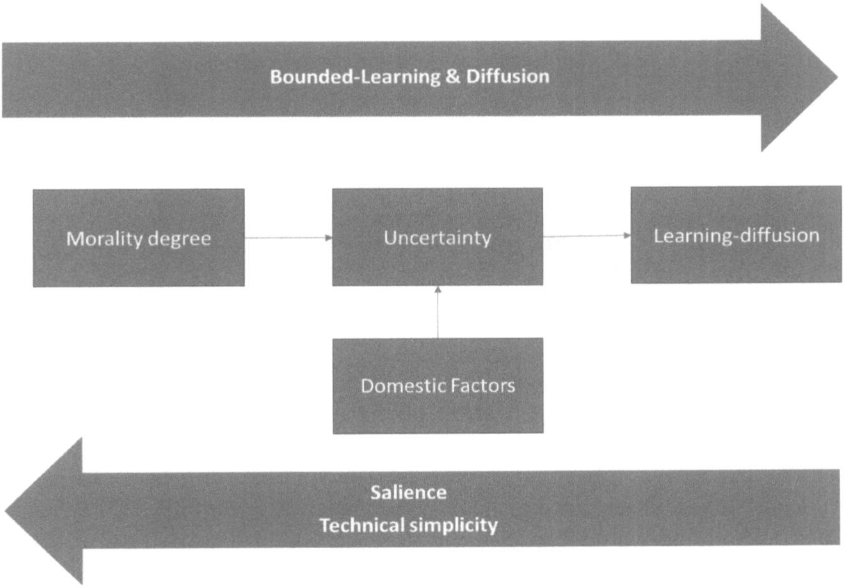

Source: Author

3.4 Domestic Factors

However, it is not plausible that factors external to the state are all that matters to the legislators. Government officials care about internal factors, e.g., how policy changes affect their odds of reelection, or about the opportunity costs associated with legislative action (Martin, Genovese, and Kern 2017, 8–9). As previously mentioned, domestic factors have been the focus of much of the extant literature on morality policy and clearly play an important role in the overall process of policymaking. For these reasons, I will incorporate previous theories into the models, although the analysis will concentrate more heavily on the effects of diffusion.

For such a task, the above-described "Unified Model of Government Innovation" (Berry and Berry 2014) will be followed as a "guiding tool" that will serve to organize inquiry (Schlager 2007, 293), just as a large number of researchers have done (Berry and Berry 2007, 243). I group covariates accordingly in the following conceptual categories: political representation, morality policy, problem severity and demographic characteristics, as elsewhere suggested (Heidt-Forsythe 2013; Kim 2016; Kreitzer 2015a; Roh and Berry 2008). A representation of this can be seen in the figure below.

Figure 2. *Extended Unified Model of Government Innovation*

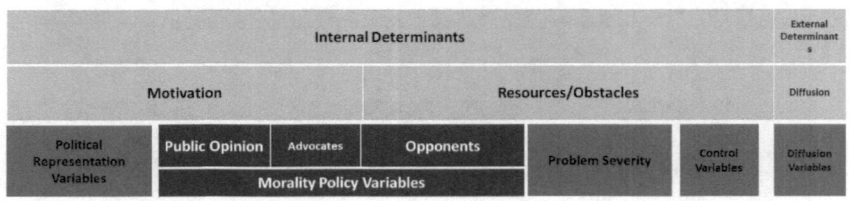

Source: author, based on (Berry and Berry 1990)

In general, one would expect liberal states to be more supportive of a liberal measure such as legalization of marijuana for medicinal purposes (Ferraiolo 2004, 188–89; Meier 1994; Mooney and Schuldt 2008), and less lenient towards a conservative measure such as banning the legality of marriages of same-sex couples (Haider-Markel 2001a; Mooney and Schuldt 2008). The relationship between the states' mood and legislation directed at controlling obesity, however, is less clear. For one, if more citizens perceived their nutrition habits as a deeply individual conduct, it might be that states with liberal constituencies—where residents favor less government involvement in social issues (Ferraiolo 2004, 188–89; Haider-Markel and Kaufman 2006, 173)—to be less supportive of laws that attempt to regulate eating behavior. This leads me to expect the following:

Citizen Ideology Hypothesis: states with more politically liberal states are more likely to enact MML and less likely to adopt SSM bans and AO

It has been shown that competitive elections affect certain types of policies but not others. Morality policies are special in this respect, in that more often than not these type of laws are an attempt to challenge predominant approaches to traditional issues (Haider-Markel 2001a; Meier 1994, 107), for instance, favoring medical marijuana laws or homosexual marriage. Supporting such legislation may damage a party's position within a competitive electoral environment (Haider-Markel 2001a, 14–15). Legislators who favor such measures are taking a major political risk. Elected officials might be willing to take such risk when the potential benefits outweigh the costs of inaction, e.g., if they perceive that they have a real chance of becoming the majority party, or that losing majority party status is a real alternative. The latter is tangible in states with more politically competitive districts. In other words, when party competition intensifies, enacting a politically-risky issue becomes more attractive (Meier 1994, 107). Since obesity is generally viewed as a "low-valence issue" (Oliver and Lee 2005, 939), AO legislation might be less politically risky; hence, I expect electoral competition to have an insignificant effect on the odds of passing AO legislation. Given the broad popular support in the analysis period for SSM bans (Pew Research Center 2011, 14) and MML (Dutton et al. 2014), states with higher electoral competition should be more likely to pass these laws as parties compete for public support and electoral success. Therefore, I hypothesize the following:

> **Electoral Competition Hypothesis**: Legislators representing competitive electoral districts will be more likely to enact SSM bans and MML, whereas it will have no significant effect on the adoption of AO.

Partisan platforms affect policy decisions especially when a given party controls the legislative and executive branches of government (a.k.a. unified government), due to party control over the agenda and party discipline (Aldrich and Rhode 2001). It has been documented, that the Republican Party is generally less supportive of legislation with strong liberal morality content than the Democratic Party (Kreitzer 2015b; Lewis 2011). In the literature it has been established, too, that in general, the Democratic Party tends to favor government intervention to address public problems (Rodriguez 2010, 75). This leads me to expect the following:

> **Republican Party Control Hypothesis**: State governments controlled by Republicans will be more likely to enact SSM bans and AO legislation, and less likely to adopt MML.
> **Democratic Party Control Hypothesis**: State governments controlled by Democrats will be less likely to enact SSM bans and AO legislation, and more likely to adopt MML.

As elected officials become more conservative in a given state, I expect them to oppose policies with more morality content, such as medical marijuana (and support bans of same-sex marriage). However, the expectation of the relationship between the ideology of the government and AO legislation is less clear. This leads me to formulate the following hypothesis:

> **Government Ideology Hypothesis**: states with more liberal officials are more likely to enact MML, less likely to adopt SSM bans and AO.

Interest groups have been found to exert substantive influence in a myriad of issues, e.g., found for assisted reproductive technologies (Heidt-Forsythe 2017), state medical savings accounts (Bowen Jr., William R. 2005, 145), stand-your-ground laws (Butz, Fix, and Mitchell 2015), abortion laws (Mooney and Lee 1995), and I will control for their influence in the models. In addition to this, I will incorporate one opposition group characterized by radical stances against legislation that reflects characteristics of morality legislation to a higher degree. The religious organizations likely to have the largest influence are those classified in the literature as "protestant fundamentalists" because their religious doctrines are in conflict with liberal behavior (Haider-Markel 2001a; Haider-Markel and Kaufman 2006; Haider-Markel and Meier 1996, 337–38; Monogan 2012; Pierce and Miller 2004).

> **Advocates Hypothesis:** states with more interest groups supportive of a specific issue (depending on the policy in question) will be more likely to adopt that legislation.
> **Opponents Hypothesis:** states with more interest groups that oppose a specific issue (depending on the policy in question) will be less likely to adopt that legislation.
> **Religious Fundamentalists Hypothesis:** states with more citizens belonging to a fundamentalist religion will be less likely to adopt legislation that reflect the theoretical characteristics of morality policy (SSM & MML); I expect this factor to be irrelevant for AO.

When a policy is enacted in order to address a given situation, policy makers monitor the evolution of the problem (Kingdon 2003); if the situation aggravates, we might expect that the pressure and incentive to enact legislation that alleviates the situation rise (Nice 1994). This situation is usually referred to as "problem-severity" in the literature (Berry and Berry 2014). The models will also control for population and education levels.

> **SSM Problem Severity Hypothesis:** states with a higher percentage of same-sex households will be less likely to pass SSM bans.
> **AO Problem Severity Hypothesis:** states with a higher percentage of obese population will be more likely to enact AO legislation.
> **MML Problem Severity Hypothesis:** states with a higher percentage of population with terminally ill diseases will be more likely to enact MM legislation.

4 Research Design

In this section, I describe the methods implemented throughout the project. I start with the logic of case selection, followed by variable operationalization. Then I turn to describe the analytical strategy implemented, followed by the model building strategy, and the comparative strategy. I conclude this section with limitations of the project.

Political scientists are confronted with the question of which setting is most appropriate so as to provide an adequate test of their hypothesis. Researchers that make use of Large-N designs can select a variety of units of observations, for instance, countries across the world, countries within regions or subnational units. A crucial factor to consider is data availability and variation across theoretically relevant variables. A large body of literature has opted to test theories in the USA for several reasons, which are captured in the following quote:

> "No two states operate under the same political institutions, have the same residents, political cultures, or histories. The wealth of variation has offered researchers a wonderful opportunity to study the relationship between these different conditions and a variety of political outcomes and behaviors. Theories and relationships that can only be poorly tested at the national level with a handful of observations under generally consistent and slow changing conditions can often be much more richly theorized and thoroughly vetted across the states [, for instance] how new policies come about and diffuse across units [is amongst] the great many questions that have been profitably studied at the state level" (Boehmke and Branton 2014, 855)

This has allowed that the literature on comparative state public policy, has amassed a large amount of knowledge of political processes—for a review see (Berry and Berry 2014)—particularly about morality policy. Indeed, although the phenomenon that this project tackles has not been studied before, the USA has been the most explored setting by morality policy scholars (Engeli, Green-Pedersen, and Larsen 2012; Tatalovich and Daynes 2011).

Although enactment of the Civil Rights Acts increased the regulatory powers of federal agencies in the enforcement of civil rights, many morality politics battles are waged at the state level in the In the USA. Issues that morality policies address are regularly executed by state bureaucracies, and, sometimes there is simply no federal law to enforce; when there exists federal guidelines, agencies may not have the personnel, the financial resources or the political will to enforce morality-related issues (Doan and McFarlane 2012, 616; Tatalovich and Daynes 2011, 35). In this vein, the 50 sub-national units of the USA offers a good setting to test my theory. Moreover, selecting the USA will allow me not only to build upon but also to contribute to an existing body of literature.

4.1 Case Selection

Once that the sub-national units of USA were selected as an appropriate setting so as to study the diffusion of morality legislation, I proceeded to choose a small but carefully selected number of policies that could allow me to make the intended contribution, closely following recommendations in the literature (Hollander and Patapan 2016; Mooney and Schuldt 2008).

However, perhaps one of the main reasons why up to date there still exists no study that has covered the gap in the literature mentioned in previous sections is due to the fact that drawing inferences from a cross-(morality) policy comparison has proven hard to be carried out. In order to compare a particular "aspect of the politics" of different policies, while keeping all other conditions as equal as possible, one faces a situation characterized by the fact that even within the same conceptual category, certain covariates will only be relevant for one policy in particular, and irrelevant for other cases. For one, models with such "policy-specific variables" would be better specified than models without them. Nevertheless, controlling for such policy-specific factors would inhibit a proper comparison across policies. In other words, the variation of determinants across policy areas makes theory development especially difficult (McNeal et al. 2003, 57), as has been pointed out regarding comparative public policy in general (Kreitzer 2015b, 59; Pierce 2009, 12), and morality policy in particular (Mooney and Schuldt 2008, 212). As an alternative, one can strive at parsimony at the expense of detailed explanations of the diffusion of different policies by disregarding the nuances of each policy (Kreitzer 2015b). Doing so will make cross-policy comparison more feasible.

Mooney and Schuldt proposed that in these circumstances, researchers should certainly be able to make relative judgments about policies' "level of morality" (2008, 212) in order to construct a morality continuum/spectrum that classifies the degree to which legislation reflect the theoretical characteristics of morality policy, as elsewhere done (Hollander and Patapan 2016, 2)[13]:

> "Clearly, there is a continuum of the political environments surrounding morality policy reform… by examining the adoption patterns of [at least] two policies relatively distant on this continuum, we can begin to understand the impact of [theoretically relevant variables] on the politics of morality policy" (Mooney and Lee 2000, 226)

4.1.1 Morality Continuum

Following such propositions[14], three policies from an assumed "morality continuum" were selected, in such a way that the whole spectrum were represented by one classical morality case—Same-Sex Marriage bans (SSM)—another one that could be situated in the middle of such scale—Medical Marijuana Laws (MML)—and another case of legislation with minimal characteristics of morality policy—Anti-Obesity Legislation (AO). Although no sample of three policies can be considered truly representative, variation along this dimension makes generalization a less hazardous enterprise (Karch 2007a, 17). The policies that will be analyzed in this project would be distributed along such a continuum as follows:

---

13 Authors justified their selection as follows: "These cases [legalization of same-sex marriage and recreational marijuana] have been chosen because they traverse the moral spectrum… They therefore provide the necessary breadth for evaluating federalism's role in morality policy innovation and diffusion." Hollander and Patapan (2016, 2). That wok, however, used a different analytical technique (qualitative case studies).

14 I am indebted to Prof. Dr. Christian Martin for his substantial feedback on my case selection

Figure 3. Morality Policy Continuum

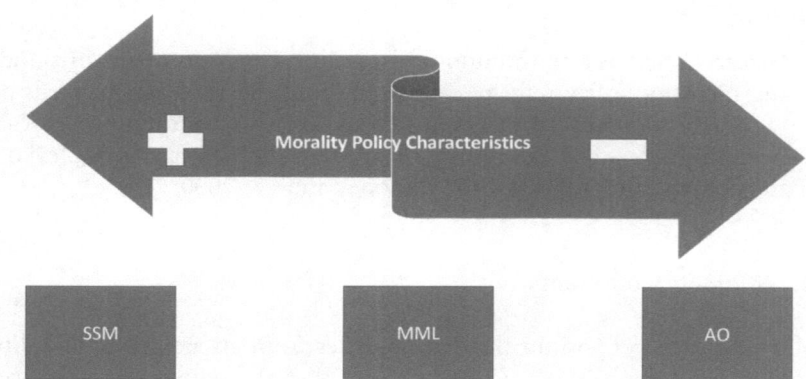

Source: Author

There is more consensus about same-sex marriage laws being on a conservative side of a morality spectrum. This type of laws has been categorized in the morality policy literature in the category of legislation that reflect all characteristics of morality policy, categorized by authors distinctly as sin- (Haider-Markel and Meier 1996; Meier 1994), manifest- (Knill 2013) and consensus morality policy (Mooney and Lee 2000). Indeed, gay marriage is consistently grouped in the category of policies that reflect most or all theoretical characteristics of morality policy (Larsen 2010; Smith 2002); it even ranks higher than abortion and death penalty (Mooney and Schuldt 2008, 202). Similarly, a recent project used same-sex marriage legislation as an example of legislation on the most conservative side of a morality policy continuum (Hollander and Patapan 2016, 2)

Opinion of where in a morality policy spectrum medical marijuana would be positioned is less clear than SSM, but evidence shows that it would be somewhere in the middle. Indeed, marijuana related legislation has been categorized in the literature as an example of policy that reflects several, but not all characteristics of morality policy, categorized by authors distinctly as redistributive- (Meier 1994), latent- (Knill 2013) and contentious morality policy (Mooney and Lee 2000). Moreover, a previous project used marijuana legislation as an example of legislation positioned differently than same-sex legislation along a morality policy continuum (Hollander and Patapan 2016, 2). For these reasons I believe that MML can serve as example of a case positioned in the middle of a morality policy spectrum.

Although obesity policy is an issue that is less likely to feature characteristics of morality policies and has even been said to generate little political debate (Oliver and Lee 2005, 939), anti-obesity legislation has been discussed as an example of morality policies' susceptibility to be reframed for instrumental reasons by one side of the involved actors (Ferraiolo 2014; Knill 2013), as occurred when the food industry's attempt to mobilize social opposition with a campaign that attempted to reframe the ban to oversized servings of sugary drinks in food-service establishments as infringement of individual liberties (Frum 2012).

These policies differ in the general support that people have shown toward them. Given the lack of complete state data on attitudes towards specific issues, previous works have resorted to national public opinion figures to proxy for general sentiment towards morality issues (Butz, Fix, and Mitchell 2015; Mooney and Lee 2000; Jensen 2003; Kim 2016, 17). If we do so, we find somehow comparable levels of support for SSM bans and MML in the period of analysis, that contrast with a less clear picture of publics receptivity of AO. Based on national polls, most people supported the ideas of restricting marriage to heterosexual couples and of medical doctors being allowed to prescribe marijuana[15] for medical purposes, whereas national figures depict tighter opinions from opponents and advocates of government intervention in obesity control. In this respect, the former two could be described as consensus morality issues, whereas AO as contentious morality issues (Mooney and Lee 2000). Opinion about legalizing marijuana for medical purposes during the period of analysis fluctuated from a ratio of supporters to opponents of 62 % to 32 %, to 77 % to 17 % (Dutton et al. 2014). The picture for same-sex marriage changed from 65 % opposed and 27 % in favor in 1996, 57 % opposed and 35 % in favor in 2001, to 53 % opposed and 36 % in favor in 2005 (Pew Research Center 2011, 14). On the contrary, national figures reveal that 54 % or respondents oppose and 42 % support government involvement in obesity control (Kam 2017, 984).

---

15 Opinion about legalizing marijuana for recreational purposes shows a markedly different picture; opinion varied from low support (27 % versus 69 %) in 1979, to higher, but evenly distributed supporters in 2014 (51 % in favor against 44 % opposed); in 2009, 41 % were in favor and 52 % opposed, in 2011, these figures were 40 % and 51 %, 47 % and 47 % in 2012, and 45 % and 45 % in 2013 Dutton et al. (2014)

4.1.2 Same-Sex Marriage (SSM) Bans

Although homosexual couples have long been barred from marrying, it has been argued that the period of adoptions of the first statutory restrictions to same-sex marriage from the 1990s has been the most visible issue in the contemporary gay rights movement (Lewis 2011). In 1993, the Hawaii Supreme Court issued a decision signaling for the first time in US-history support for the argument that denying marriage licenses to same-sex couples was discriminatory (Hollander and Patapan 2016, 5–6). The Hawaii Supreme Court ruled that prohibiting same-sex marriage constituted a violation to the Hawaii Constitution's ban on sex discrimination. Given that states are required to recognize marriages (and legal contracts in general) from other states as indicated by the "full faith and credit" clause of the Constitution, a group of opponents quickly mobilized to outlaw recognition of outer-state SSM in their states (Haider-Markel 2001a; Hollander and Patapan 2016, 7; Lewis 2011). In the chapter on SSM bans, I will examine such state laws/constitutional amendments enacted between 1995 until 2006.

The empirical record on SSM bans is mixed. For instance, there is evidence that SSM bans diffuse across borders, that electoral competition increases and the levels of education attainment decreases the odds of SSM ban adoption (Lewis 2011), although these effects were null for the first ban enactments (Haider-Markel 2001a); religious fundamentalists were not substantially linked to the probability of SSM ban passage (Barclay and Fisher 2003; Lewis and Oh 2008), although some evidence points to the contrary (Haider-Markel 2001a; Lewis 2011); LGBT interest groups were negatively associated with SSM bans (Barclay and Fisher 2003; Haider-Markel 2001a), although see Lewis (2008, 49); also the Democratic partisanship was found negatively associated with the odds of enacting SSM bans (Lewis and Oh 2008, 49), although see Haider-Markel and Lewis (2001a; 2011).

4.1.3 Medical Marijuana Laws (MML)

The use of marijuana has long been understood as a moral question in the United States (Bewley-Taylor 2009; Hollander and Patapan 2016, 15). Similar to arguments against alcohol, drug opponents in the US have traditionally linked drug use with moral dissipation and crime (Ferraiolo 2007; 2009). Between 1996 and 2011, 16 states enacted medical marijuana laws, after the adoption of the first policy addressing this issue occurred in 1996 in California. Basically, having medical marijuana legislation implies to instruct state law enforcement bodies not to enforce the federal Controlled Substances Act—which makes marijuana an illicit substance with no accepted medical value and instead assigns it an elevated potential for abuse, equated to narcotics such as heroin and LSD (Musto 1987). In this study, medical marijuana policy refers to legislation that provides meaningful protection for patients; for this, it is necessary that the policy a) removes state-level criminal penalties for possession and use of marijuana for medical purposes and b) provides a means of access (Marijuana Policy Project 2013). In other words, marijuana legislation allows patients to use and possess medical marijuana if approved by a medical doctor.

I identified a strikingly low number of academic research on state-level medical marijuana policy. These studies found out that the first MML did diffuse across borders and that states governed by the Republican party were less likely to pass MML (Ferraiolo 2004, 201), that citizen ideology is positively associated with medical marijuana enactments, whereas states' evangelical rate or share of religious fundamentalists decrease the odds of MML enactment (Bradford and Bradford 2016; Hannah and Mallinson 2017; Kim 2016).

4.1.4 Anti-Obesity (AO) Laws

Obesity is commonly defined as a body mass index (hereafter BMI) of at least 30 (Marlow 2013, 84). Obesity has climbed rapidly among the population of the United States (Boehmer et al. 2008; Dodson et al. 2009; Lankford et al. 2013; Marlow 2013). In the face of this, policymakers have sought effective means of slowing and reversing these trends, especially at the state level. The analysis of AO legislation examines a data set containing 105 laws enacted over 1998 to 2010 by state legislatures.

Scholarly work on obesity legislation has focused for the most part on legislation aimed at addressing childhood obesity over relatively narrow periods of time. These works concluded that enacting legislation to control child obesity was negatively associated with the number of lobbyists of companies that produce unhealthy foods (Dodson et al. 2009), although Boehmer et. al. does not find the same (Boehmer et al. 2008, 333); whereas Democratic control of both chambers decreases the odds of enacting childhood AO laws (Boehmer et al. 2008, 333), Democratic governors were found to increase the odds of enactment (Cawley and Liu 2008).

Scholarship from political science on obesity legislation targeted at the general public is less numerous. In general, these works point towards the lack of explanatory power of political factors (Marlow 2013, 86; Oliver and Lee 2005, 939; Rodriguez 2010). None of these works explored whether anti-obesity laws exhibit interdependence.

4.2 Variable Operationalization

Karch claims that, for a variety of reasons, legislators draw lessons from some models more than from others, and that the prevailing political circumstances has implications for the examples upon which they rely in the process of policy diffusion (Karch 2007b, 56). Such "variety of reasons" that the author refers to is of crucial importance in the field. It refers to the theoretical specification and the nature of interdependence that might exists amongst jurisdictions.

> "[the definition of] connectivity... is a matter of theory. It depends on the theoretical argument that is used in order to establish interdependence between units. The degree of connectivity between i and j cannot be estimated statistically, because there are insufficient degrees of freedom. The assumptions used to justify... interdependence are typically fairly strong ones that require a solid theoretical foundation" (Martin 2010, 10)

In this line, in order to investigate whether diffusion is driven by the mechanism described above—bounded-learning, one needs an indicator that can capture such effect, i.e., the diffusion variables in the models should reflect that information from specific sources are weighted more heavily. If the covariate reaches traditional statistical significance levels—accounting for internal determinants—it can be inferred that there is evidence that diffusion was preceded by a bounded-learning mechanism, all other things being equal (Gilardi 2004; Meseguer 2006).

So, how can we construct a morality-policy-theory-guided connectivity matrix? In other words, how can we model interdependence for this type of legislation? As mentioned above, if legislators are interested in gauging how their electorate might react to the enactment of a given morality policy based on the electoral consequences observed in morality policy adopting jurisdictions, and that this learning is bounded to a biased sample of jurisdictions selected on the basis of homophily, I believe that law makers will look for information in jurisdictions that reflect similar attributes related to morality legislation, i.e., namely values, culture and ideology (Butz, Fix, and Mitchell 2015; Doan 2014; Mooney and Schuldt 2008). This, in turn, requires the development of indicators that reflect that information was drawn from jurisdictions with similar scores on these characteristics. I will do this with two measures. One is a variable that reflects similarity regarding one specific aspect, and the other one reflects similarity in general. I now turn to describe these.

4.2.1 General Diffusion

The first diffusion variable draws on the propositions that geographical neighboring states in the USA share similar culture and values (Foster 1978; Gray 1994; Karch 2007b; Lutz 1987; Mooney 2001a; Mooney and Lee 1995; Seljan and Weller 2011, 353; Stream 1999) and that state morality policies reflect regional cultures in the US (Berry and Berry 2007; Haider-Markel 2001a). Moreover, it has been documented that information from neighboring jurisdictions is especially relevant in policy domains that involve "dramatic moments" (Butz, Fix, and Mitchell 2015; Hays and Glick 1997; Karch and Cravens 2014, 472), such as some of the responses that certain morality policies generate, e.g., people chaining themselves to cars or committing murder over abortion regulation and other laws with high moral content (Mooney and Schuldt 2008, 201).

Moreover, this literature has documented that there exists a constant cross-mixing of population and media amongst neighbors (Mintrom 1997), which more often than not alerts citizens and government officials about the existence of legislation in nearby states (Karch 2007b, 57–58), and which at times triggers changes in public opinion in adjacent states (Karch and Cravens 2014, 472; Pacheco 2012). The literature argues that all these reasons have created a historical pattern of looking at geographically proximate polities to retrieve information (Karch 2007b, 61; 2007b; 2007b, 57–58; Mooney 2001a; Sponsler 2010, 59–60).

In line with these arguments, I operationalize diffusion bounded to states that are similar in culture and values with a spatially-lagged dependent variable. Such operationalization goes in line with the reasoning of bounded learning, i.e., not all previous enactments are equal, rather, legislators use cognitive heuristics in that they give heavier weight to information from a specific group of states: states with similar cultures and values.

I will construct four measures to reflect alternative geographical diffusion effects as follows. On the one hand, I measure the number (i.e., sum) of adjacent neighbors that have adopted the same policy (component in the case of AO) before the current year, following the original coding of from Berry and Berry (1990). However, the latter measurement ignores potential effects from the non-continental states (Alaska & Hawaii) by assigning zeroes in all years. One alternative for this previously implemented in the literature is to include Alaska and Hawaii in the data set by coding the states in their nearest proximity as theoretical "virtual neighbors" (Sylvester and Haider-Markel 2016); given that they are the physical point-of-departure from the contiguous states and, it has been suggested that they might act as conduit for retrieving information on policies (Chamberlain and Haider-Markel 2005, 454). In this vein, I construct a second variable that considers Washington and Oregon as neighboring states of Alaska; whereas Washington, Oregon, and California were counted as neighboring states for Hawaii. A third coding criterion proposed in the literature (Imhof, 2006, 69; Kim 2016; King, Zeckhauser, and Kim 2004, 15–16) suggests coding the states that belong to the Pacific states region, Washington, Oregon, and California (U.S. Census Bureau), as the neighboring states of AK and HI. Therefore, I construct a third variable that uses the states of the Pacific region as a crude proxy to define the neighbors of the two non-continental states.

It is also conceivable that diffusion is occurring at levels that go beyond adjacency. Due to demographic and political differences, it seems unlikely that one state from a given region, e.g., a state from the south, looks to an adjacent state that belongs to another regions, e.g., east, for policy cues. Moreover, it is plausible that states consider and look at policy activity within their regions, especially now that advances in information and communication technologies and greater access to internet technology in general allow legislators to more easily observe policy innovation in states throughout the country. Therefore we need a variable that implies that state leaders are attuned to the politics and policy actions of the region (Berry and Berry 2007; Chamberlain and Haider-Markel 2005; Mooney 2001a). For this, one needs first to come up with divisions whose states actually share relevant characteristics. To do this, the literature has relied on divisions as defined by the U.S. Census Bureau (Chamberlain and Haider-Markel 2005, 450 {Bright 2013 #299; Doyle 2006; Mooney 2001a; Paynter 2008; Stoutenborough and Beverlin 2008)} (Berry and Berry 2007; Haider-Markel 2001a), which divides the country in nine divisions (U.S. Census Bureau).

To account for possible diffusion effects from policy activity in a region, I calculate the sum of neighbors from the same Census division that have adopted the same policy before the current year. Moreover, such a regional variable is suggested to best capture the concept of localized communications networks of policy experts (Haider-Markel 2001a, 23).

Passage or rejection of a morality policy in a nearby jurisdiction, however, can motivate future enactments, or have the opposite effect, depending on the consequences that the policy maker had observed (Mooney 2001a, 105–6). For one, it can encourage policymakers to follow though if the electoral consequences of passage observed in proximate units are desirable. It can help lawmakers overcome opposition in their own state by pointing to the beneficial consequences of (not) adopting a given policy in other states (Mooney and Lee 1995). However, if the information retrieved from neighboring states is negative, policy activity in neighboring states can have the opposite effect.

In addition to revealing information about electoral repercussions of morality policy adoptions, a spatially-lagged variable could also capture information about media coverage in neighboring states, since they often share media markets. The direction here also depends on whether publicity about the policy in question was negative or positive. If a given morality law drew negative attention from the media, it is likely that the electoral repercussions are undesirable from the perspective of an electorally-minded policy maker, which in turn could decrease the likelihood of future enactments in neighboring states. Another reason why a spatial lag could exert a negative influence is when a legislator from a focal state learns from their neighbors that, although electoral repercussions might be associated with the enactment of a given morality policy, adoption of less extreme versions of the policy were not accompanied with electoral externalities, as observed in the diffusion of two morality policies: stand-your-ground laws (Butz, Fix, and Mitchell 2015, 368) and living-will laws (Hays and Glick 1997, 509)

A spatial lag could also capture public opinion spillover effects. Residents from a focal state might react to a policy enacted in a neighboring state by changing their aggregate opinions on that policy; if opinion in the focal state becomes supportive, electorally-minded officials from that state have an incentive to respond by enacting the that policy. This can be empirically tested—as already done regarding antismoking legislation (Pacheco 2012)—however, to do that, one requires issue-specific public opinion data, which is not available for the policies analyzed in this dissertation.

4.2.2 Specific Diffusion

The general diffusion measures yield evidence that information was drawn from jurisdictions that are similar regarding any of the moral attributes that contiguous states in the US share; however, we can isolate one.

I mentioned previously that morality policy engenders electoral uncertainty, and for that reason, law makers are interested in learning from reactions of the citizenry of other units with similar moral attributes regarding a given morality policy, as to gauge how their own constituents might react to a given morality policy. The ideology of previous adopters could be of special interest in this respect. Assuming that the enactment of a given policy can be seen by other governments and is interpreted as a signal that the policy is close to the adopting state's ideological ideal point, potential adopters could infer where a given policy lies on an ideological scale, based on the ideology of previous adopters (Carley, Nicholson-Crotty, and Miller 2017, 438). The dominance of the two-party system and the associated rhetoric of liberal versus conservative ideas in the US makes one expect that an ideological dimension is a plausible reference on which policymakers assess potential policies (Grossback 2004):

> "States of similar ideology share preferences on a host of policy issues. Thus, if a state sees that others of like ideology have adopted a policy, it can have confidence that the policy lies somewhere close to its own preferences and will be acceptable to its lawmakers and citizens." (Grossback 2004, 529)

In order to capture diffusion amongst ideologically similar states, I measure the absolute value of the ideological distance between a potential adopter and the governments of all states that have previously adopted the legislation in question. To measure the ideology of the states, I use the "NOMINATE measure of state government ideology" (Berry et al. 2010), which measures the average location of elected officials in each state on a liberal-conservative continuum. The value for the previous adopter(s) is represented by the ideology of the state(s) in the year of enactment. The previous adopters' ideology is a weighted average wherein the most recent state to adopt has the same weight as all other adopters. The formula is as follows:

Equation 1. Ideological Distance

Ideological Distance = ABS([(MostRecentAdopterIdeo.+ AllOtherAdopterIdeo.) / 2] − PotentialAdopter).

Source: Grossback (2004), Cruz-Aceves and Mallinson (2019)

The ideological diffusion variable is in line with the reasoning of bounded-learning through cognitive heuristics from homophilous units, where legislators give heavier weight to information from a specific group of states, where such reference group is defined by similarity, but on one specific attribute: ideology. This variable, moreover, not only reflects a state's prior beliefs about what constitutes proper policy, but also will not ignore the potential role of non-geographically adjacent polities. Last, it has been suggested that ideological information might be of special relevance for policy decisions regarding issues that may not be easily placed on a liberal-conservative scale (Grossback 2004, 525–26).

4.2.3 Domestic Factors

Unfortunately, there exists no data on citizens' opinion regarding all issues neither for all years nor states. Moreover, introducing issue-specific covariates would hinder cross-policy comparison, as discussed above. To overcome this, I will follow the strategy implemented in previous works that have opted to use an indicator of citizen ideology as a (broad) measure of state public opinion (Berry et al. 2010, 117; Haider-Markel and Kaufman 2006; Kim 2016; Lewis 2011; Mooney and Lee 2000). The ideology of the citizenry is certainly not the most accurate indicator of opinion on specific policy questions, especially because the general public more often than not has less defined political ideology than, for instance, interest groups or political activists, however, given that sometimes communication between citizen and policy maker is moderated by activists and interest groups, more often than not there are slippages in the communication process, for which, state public opinion and state policy are can be less congruent than general public ideology and the overall ideological slant of a state's policy regime (Mooney and Lee 2000, 229). In fact, public opinion about morality policies tends to be along the same line as the liberal-conservative continuum of mass public ideology (Kim 2016, 23–24).

For these reasons, I will use the "revised 1960–2010 citizen ideology series" variable (Berry et al. 2010, 117), which is calculated from the estimated ideologies of major party candidates for Congress, weighted by their electoral support. Higher scores indicate more liberal citizen ideologies (or public moods). This indicator reflects the average location of the active electorate in each state on a liberal-conservative scale. I also control for elected officials' liberalism, with the same measure used in the calculation of ideological diffusion (described above), as suggested elsewhere (Grossback 2004). The underlying (liberal-conservative) continuum for these indicators is defined by the authors as "operational ideology" or "policy mood", which reflect the kinds of policies preferred by citizens or elected officials, rather than self-identification (also known as "symbolic ideology").

To account for how competitive political environments and electoral pressure facing state legislatures influence policymaking, I will use the index (four-year moving average thereof) of district-level electoral competition (Holbrook and van Dunk 1993). This variable is constructed by averaging the winning candidates' share of the popular vote, the margin of victory, whether the seat is safe, and whether the election is contested. To account for the partisan influences, the analyses include two binary covariates indicating whether Republicans or Democrats control both the executive and legislative branches of government. The omitted reference category is divided-party government.

Churches play an important role for interest aggregation in the USA, in that they basically cluster like-minded individuals, and as such, they play a central role in morality policy debates (Meier 1994, 98). I follow previous comparative state policy studies that have tackled the difficulty to measure the extent of activity among religious groups by including a measure reflecting adherence to fundamentalist religious groups as proxy measure[16] (Berry and Berry 1990; Haider-Markel and Meier 1996; Mooney

---

16 Just as previous works Haider-Markel and Meier (1996); Pierce and Miller (2000){, I include in this variable the following denominations: Beachy Amish Mennonite Churches, Church of God General Conference, Church of God in Christ, Church of God of Prophecy, Church of Jesus Christ of Latter day Saints, Church of the Nazarene, Community Church of Christ, Conservative Baptist Association of America, Conservative Mennonite Conference, Evangelical Mennonite Church, Independent Free Will Baptists Associations, International Pentecostal Church of Christ, International Pentecostal Holiness Church, Mennonite

and Lee 1995; Pierce and Miller 2000; Pierce and Miller 2004). Given that the values of this variable (measured every ten years) have varied so minimally in the US states across in the last decades, that using the figures from 1990 or 2000 has proven inconsequential (Gibson 2004, 1139; Monogan 2012; Pierce and Miller 2000; Taylor 2007, 43), I will use figures from year 2000 (Jones et al. 2002).

Finding time-series cross-sectional advocacy/opposition data for all the 50 states has proven difficult (Haider-Markel and Meier 1996, 336; Yackee 2009). In order to test the influence of advocates and opponents, I will use the number of organizations registered to lobby, i.e., state interest groups (Gray and Lowery 1996; 2001, 267; Lowery et al. 2013)[17]. While the number of a state's interest groups does not automatically translate into activity, I believe that it does gauge the relative prevalence of advocacy and opposition vis-à-vis certain issues, as elsewhere suggested (Butz, Fix, and Mitchell 2015; Heidt-Forsythe 2017). In addition to being available for all states across two decades (recorded in 1990, 1997 & 2007), one further advantage of using this variable is that, although the number of interest groups relevant to each policy still differ, doing so allows one to represent, for all the policies analyzed in this project, advocacy and opposition with the same measure[18]. This makes the cross-policy comparison a less hazardous enterprise.

Brethren Churches, Mennonite Church USA, National Association of Free Will Baptists, Old Order Mennonite, Original Free Will Baptists, Pentecostal Church of God, Reformed Mennonite Church, Salvation Army, Seventh Day Adventist Church, Southern Baptist Convention, United Church of Christ.

17 Obtained directly from Prof. David Lowery (personal communication, July 2017). Data reflects organizations registered to lobby (rather than the lobbyist), assigned to 27 categories of substantive interests; data for 1990 1997 were gathered from state lobby registration lists from all 50 states; data for 2007 was collected from the National Institute on Money in State Politics. A "translation table" was used to match the most recent data with that from 1990 and 1997 Gray and Lowery (2001, 266–67); Lowery et al. (2013, 582–83).

18 A popular strategy to measure advocacy and opposition to certain policies is to use employment figures in specific sectors Mooney and Lee (1995); Ferraiolo (2014); Heidt-Forsythe (2013); Stream (1999); Meier (1994); Jacoby and Schneider (2001). This can be implemented when the literature has identified specific industries that might be (more or less) affected by the enactment of a given policy; in such scenario, the number of employees in such industries might serve as a proxy for advocacy/opposition vis-à-vis given laws. The population affected by same-sex related legislation, however, does not tend to cluster in a specific industry, which impedes using employment figures for this purpose. Instead, authors more often than not proxy advocacy/opposition to same-sex related legislation

In order to identify the most relevant interest groups for the policies analyzed in this project, I turned to policy-specific literature. It has been documented that the fiercest opposition to medical marijuana has come from state law enforcement (Ferraiolo 2004; 2007; 2009; 2014; Meier 1992; 1994); hence, I will measure opposition to MML with the number of state police & sheriff interest groups per 1 million population. Opposition to anti-obesity legislation has come mainly from interest groups that represent a specific group of enterprises (Goldman et al. 2014, 1); I will use the number of these state interest groups to measure opposition to AO legislation per 1 million population[19]. Advocacy for both medical marijuana and anti-obesity legislation has mainly been carried out by medical interest groups (Ferraiolo 2004; 2007; 2009; 2014; Heidt-Forsythe 2013; Rodriguez 2010); in this vein, I will measure advocacy for these two policies with the number of medical doctors', health professionals' and physicians' state interest groups per 1 million population. Finally, I measure opposition to same-sex marriage bans with the number of Lesbian, Gay, Bisexual and Transgender state interest groups.

To capture "problem severity" in the states, I also turn to policy-specific literature. The number of deaths caused by illnesses, whose derived pains have been argued to be alleviated by marijuana should serve as an indicator of the magnitude of the state's demand for Medical Marijuana Legislation (Imhof and Kaskie 2008). For this reason, in order to represent the number of people who may be eligible to benefit from having medical marijuana policy enacted, I use annual cancer death rates in a state (United States Census Bureau Various Years). I would have liked to include deaths caused by AIDS, however, data was missing for several states and years. Given that anti-obesity laws strive to reduce obesity rates—and in fact, states cover a high proportion of the costs of obesity—it is intuitive to represent the state context for anti-obesity legislation with numbers on obesity cases. In this vein, I use the percentage of a state's population that is obese (Centers for Disease Control and Prevention), as has been

---

with state membership in two national—vis-à-vis state—groups, namely "National Gay and Lesbian Task Force" and/or "Lambda Legal" Haider-Markel (2001a); Haider-Markel and Meier (1996); Lewis and Oh (2008), which is available only for year 1990. For these reasons, I do not use this alternative measurement.

19 These interest groups are: American Beverage Association, Campbell Soup Company, Coca-Cola Company, Corn Refiners Association, Del Monte Corporation, General Mills, Grocery Manufacturers Association, Hershey Company, Kraft Foods, Mars, Mondelēz International, National Confectioners Association, Nestlé, PepsiCo & Snack Food Association.

use in the past (Rodriguez 2010). For same-sex marriage bans, I use the percentage of coupled households that are same-sex partner households from the 2000 Census (United States Census Bureau Various Years).

Finally, education attainment is measured as the percent of the population over 25 years old with at least a BA degree (American Community Surveys). In the figure below, I show how each explanatory variable fits into the conceptual framework (see **A-Table 1** for a summary).

Figure 4. Independent Variables, according to the "Unified Model".

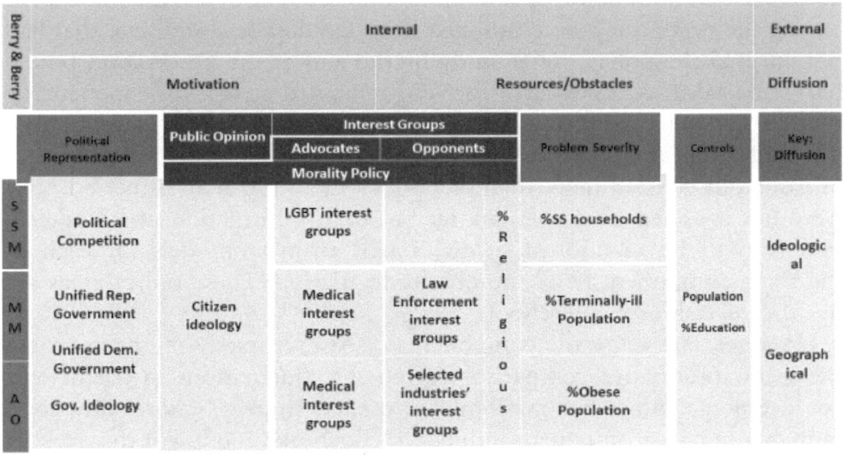

Source: author, based on (Berry and Berry 1990)

4.3 Event History Analysis (EHA)

Whereas there are several empirical strategies available to researchers to study diffusion, EHA has been recognized by political scientists as a particularly useful method to capture not only the impact of my key explanatory variable—diffusion—on legislative events, but also a more extensive set of questions, in that other theoretically relevant state characteristics can be accounted for in the statistical models (Box-Steffensmeier and Jones 2004; Heidt-Forsythe 2013; Sabatier 2007).

Using EHA implies to study the occurrence of the adoption of MML, SSM & AO legislation at a particular point in time using panel data (multiple-record-per-subject data). The outcome variable in the analyses is dichotomous, where states were assigned a value of zero for every year in which the event of interest (enactment of SSM, MML or AO) had not taken place and a value of one otherwise. Time was measured in years (discrete units). The analysis period starts in the year of the first event occurrence, i.e., 1996 for MML (California); 1995 for SSM (Utah); and 1998 for AO (Louisiana).

For the SSM, MM cases, single-spell EHA will be used, where the interest lies in the time until the enactment of the corresponding law occurs. The units of observation in these EHAs (and in models of AO components) are "state-year" observations, i.e., each of the 50 states in a given year. In these cases, once subjects were no longer "at risk" for experiencing the event, they were dropped from the data set. Any state that had not enacted the policy under study by the end of the observation period (2011 for MML & SSM, 2010 for AO) remained at risk for experiencing the event. Due to the high degree of legislative activity regarding AO, however, "repeated-spell" analyses were estimated for this policy, i.e., if jurisdictions enacted more than one policy in all the analysis period, they were not dropped from the data set but such information was modeled, too. As will be mentioned below, I will estimate models for each of the three components[20] of anti-obesity legislation. These policy areas are healthcare, taskforce and school.

However, analyzing the components of AO separately might not yield the most informative comparison, given that fluctuations in coefficients could emerge somewhat randomly, and such strategy ignores any commonality or cross-component influences. (Boehmke 2009). For that reason, I also present results of single and repeated spell pooled EHAs, which include the information of all components of AO. In these analyses, the unit of observation changes from state-year to state-year-component.

Discrete-time Specification

Now there are several alternatives of discrete-time EHA[21]. The one that I opted for in this work is the complementary log log (cloglog) function for

---

20 I will use the following terms interchangeably: policy component, policy area
21 One option that has gained attention recently are Cox models (Box-Steffensmeier and Jones 2004). Such semi-parametric tool allows (and requires) researchers to test whether the model violates the proportional hazards (PH) assumptions (Box-Steffensmeier and Jones 2004). There are graphical tests (by looking at martin gale residuals) and numeric tests (through the global and covariate specific Grambsch and Therneau tests). Given that the latter showed several violations

several reasons. On the one hand, the cloglog link function is theoretically more adequate for survival data than traditional functions such as logit or probit. Event history data in general and especially duration data of policy diffusion are right censored, in other words, observations for which the outcome is coded as 1 are relatively rare compared to observations for which $Y = 0$. However, the attributes of the cloglog distribution are appropriate to handle these types of data sets (Buckley and Westerland 2004).

One advantage of the cloglog function is that it is asymmetric, i.e., with a fat tail near probability = 0 and increasing rapidly approaching probability = 1 (Box-Steffensmeier and Jones 2004; Buckley and Westerland 2004; Leiser 2015, 28; Stoutenborough 2010; Stoutenborough and Beverlin 2008). In short, the slope of the curve for a complementary log log is more vertical than a logit or probit (Agresti 1990), which is desirable for this type of data sets (Buckley and Westerland 2004). The probability of the cloglog is:

Equation 2. Cloglog

$$\Pr(y_{it}, x_{it}\beta) = 1\text{-exp}\left[-\exp(x_{it}\beta)\right]$$

4.4 Cross-Case comparison

In the last section of the **Analysis** chapter, I will compare the diffusion of policies that differ in the degree to which they feature the characteristics of morality policy. I will do so by comparing the three policies analyzed in previous chapters. However, there is no consensus in the statistical literature whether coefficient estimates of dependent variables with different N are actually comparable (Allison 1999; Buis 2017; Mood 2010). In political science, few works have actually compared the coefficients of similar sets of independent variables for different response variables (Imhof, 152–54; Makse and Volden 2011, 119; Mitchell and Petray 2016, 293; Pacheco and Boushey 2014, 582; Pierce and Miller 2004, 165; Taylor et al. 2012).

In order to make the cross-case comparison more feasible, I implement a two stage seemingly unrelated estimation procedure (Weesie 1999, 34)—as

---

of the (PH) assumptions, I opted to estimate discrete-time EHA models instead. the complementary log-log model is very similar to the Cox model (Wong and Langevin 2007, 10; Jones and Branton 2005, 440); Allison 2014) elsewhere done (Philander and Abarbanel 2014; Taylor et al. 2012, 81)—without the policy-specific variables (opponents, advocates nor problem severity) and compare the magnitude of hazard ratios (exponentiated beta coefficients) across policies (Buis 2017, 11). In the first stage, I estimate single-spell models for SSM, MML and (pooled) AO using cloglog regression; models that exhibit duration dependency control for it with the best fitting specification thereof. Next, I combine the parameter estimates and variance covariance matrices into a single parameter vector and simultaneous covariance matrix to jointly estimate robust standard errors clustered by state; finally, I conduct Wald tests of equality for selected covariates across the equations. The latter tests will show whether the effect of variables differ significantly across models. For instance, if the hazard ratio for variable $X1$ resulting from seemingly unrelated estimation $M1$ is larger than the hazard ratio for variable $X1$ resulting from seemingly unrelated estimation $M2$, and if the Wald test of difference of the coefficients for variable $X1$ across models $M1$ and $M2$ reach traditional levels of statistical significance, one can conclude that the hazard ratio of $X1$ exerted a statistically significant larger effect on $M1$ than on $M2$ (Weesie 1999, 34; Philander and Abarbanel 2014; Taylor et al. 2012, 81).

4.5 Model Building

The path towards the selection of the best fitting model followed steps described in the literature of statistical modeling in general (Cleves 2010; Garson 2013; Hosmer, Lemeshow, and May 2008) and for social science in particular (Allison 2014; Box-Steffensmeier and Jones 2004). Briefly:
1. Analysis of multicollinearity
2. Analysis of duration dependency
3. Model Selection

4.5.1 Multicollinearity

The first step in selecting a final model consists of checking for multicolinearity. I do this by computing pairwise correlation coefficients for all variables. What we are looking for at this step is whether pairs of variables are correlated above the 0.75 level (Nelson 2007).

4.5.2 Duration Dependency/Time Specification in EHA Models

Discrete-time models have to deal with the issue of "duration dependency". An adequate measurement of temporal dependence is a recent area of scholarly inquiry in the study of policy diffusion (Box-Steffensmeier and Jones 2004; Leiser 2015). The main reason for modeling duration dependence in discrete-time models is the unrealistic expectation of a flat hazard rate for event occurrence over time (Box-Steffensmeier and Jones 2004; Wong and Langevin 2007). Accounting for temporal dependence among observations and across the cumulative risk set allows one to enhance the explanatory power of discrete event history models (Buckley and Westerland 2004).

Recently, a strategy to model duration dependency that allows to conserve degrees of freedom with the least number of assumptions about the functional form of time has been proposed in the literature: estimate full[22] models that incorporate control variables from a locally weighted regression (lowess) of the probability of adopting a given policy on the linear time counter variable, splines, logarithmic-, quadratic-, cubic- transformation of- or linear time (Box-Steffensmeier and Jones 2004; Buckley and Westerland 2004; Beck, Katz, and Tucker 1998; Wong and Langevin 2007). In order to discriminate amongst and select the best fitting form of time I perform Wald tests[23], which is commonly used to evaluate the difference between nested models[24] (Chen et al. 2003; Doyle 2006; Wong and Langevin 2007).

---

22 the duration dependency analyses result from estimating full models including the ideological diffusion variable and the geographical measure that includes AK and HI by coding the states that belong to the Pacific states region as their neighboring states (Washington, Oregon, and California) as elsewhere done (Imhof and Kaskie 2008, 69; Kim 2004, 15–16). Which geographical diffusion variable is included in the duration dependency analyses is inconsequential, because, as will be shown, the spatial and regional lag variables are highly correlated

23 Due to the methodological limitations of the likelihood-ratio test within cluster-correlated data Williams (2000) and the similarity of both model specification tools, I will follow the routine from the literature and rely on the Wald test to assess correct model specification through rejection of the null hypothesis (Wong and Langevin 2007);; Doyle 2006). Moreover, given my strategy to account for serial autocorrelation by clustering observations on each state in order to correct standard errors and make model performance reliable (Wong and Langevin 2007) described below, computation of such standard errors impedes the software to execute LR tests

24 One model is considered nested in another one if the former can be generated by imposing restrictions on the parameters of the latter.

This test allows researchers to determine whether constraining a given set of parameters to zero (leaving them out of the equation) significantly reduces the fit of a given model. Basically, the Wald test assesses the null hypothesis that the coefficients of a given set of covariates are zero by generating a chi-squared value and a corresponding p-value, if the latter is smaller than one, it is evidence that including the variables for which the null hypothesis was tested produces a statistically significant improvement in the fit of the model (Chen et al. 2003).

4.5.3 Model Selection

Models were adjudicated following the Akaike Information Criterion (AIC) and Bayes Information Criterion (BIC), as suggested in the literature (Box-Steffensmeier and Jones 2004; Karch and Cravens 2014; Leiser 2015; Paynter 2008; 2008; Wong and Langevin 2007; Wong and Shen 2002), because I am basically comparing different models with different specifications of geographical policy diffusion. The Bayes Information Criterion presents us with an alternative strategy for reviewing model performance relative to the maximum likelihood parameters and the total number of observations. The AIC imposes a penalty when parameters are added and the BIC penalizes additional parameters even more harshly than AIC; hence, parsimony is rewarded. In general, the models with the smallest AIC or BIC are considered to be the best fitting models. I follow the literature (Raftery 1996; Wong and Langevin 2007, 461) in calculating the BIC based on the number of state enactments. Formally:

Equation 3. Bayes Information Criterion

$$BIC = Deviance + [(1n (Number of Policy Enactments)) p)]$$

5. Analysis

The sections **Same Sex Marriage Bans**, **Medical Marijuana Laws**, **Anti-Obesity Legislation** are divided into four primary categories: dependent variable, descriptive statistics, model selection, results (of reduced and full models) and discussion: each analysis begins with descriptions of the response variable, followed by means, standard deviations, etc., of the independent variables; afterwards, correlation coefficients for the independent variables and duration dependency analyses are presented. Next, full models are presented and their empirical results are described; finally, the full models are discussed in the context of the hypotheses. Moreover, the final model will be accompanied by four reduced models (for SSM and MML, five for AO). Reduced models are to illustrate the relative effects of the categories of the "unified model" as follows: the first subset looks only at the variables for political representation, the second one includes only variables from the "morality policy" category. The third subset estimates models with variables from the latter two categories, followed by a fourth model that adds "problem severity" and "controls". Results of these reduced models will be briefly described, too.

5.1 Same Sex Marriage Bans

5.1.1 Dependent Variable

The response variable was obtained from Lewis (2011); it indicates whether a polity enacted its first SSM ban in each year from 1994 to 2006. I follow previous studies and disregard whether the first SSM ban was enacted as a statutory law or through constitutional amendment, and if the law/amendment was passed by legislatures or citizen legislation (Haider-Markel 2001a; Lewis 2011). Moreover, throughout the period under examination, SSM has been primarily addressed with legislative vehicles rather than through the judicial process or citizen initiatives[25]. Once an

---

25 In the analysis period, only five states used citizen legislation to pursue their initial prohibitions (less than 12 %), whereas the other (38) jurisdictions passed their initial SSM bans through traditional legislative means. However, ballot

event occurs, the adopting state is dropped out of the analysis. In the analysis period, 43 states passed laws prohibiting recognition of SSM, as can be seen in the following map.

Figure 5. Year of Enactment of SSM ban

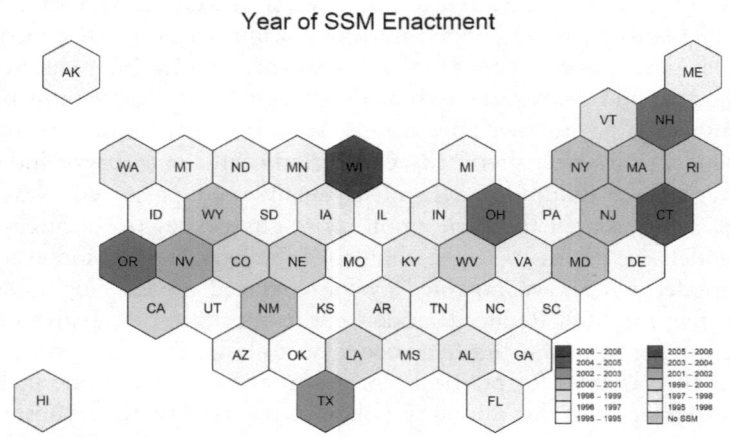

Source: Author

5.1.2 Descriptive Statistics

The table below presents the number of observations, mean, standard deviation, minimum and maximum values for all variables for the analysis period.

Table 1. Descriptive Statistics Same-Sex Marriage Bans

Variable	N	Mean	SD	Min	Max
SSM Adoption	316	0.14	0.34	0.00	1.00
Electoral Competition	316	40.69	10.59	16.39	63.56
Unified D. Government	316	0.18	0.39	0.00	1.00

initiatives were enormously successful when employed: only one of these failed to pass Lewis (2011)

Variable	N	Mean	SD	Min	Max
Unified R. Government	316	0.20	0.40	0.00	1.00
Government Ideology	316	49.81	21.10	4.05	89.00
Citizen Ideology	316	50.94	15.78	9.25	88.19
Opponents	316	0.65	1.79	0.00	8.52
Relig. Fundamentalists	316	10.81	9.52	1.46	67.60
Problem Severity	316	0.25	0.21	0.02	0.80
Population	316	15.06	1.04	13.08	17.34
Education	316	23.96	5.74	12.30	40.40
Time control (spline1)	316	4.80	3.39	1.00	13.00
Time control (spline2)	316	1.27	2.02	0.00	7.64
Time control (spline3)	316	0.40	0.73	0.00	2.83
Ideol. Dissimilarity	316	15.80	16.73	0.00	70.45
Spatial Lag	316	1.31	1.69	0.00	6.00
Spatial Lag_II	316	1.31	1.69	0.00	6.00
Spatial Lag_III	316	1.31	1.69	0.00	6.00
Regional Lag	316	1.53	1.94	0.00	7.00

Source: Author

Let us focus on the variable from which the ideological distance is calculated. In Figure 6, I plot the average of the ideology of the governments of non and adopter states (bottom panel) and the average ideology of all governments during analysis time (upper panel). In the bottom panel, we observe that in average, governments of states that adopted same-sex marriage bans are more conservative than SSM-bans non-adopters. Amongst SSM-ban adopters, however, we see in the upper panel of Figure 6 that some of their governments are rather liberal.

Figure 6. Government Ideology by (Non- & Adopter) State

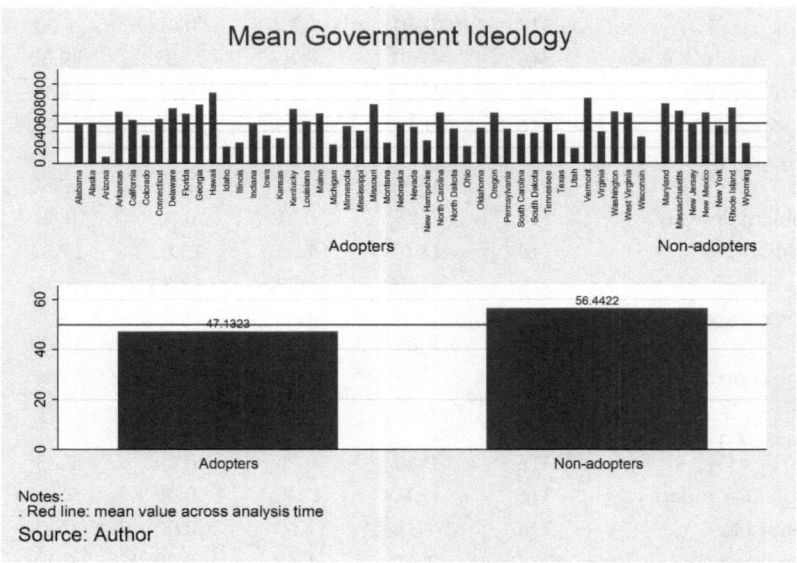

In Figure 7, I plot the ideology of the governments measured at the year of enactment of a same-sex marriage ban (bottom panel). Given that several states enacted bans in the same year, I also show the average government ideology by year (upper panel). In the bottom panel, we see that a handful of governments of ban adopters actually exhibited liberal ideologies. However, if we consider the annual average government ideology, the upper panel of Figure 7 shows that only in years 1998, 1999 and 2005 governments of SSM ban adopters were (on average) more liberal.

Figure 7. Government Ideology by (Adopter) State

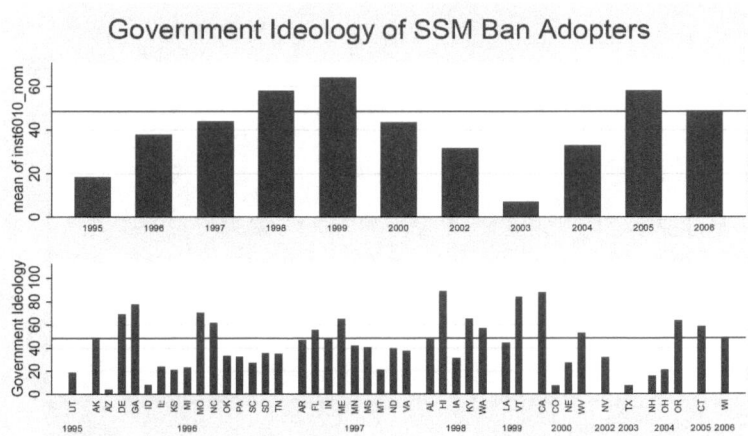

Notes:
. Red line: mean government ideology of all states during SSM ban adoption years
. Top Panel: Bars represent mean ideology of ban adopters measured at time of enactment
. Bottom Panel: Bars represent ideology measured at time of enactment
Source: Author

Let us explore the diffusion variables. Below, I show maps[26] with the values of two diffusion measures for years 1998 and 2005. For the ideological dissimilarity variable, hexagons with darker colors have larger ideological distances regarding jurisdictions that enacted the policy in question in previous years. For instance, in year 2005, Nevada, Colorado, North Dakota and the other 5 states with the same color were ideologically very similar to the jurisdictions that between 1994 – 2004 enacted a SSM. For the geographical measure, I used the specification that uses the states of the "Pacific region" —WA, OR & CA (U.S. Census Bureau)—to define the neighbors of the two non-continental states, AK and HI (Imhof, 69; Kim 2016; King, Zeckhauser, and Kim 2004, 15–16); darker colors indicate a higher number of adoptions by neighbors in *t-1*.

---

26 I opted to use maps with hexagonal units in order to have a clearer picture of the covariates in question, especially for jurisdictions with relatively small territories, e.g., the polities from the north east.

Figure 8. Maps of Diffusion of Same-Sex Marriage Bans in years 1998 & 2005

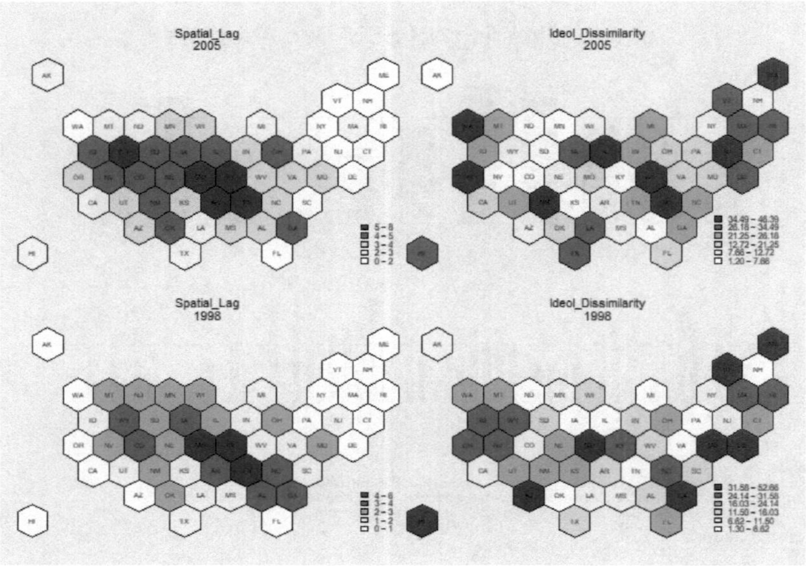

Source: Author

5.1.3 Model Selection

I will guide the reader through the model building process, as described in the section Model Building.

The first step in selecting a final model consists of checking for multicolinearity. I found no evidence of multicolinearity amongst the variables (see A-Table 2), i.e., pairwise correlation coefficients did not show that any pair of variables were correlated above the traditional 0.75 level (Nelson 2007). The spatial diffusion variables are highly correlated (0.85). This is obvious, since they are similar versions of themselves, and represents no problem, since none of these covariates will be included in the same model. Splines are also highly correlated, which is also to be expected and represents no problem for estimation (Allison 2014; Box-Steffensmeier and Jones 2004).

The next step consists in identifying if the data exhibits duration dependency and how to account for it (Box-Steffensmeier and Jones 2004; Buckley and Westerland 2004; Carter and Signorino 2010; Beck, Katz, and

Tucker 1998; Wong and Langevin 2007, 454–55). To test for different specifications of duration dependency, I estimated several models and tested
the fit against a null model where no duration dependency was assumed,
namely, I estimated models with internal and external determinants[27] with
six functional forms for the baseline duration dependence, specifically linear, logarithmic, quadratic, cubic, splines and locally weighed regression
(lowess). To evaluate which of these characterizations of duration dependency best fits the data, I computed the Wald test against the null model
(which assesses the null hypothesis that the coefficients of each measure of
time are zero); if the resulting p-value of a given estimated statistic is lower
than.1, it can be considered as evidence that such characterization of time
produces a statistically significant improvement in the fit of the model
(Chen et al. 2003; Wong and Langevin 2007). If more than one functional
forms of time provide superior fit to the data than when compared to
the null model, one would prefer the model with the largest chi square
from the Wald tests (Box-Steffensmeier and Jones 2004). Time represented
with cubic splines provides a better fit for the SSM ban models, as can be
seen in A-Table 8. I will proceed with the model adjudication routine by
including such best fitting transformation of time.

Finally, one needs to compare the AIC and BIC statistics of nested
models with internal and external determinants that differ in the characterization of geographical diffusion; I include these statistics at the bottom
of **Table 2**, which presents coefficients from the best fitting cloglog models
(A-Table 5 for exponentiated coefficients; see A-Table 21 for a summary).
In that table, we observe consistency for the most part across models.
Regardless of how we model geographic diffusion effects, internal determinants and the ideological similarity behave in a consistent manner.
The only difference in the models is that when geographic diffusion is
represented with a covariate that captures policy activity in the region we
observe (last column) that the 90 % confidence interval for the regional
diffusion variable includes zero. The AIC and BIC statistics, however, indi-

---

27 As previously mentioned, the spatial and regional lag variables are highly corre-
    lated; hence, which geographical diffusion variable is included in the duration
    dependency analyses is inconsequential. Hence, the external determinants includ-
    ed in the all duration dependency analyses are the ideological diffusion variable
    and the geographical measure that includes AK and HI by coding the states
    that belong to the Pacific states region as their neighboring states (Washington,
    Oregon, and California) following Imhof (2006, 69) and King, Zeckhauser, and
    Kim (2004, 15–16)

cate that any of the models with spatial lags (columns 1 to 3) are preferred; in fact, the results of the first three columns are identical.

Table 2. Same-Sex-Marriage Bans Diffusion Models

	SSM	SSM	SSM	SSM
Electoral Competition	0.05	0.05	0.05	0.05
	(0.02)**	(0.02)**	(0.02)**	(0.02)**
Unified D. Government	-0.04	-0.04	-0.04	-0.31
	(0.77)	(0.77)	(0.77)	(0.74)
Unified R. Government	1.82	1.82	1.82	1.77
	(0.71)**	(0.71)**	(0.71)**	(0.71)**
Government Ideology	0.02	0.02	0.02	0.02
	(0.02)	(0.02)	(0.02)	(0.02)
Citizen Ideology	-0.02	-0.02	-0.02	-0.01
	(0.02)	(0.02)	(0.02)	(0.02)
Opponents	-1.62	-1.62	-1.62	2.12
	(9.58)	(9.58)	(9.58)	(10.15)
Relig. Fundamentalists	0.10	0.10	0.10	0.10
	(0.03)***	(0.03)***	(0.03)***	(0.03)***
Problem Severity	1.71	1.71	1.71	2.53
	(1.74)	(1.74)	(1.74)	(1.85)
Population	0.11	0.11	0.11	0.13
	(0.19)	(0.19)	(0.19)	(0.22)
Education	-0.05	-0.05	-0.05	-0.02
	(0.06)	(0.06)	(0.06)	(0.05)
Ideol. Dissimilarity	-0.01	-0.01	-0.01	-0.00
	(0.02)	(0.02)	(0.02)	(0.02)
Spatial Lag	-0.33			
	(0.16)**			
Spatial Lag_II		-0.33		
		(0.16)**		
Spatial Lag_III			-0.33	
			(0.16)**	
Regional Lag				0.04
				(0.16)
Chi2	80.86	80.86	80.86	80.15
Df_M	15	15	15	15
P	0.00	0.00	0.00	0.00

	SSM	SSM	SSM	SSM
Ll	-87.97	-87.97	-87.97	-89.85
N	316	316	316	316
AIC	207.9455	207.9455	207.9455	211.7054
BIC	236.1247	236.1247	236.1247	239.8846

* $p<0.1$; ** $p<0.05$; *** $p<0.01$
Notes:
Coefficients from cloglog models with robust standard errors clustered on state.
Models control for time dependency with cubic splines (not shown, significant in all models).
A- & BIC calculated based on 43 events.
All significance tests are two-tailed.

5.1.4 Results

This section is divided in two parts. In section Reduced Models, I will provide a brief description of results of models that include different vectors of variables according to the conceptual categories of the Unified Model (columns 1–4 of **Table 3**). In section Final Model, I will describe results of the model that includes all covariates, included in last column of Table 3.

All models control for serial autocorrelation in the unobserved relationships among state-year observations by clustering observations on each subject (state), which yields corrected standard errors and reliable model performance (Buckley and Westerland 2004; Wong and Langevin 2007, 18). Although not shown for space limitations, all models also control for time dependency according to the best fitting specification of time, i.e., cubic splines (see A-Table 8).

Table 3. Reduced and Final Models of Same-Sex Marriage Bans

	1	2	3	4	5
Electoral Competition	1.00		1.05	1.05	1.05
	(0.02)		(0.03)**	(0.02)**	(0.02)**
Unified D. Government	1.57		0.69	0.69	0.96
	(0.92)		(0.42)	(0.45)	(0.74)
Unified R. Government	1.97		4.20	5.85	6.15
	(1.13)		(2.59)**	(4.23)**	(4.40)**
Government Ideology	0.99		1.02	1.02	1.02
	(0.01)		(0.02)	(0.02)	(0.02)

	1	2	3	4	5
Citizen Ideology		0.99	0.99	0.99	0.98
		(0.02)	(0.02)	(0.02)	(0.02)
Opponents		0.97	1.01	1.02	0.98
		(0.10)	(0.08)	(0.10)	(0.09)
Relig. Fundamentalists		1.05	1.10	1.11	1.10
		(0.02)**	(0.03)***	(0.03)***	(0.03)***
Problem Severity				10.77	5.54
				(19.69)	(9.66)
Population				1.14	1.11
				(0.23)	(0.21)
Education				0.98	0.95
				(0.05)	(0.06)
Spatial Lag					0.72
					(0.11)**
Ideol. Dissimilarity					0.99
					(0.02)
Chi2	37.93	71.84	73.13	67.93	80.86
Df_M	7	6	10	13	15
P	0.00	0.00	0.00	0.00	0.00
Ll	-103.62	-99.88	-91.28	-89.93	-87.97
N	316	316	316	316	316

$* p<0.1; ** p<0.05; *** p<0.01$

Notes:

Hazard Ratios from cloglog models with robust standard errors clustered on state.
Models control for time dependency with splines (not shown).
All significance tests are two-tailed.

5.1.4.1 Reduced Models

The model with only political representation variables (column one of Table 3) indicates that, if we ignore diffusion effects, demographic and morality policy factors, none of the coefficients for the political predictors reaches traditional levels of statistical significance. If we focus only on factors pointed out in the morality policy literature (column 2), only the coefficient for religious fundamentalists is significantly associated with the outcome variable: a 1-unit increase in the latter is substantially correlated (p<0.05) with an estimated 5 % increase in the odds[28] of adopting a same-sex marriage ban.

When we combine morality policy and political representation covariates in a model (column three), but still ignore demographic and diffusion factors, the results from the model with morality policy variables hold— although the estimated effect of religious fundamentalists and its corresponding significance level increases to a positive 10 % (p<0.01) association with the odds of event occurrence; in addition to that, two factors from the political representation category turn out significant: electoral competition and unified Republican governments are now positively associated with the dependent variable (p<0.05). A one-unit increase of the former is associated with an estimated 5 % increase in the hazard of adopting a same sex marriage ban, whereas polities controlled by Republicans face a 4.20 greater hazard of enacting a SSM ban.

If we add demographic factors to the equation, we observe in column four of Table 3 that the confidence interval of the hazard ratios for the population, education attainment, and the percentage of same-sex coupled households includes 1; however, the results from the reduced model from column three that ignored demographic factors hold, the only differences are that unified Republican governments face a 5.85 greater hazard of enacting same sex marriage bans (p<0.05) and a one-unit increase in the religious fundamentalists variable is significantly associated with an 11 % hazard of event occurrence (p<0.01).

Interestingly, in any of the reduced models (columns 1 to 4 of Table 3) did I find evidence that neither Democratic governments, ideology (neither of the government nor of the citizenry) nor interest groups were substantially associated with the hazard of passing same sex marriage bans.

5.1.4.2 Final Model

When we add diffusion effects to the equation, we observe in column 5 of Table 3 that a similar vector of domestic factors that turned out statistically significant in models that combined variables from political representation

---

28 Hazard ratios are obtained by exponentiating regression coefficients, and have a similar interpretation as "odds ratios", i.e., hazard ratios greater (less) than one indicate that a unit increase in the covariate corresponds to an increase (decrease) in the hazard of experiencing the event (enacting the corresponding legislation), all else equal (Cleves 2010).

and morality policy, with and without demographic factors (columns 3 and 4) also reached levels of statistical significance: electoral competition (alpha level 0.05), unified republican government (p<0.01) and religious fundamentalists (p<0.01). Controlling for internal and external factors, a one-unit increase in the level of electoral competition increases the hazard of banning SSM by an estimated 5 %; each additional adherent to a fundamentalist doctrine is associated with an estimated 10 % increase of the hazard of banning the recognition of SSM. We also see that the estimated hazard of enacting a same-sex marriage ban for those jurisdictions with unified Republican governments is 6.15 times the hazard of passing the same law for jurisdictions without unified Republican governments. The rest of the variables did not reach traditional levels of statistical significance.

Figure 9. Coefficient Plot of Diffusion Variables, Controlling for Domestic Factors

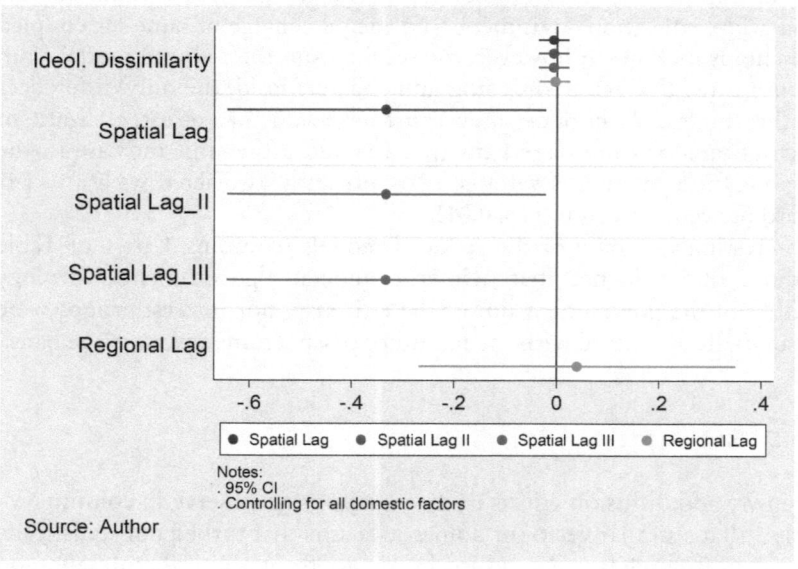

Turning to our key dependent variables, contrary to my expectations, the coefficient for the ideological diffusion variable did not reach traditional levels of statistical significance. On the other hand, geographic diffusion turned out statistically significant and negative—as hypothesized; except for when geography is captured with a regional instead of an adjacency-lagged variable, as can be seen in Figure 9[29], which plots the coefficients for the diffusion variables and their 95 % confidence intervals, controlling for all domestic factors. If we exponentiate the coefficients for the three spatial lagged variables, we observe that a one additional adjacent state that enacts a law that bans homosexual marriage is significantly associated with a 28 % decrease in the hazard of banning same-sex marriage in a given state.

In the model that incorporates all covariates, the rest of the variables did not reach traditional levels of statistical significance.

5.1.5 Discussion

The case of same-sex marriage bans shows for the most part consistency with the theoretical expectations. We observe that more factors highlighted in the literature on morality policy have predictive power for the enactment of SSM; however, the picture would be incomplete without the effect of political representation and diffusion variables.

Passage of this policy—that was included in this project as an example of legislation that reflects all theoretical characteristics of morality policy— in a nearby jurisdiction j could have discouraged policymakers from unit i to ban homosexual marriage for several reasons. On the one hand, officials might have observed that passage of this law in units with similar culture and values had negative electoral consequences, e.g., they might have observed "electoral retaliation" in neighboring polities (Butz, Fix, and Mitchell 2015, 368; Haider-Markel 2001b, 44; Mooney 2001a, 105–6; Sponsler 2010, 54; 2011, 121–22). In other words, legislators might have learned from SSM ban enactments in similar states that the political risks of doing so were high, which in turn inhibited future ban enactments. This goes in line with the negative geographic diffusion pattern observed in another subnational analysis of legislation in the US involving moral content, namely living-will laws (Hays and Glick 1997, 511)—which were adopted between years 1976 and 1991 by a comparable number of states (45). Other policy areas that did not involve a high moral content also

---

29 The interpretation of coefficient plots is straightforward. The length of the lines mirrors the magnitude of confidence intervals (CI) of regression tables, and the location of the point estimates (indicated by a dot) indicates the magnitude of the coefficient; if a given CI includes zero, it can be considered as evidence of a non-statistically significant effect of that covariate on a given outcome variable.

exhibited this pattern, i.e.,, R&D tax credit (Miller and Richard 2010, 22), finance innovations (Lacy and Tandberg 2014, 641), renewable energy policy (Stoutenborough 2010, 166), film incentives (Leiser 2014, 33), inpatient health care transparency laws (Eaton 2013, 103), undocumented student tuition policies (Sponsler 2011, 96) performance funding to incentivize student retention (Li 2017, 766) and merit-based student grant programs (Doyle 2006, 273).

Another explanation for the negative diffusion effect is that legislators might have decided to support more nuanced versions of SSM bans instead, based on what they observed in their moral peers. Policy makers could have learned from their neighbors that this policy generated undesirable consequences, e.g., negative press coverage, divisive controversies, hence, SSM bans in i could have motivated adoption of less extreme measures in j, similar to what was observed in the diffusion of another policy with moral content, i.e., stand-your ground laws (Butz, Fix, and Mitchell 2015, 356). The national figures on public opinion on same-sex marriage can to some extent support the interpretation of legislators learning either not to support SSM bans or to adopt less extreme versions of it. As I commented earlier, although the majority of the people were supportive of SSM bans at the time the first bans were enacted, negative attitudes towards same-sex marriage actually decreased from 65 % in 1996 to 53 % in 2005, whereas support for homosexual marriage grew from 27 % to 36 % in the same period (Pew Research Center 2011, 14). In other words, the retrenchment in the group of people that supported SSM bans was larger than the expansion of SSM-bans opponents—3 percentage points, which might indicate that the electoral retaliation from the growing number of people against SSM bans could have become more tangible. In other words, although marginally informative because they reflect national figures, these trends could support the idea that enactments of SSM bans could have brought about negative electoral consequences, in that although SSM bans were preferred by the majority, a growing number of gay-marriage supporters could have responded with electoral retaliation, which was in turn observed by legislators from neighboring jurisdictions, who ultimately were discouraged to enact these laws or motivated to enact less comprehensive versions thereof.

When we shift our attention to a specific group of similar states, namely, ideologically aligned jurisdictions, it seems that information retrieved from this group was not relevant for future enactments of SSM bans, as observed by the statistically insignificant coefficient for adoptions by ideologically dissimilar states. In other words, legislators responded to the uncertainty generated by this policy by looking at the aftermath of adopting SSM bans only in states with similar values and culture. The fact that information from ideologically similar states was not relevant is not all too surprising, though. On the one hand, legislators could have believed that the information that they retrieved from their neighboring states was enough so as to make a decision of a policy that is highly salient and that involves relatively little technical complexity. Moreover, it has been suggested that lawmakers might observe the aftermath of policy enactment in ideologically similar jurisdictions so as to gauge how their electorate might react to a given policy based on how the electorate of other units reacted, but especially for policies that cannot be easily identified as liberal or conservative, because estimating how the home electorate might react to these policies becomes more difficult (Grossback 2004, 523). All of the works reviewed in the literature classified same-sex marriage-related laws clearly as conservative policies; hence, there might have been little reasons to factor in how the electorate would react to a policy that would be clearly supported by conservative citizens and elites.

Contrary to morality policy scholarship that emphasizes the role of organized interests and the ideology of the elite, the variables of opposition to SSM bans and government ideology did not turn out statistically significant; however, religious-based advocacy did turn out as expected. This can indicate that during the analysis period (1995–2006), local opposition to SSM bans was not as well organized as their advocates. On the other hand side, if we assume that support for SSM bans was higher in the analysis period—based on the national figures earlier mentioned—this finding gives partial support to the claim that when a majority of the population supports a given morality policy—also known as "consensus morality policy", there is more room for activists and the ideology of the elected officials to exert influence on the odds that the policy is enacted (Mooney and Lee 2000, 230), although, as mentioned above, I did not find that SSM-bans opponents nor the government's ideology exerted a significant influence.

The positive and significant coefficient for electoral competition supports the arguments that consensus morality policies can give rise to entrepreneurial politics (Lewis 2011; Mooney and Lee 2000), and that this is especially likely when the level of electoral insecurity is high (Mooney and Lee 1995). If public support in the states actually mirrors the national figures mentioned above, legislators might have had clearer signals that a majority of the population supported SSM bans, for which there existed great incentive for them to compete for public favor by showing their support regarding this policy. It was also suggested that the likelihood that politicians react in such an entrepreneurial fashion should be higher as the level of electoral competition in a state rises, given that the latter indicates greater insecurity of their electoral status. This seems to be confirmed by the influence of electoral competition that I identified, contrary to previous works that did not find discernible effects of electoral competition and same-sex related legislation (Haider-Markel 2001a; 2001b, 44).

Last, my results indicate that states with unified Republican governments, but not states controlled by the Democratic party were more likely to enact SSM bans, which goes in line with the claims that, on the one hand, the Republican party is not only especially active in their opposition same-sex marriage (Haider-Markel 2001a, 14), but that opposing such issues represent an electoral opportunity for the Republican but not for the Democratic party (Engeli, Green-Pedersen, and Larsen 2012, 168; Tatalovich and Daynes 2011).

5.2 Medical Marijuana Laws

5.2.1 Dependent Variable

The response variable indicates whether a polity enacted its first MML —through which citizens are allowed to possess and use marijuana for medical purposes if approved by a medical doctor—in each year from 1996 to 2011. It was obtained from a comprehensive report (Marijuana Policy Project 2013) and crosschecked in states' government websites. Once an event occurs, the adopting state is dropped out of the analysis. In the analysis period, 16 states passed laws allowing medical use of marijuana, as can be seen in the following map.

Figure 10. Year of Enactment of MML

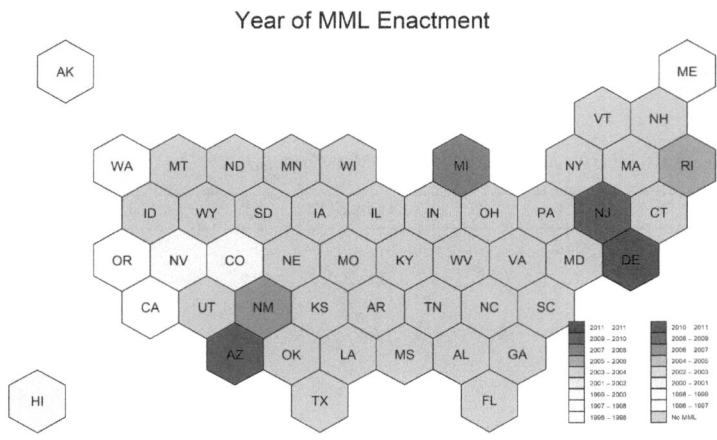

Source: Author

MML were enacted by the initiative process and by state legislatures[30] (see A-Figure 1). However, consistent with previous research (Bradford and Bradford 2016; Hannah and Mallinson 2017; Witte 2013; 2013), the method of passage was not reflected in the construction of the dependent variable, for the event of interest is the propensity of states to enact medical marijuana legislation. Although MML are similar in terms of qualifying conditions, allowance of personal production, permissible amounts of marijuana possession and plant counts per patient (Crawford 2013, 9; Marijuana Policy Project 2013), there is variation in design and implementation, e.g., depending on the state, patients may cultivate their own marijuana, designate a caregiver to do so, and/or obtain marijuana from a dispensary (Marijuana Policy Project 2013). Such variations are not the main focus of the present study; instead, the initial passage of these laws is the primary focus, representing a puzzling decision to liberalize/reform laws related to access and use of a historically and federally strictly prohibited substance.

---

30 In the analysis period, ten states have used citizen legislation to pursue their initial MML, whereas the other (6) jurisdictions passed their initial MML through traditional legislative means (Washington, D.C. also enacted a MML in this time span. New Mexico enacted its MML through the legislature, although the state has direct democracy means available.

5.2.2 Descriptive Statistics

The table below presents the number of observations, mean, standard deviation, minimum and maximum values for all variables for the analysis period.

Table 4. Descriptive Statistics Medical Marijuana Laws

Variable	N	Mean	SD	Min	Max
MML Adoption	673	0.02	0.15	0.00	1.00
Electoral Competition	673	37.78	10.97	12.05	62.22
Unified D. Government	673	0.18	0.39	0.00	1.00
Unified R. Government	673	0.30	0.46	0.00	1.00
Government Ideology	673	46.09	22.89	0.00	91.03
Citizen Ideology	673	48.99	15.37	8.45	95.97
Opponents	673	10.96	10.57	0.00	62.55
Relig. Fundamentalists	673	15.00	12.83	1.46	67.60
Problem Severity	673	171.30	33.41	84.90	233.90
Population	673	15.13	0.96	13.08	17.27
Education	673	25.84	5.25	14.20	44.40
advocates	673	18.15	15.78	0.00	94.69
Ideol. Dissimilarity	673	18.69	14.51	0.00	60.22
Spatial Lag	673	0.42	0.85	0.00	4.00
Spatial Lag_II	673	0.40	0.84	0.00	4.00
Spatial Lag_III	673	0.41	0.85	0.00	4.00
Regional Lag	673	0.40	0.97	0.00	5.00

Source: Author

Let us focus on the variable from which the ideological distance is calculated. In Figure 11, I plot the average of the ideology of the governments of non and adopter states (bottom panel) and the average ideology of all governments during analysis time (upper panel). In the bottom panel, we observe that in average, governments of states that adopted a medical marijuana policy are more liberal than non-adopters. Amongst MML adopters, however, we see in the upper panel of Figure 11 that several governments of these polities are rather conservative (e.g., AZ, CA, CO and MT).

Figure 11. Government Ideology by (Non- & Adopter) State

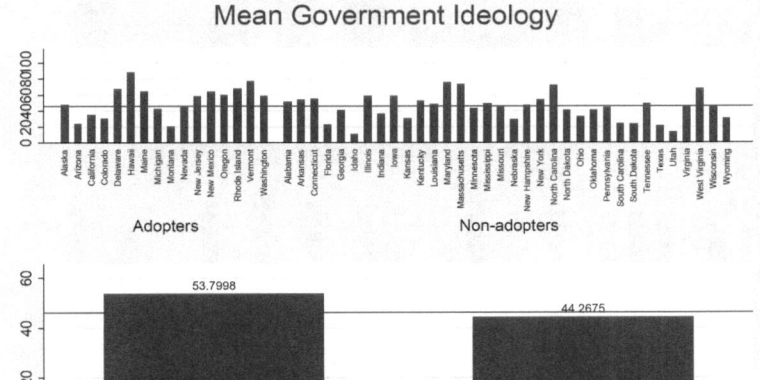

Notes:
. Red line: mean value across time
Source: Author

In Figure 12, I plot the ideology of the governments measured at the year of enactment of a medical marijuana policy (bottom panel). Given that some states enacted bans in the same year, I also show the average government ideology by year (upper panel). In the bottom panel, we see that some governments of MML adopters actually exhibited conservative ideologies. However, if we consider the annual average government ideology, the upper panel of Figure 12 shows that only in year 2010 the average government ideology of MML adopters was conservative, although the average government ideology of adopters in years 2000 and 2004 was below the mean, too. Interestingly, we also see that the ideology of the government of the first MML adopter (CA) actually scored below the mean.

Figure 12. Government Ideology by (Adopter) State

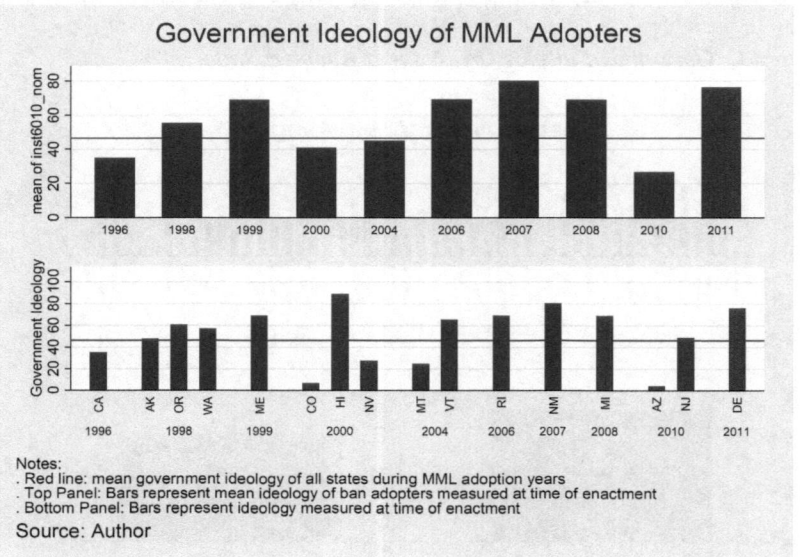

Let us explore the diffusion variables. Below, I show maps with the values of two diffusion measures for years 2005 and 2010. For the ideological dissimilarity variable, hexagons with darker colors have larger ideological distances regarding jurisdictions that enacted the component in question in previous years. For instance, in 2010, Montana, Kentucky, Ohio and the other 5 states with the same color were ideologically very similar to the jurisdictions that between 1996 – 2009 enacted a MML. For the geographical measure, I used the specification that uses the states of the "Pacific region" —WA, OR & CA (U.S. Census Bureau)—to define the neighbors of the two non-continental states, AK and HI (Imhof, 2006, 69; Kim 2016; King, Zeckhauser, and Kim 2004, 15–16); darker colors indicate a higher number of adoptions by neighbors in *t-1*.

*Figure 13. Maps of Diffusion of Medical Marijuana Policy in years 2005 &
2010*

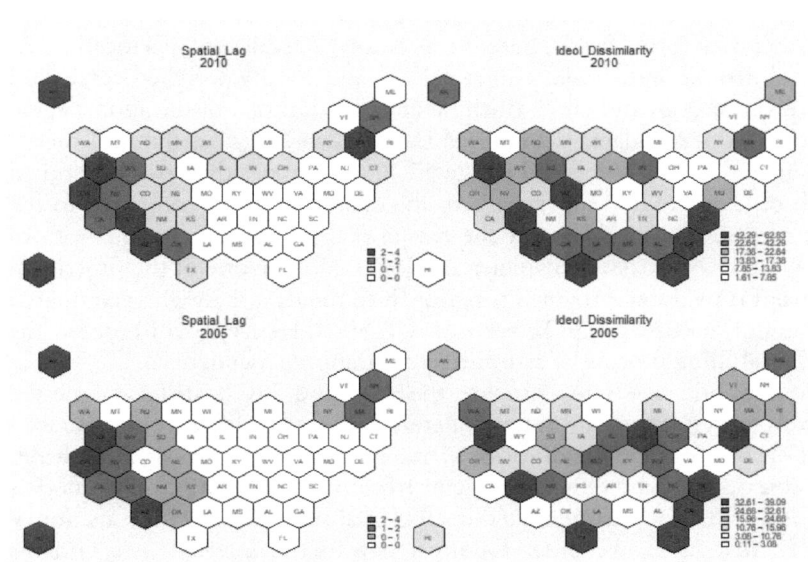

Source: Author

5.2.3 Model Selection

I will guide the reader through the model building process, as described in
section **Model Building.**

The first step in selecting a final model consists of checking for multicolinearity. I found no evidence of multicolinearity amongst the variables (see
A-Table 3), i.e., pairwise correlation coefficients did not show that any pair
of variables were correlated above the traditional 0.75 level (Nelson 2007).
The spatial lag variables are almost perfectly correlated (0.98); the regional
lag is highly correlated with the spatial lags (0.76 – 0.80). This is obvious,
since they are similar versions of themselves, and represents no problem,
since none of these covariates will be included in the same model.

The next step consists in identifying if the data exhibits duration de-
pendency and how to account for it (Box-Steffensmeier and Jones 2004;
Buckley and Westerland 2004; Carter and Signorino 2010; Beck, Katz, and
Tucker 1998; Wong and Langevin 2007, 454–55). To test for different spe-

cifications of duration dependency, I estimated several models and tested the fit against a null model where no duration dependency was assumed, namely, I estimated models with internal and external determinants[31] with six functional forms for the baseline duration dependence, specifically linear, logarithmic, quadratic, cubic, splines and locally weighed regression (lowess). To evaluate which of these characterizations of duration dependency best fit the data, I computed the Wald test against the null model (Chen et al. 2003; Wong and Langevin 2007). If more than one functional form of time provide superior fit to the data than when compared to the null model, one would prefer the model that the largest chi square from the Wald tests (Box-Steffensmeier and Jones 2004). None of the functional forms of time tested provided superior fit to the data than when compared to the null model, as can be seen in A-Table 8. Hence, I will proceed the model building process by assuming no duration dependency.

Finally, one needs to compare the AIC and BIC statistics of nested models with internal and external determinants that differ in the characterization of geographical diffusion; I include these statistics at the bottom of Table 5, which presents coefficients from the best fitting cloglog models (see A-Table 6 for exponentiated coefficients; see A-Table 21 for a summary). In that table, we observe consistency in the internal determinants across models. Regardless of how we model geographic diffusion effects, internal determinants and the ideological similarity behave in a consistent manner. The only difference in the models is that when geographic diffusion is represented with a covariate that ignores potential effects from the non-continental states, and with a variable that considers WA and OR as neighboring states of AK; and WA, OR, and CA as neighboring states for HI, as done elsewhere (Chamberlain and Haider-Markel 2005, 454; Sylvester and Haider-Markel 2016), we observe in columns two and three that the 90 % confidence interval for variables "Spatial Lag_II" and "Spatial Lag_III" includes zero. The AIC and BIC statistics, however, indicate that the model with regional lag (last column) is preferred, followed by the

---

31 As previously mentioned, the spatial and regional lag variables are highly correlated; hence, which geographical diffusion variable is included in the duration dependency analyses is inconsequential. Hence, the external determinants included in the all duration dependency analysis are the ideological diffusion variable and the geographical measure that includes AK and HI by coding the states that belong to the Pacific states region as their neighboring states (Washington, Oregon, and California) (Imhof 2006, 69; King, Zeckhauser, and Kim, 2004, 15–16)

model in column one. In fact, the coefficient estimates of internal determinants amongst these two preferred models differ minimally.

Table 5. Medical Marijuana Laws Diffusion Models

	MML	MML	MML	MML
Electoral Competition	0.06	0.06	0.06	0.06
	(0.03)**	(0.03)**	(0.03)**	(0.03)**
Unified D. Government	-0.51	-0.39	-0.49	-0.50
	(0.80)	(0.85)	(0.81)	(0.75)
Unified R. Government	-2.20	-2.29	-2.24	-2.30
	(0.95)**	(0.94)**	(0.95)**	(1.06)**
Government Ideology	-0.02	-0.03	-0.03	-0.02
	(0.02)	(0.02)	(0.02)	(0.02)
Citizen Ideology	0.01	0.02	0.01	0.01
	(0.02)	(0.02)	(0.02)	(0.02)
Opponents	-5.29	-5.98	-5.49	-5.20
	(2.72)*	(2.85)**	(2.81)*	(3.13)*
Relig. Fundamentalists	-0.14	-0.12	-0.13	-0.17
	(0.06)**	(0.05)**	(0.06)**	(0.07)**
Problem Severity	-0.01	-0.01	-0.01	-0.01
	(0.01)	(0.01)	(0.01)	(0.01)
Population	-0.16	-0.21	-0.18	-0.01
	(0.38)	(0.38)	(0.39)	(0.41)
Education	0.00	0.01	0.01	-0.03
	(0.06)	(0.06)	(0.06)	(0.07)
advocates	3.92	3.99	3.96	4.61
	(2.07)*	(1.98)**	(2.05)*	(2.45)*
Ideol. Dissimilarity	0.05	0.05	0.05	0.04
	(0.02)***	(0.02)***	(0.02)***	(0.02)***
Spatial Lag	0.43			
	(0.26)*			
Spatial Lag_II		0.22		
		(0.27)		
Spatial Lag_III			0.37	
			(0.26)	
Regional Lag				0.64
				(0.23)***
Chi2	61.70	38.91	50.74	122.09

	MML	MML	MML	MML
Df_M	13	13	13	13
P	0.00	0.00	0.00	0.00
Ll	-58.44	-59.38	-58.78	-55.74
N	673	673	673	673
AIC	144.8870	146.7583	145.5535	139.4837
BIC	155.7033	157.5745	156.3698	150.2999

$* p<0.1; ** p<0.05; *** p<0.01$
Coefficients from cloglog models with robust standard errors clustered on state. Wald tests indicated no time dependency, hence, models do not control for it. A- & BIC calculated based on 16 events. All significance tests are two-tailed.

5.2.4 Results

This section is divided in two parts. In section **Reduced Models**, I will provide a brief description of results of models that include different vectors of variables according to the conceptual categories of the Unified Model (columns 1–4 of Table **6**). In section **Final Model**, I will describe results of the model that includes all covariates, included in last column of Table **6**.

All models control for serial autocorrelation in the unobserved relationships among state-year observations by clustering observations on each subject (state), which yields corrected standard errors and reliable model performance (Buckley and Westerland 2004; Wong and Langevin 2007, 18).

Table 6. Reduced and Full Models of Medical Marijuana Policy

	1	2	3	4	5
Electoral Competition	1.08		1.06	1.05	1.07
	(0.03)***		(0.03)**	(0.03)*	(0.03)**
Unified D. Government	0.77		1.40	1.64	0.61
	(0.67)		(1.28)	(1.53)	(0.46)
Unified R. Government	0.43		0.18	0.17	0.10
	(0.38)		(0.19)*	(0.17)*	(0.11)**
Government Ideology	1.00		0.97	0.97	0.98
	(0.02)		(0.02)	(0.03)	(0.02)
Citizen Ideology		1.00	1.01	1.02	1.01
		(0.02)	(0.02)	(0.02)	(0.02)
Opponents		0.99	0.97	0.96	0.95

	1	2	3	4	5
		(0.03)	(0.03)	(0.03)	(0.03)*
advocates		1.02	1.03	1.02	1.05
		(0.01)	(0.02)*	(0.02)	(0.03)*
Relig. Fundamentalists		0.87	0.91	0.91	0.84
		(0.04)***	(0.05)*	(0.05)*	(0.06)**
Problem Severity				0.99	0.99
				(0.01)	(0.01)
Population				0.72	0.99
				(0.26)	(0.41)
Education				1.02	0.97
				(0.05)	(0.06)
Regional Lag					1.90
					(0.43)***
Ideol. Dissimilarity					1.05
					(0.02)***
Chi2	16.50	28.91	30.70	37.11	122.09
Df_M	4	4	8	11	13
P	0.00	0.00	0.00	0.00	0.00
Ll	-69.15	-68.43	-64.90	-63.82	-55.74
N	673	673	673	673	673

* $p<0.1$; ** $p<0.05$; *** $p<0.01$
Notes:
Hazard Ratios from cloglog models with robust standard errors clustered on state.
Models control for time dependency with splines (not shown).
All significance tests are two-tailed.

5.2.4.1 Reduced Models

If we ignore diffusion effects, demographic and morality policy factors, the model with only political representation variables (column one of **Table 6**) that indicates that only the level of electoral competition in a state exerts a positive and significant ($p<0.01$) effect on the hazard of enacting a medical marijuana policy; a one-unit increase in the scale of electoral competition is correlated with an estimated.8 % increase in the hazard[32] of enacting a

---

32 Hazard ratios are obtained by exponentiating regression coefficients, and have a similar interpretation as "odds ratios", i.e., hazard ratios greater (less) than one

medical marijuana policy. If we focus only on factors pointed out in the morality policy literature (column 2), only the coefficient for religious fundamentalists is significantly associated with the outcome variable: a 1-unit increase in the latter is substantially correlated ($p<0.01$) with a 13 % decrease in the odds of adopting a medical marijuana policy. When we combine morality policy and political representation covariates in a model (column three), but still ignore demographic and diffusion factors, the two latter results hold—although the estimated effects and statistically significant are slightly reduced; in addition to that, two more factors turn out significant: unified Republican governments is negatively and medical doctors interest groups positively associated with the occurrence of the dependent variable. A one-unit increase of the former variables is associated with estimated 92 % decrease and 3 % increase, correspondingly, in the hazard of adopting a MML (although marginally significant).

If we add demographic factors to the equation, we observe in column four of **Table 6** that the confidence interval of the hazard ratios for the selected controls and problem environment includes 1; moreover, the estimated magnitude of two variables from the political representation category (electoral competition and Republican government) and one from the morality policy category (religious fundamentalists) remain technically unchanged; however, the hazard ratio for advocates now includes 1.

Interestingly, in none of the reduced models (columns 1 to 4 of **Table 6**) did I find evidence that neither Democratic governments, ideology (neither of the government nor of the citizenry) nor opponent interest groups were substantially associated with the hazard of passing medical marijuana legislation.

5.2.4.2 Final Model

When we add diffusion effects to the equation, we observe in column 5 of **Table 6** that a similar vector of domestic factors that turned out statistically significant in reduced models also reached levels of statistical significance: in a positive direction, electoral competition (alpha level 0.05) and advocates ($p<0.1$); in a negative direction, unified republican government ($p<0.05$), opponents ($p<0.1$) and religious fundamentalists ($p<0.05$).

---

indicate that a unit increase in the covariate corresponds to an increase (decrease) in the hazard of experiencing the event (enacting the corresponding legislation), all else equal (Cleves 2010).

Controlling for internal and external factors, a one-unit increase in the level of electoral competition increases the hazard of enacting a MML by an estimated 6 % in model one, and 7 % when geographic diffusion is accounted for regionally; each additional medical interest group is associated with an estimated 4 % increase in the hazard of adopting a medical marijuana law (5 % when regional diffusion is controlled for). Each additional adherent to a fundamentalist doctrine is associated with an estimated 13 % decrease (16 % if regional diffusion is instead included in the equation) of the hazard of enacting a medical marijuana law. We also see that the estimated hazard of enacting a medical marijuana policy for jurisdictions with unified Republican governments is 89 % (90 % for models accounting for regional diffusion) lower than polities without unified Republican governments. Finally, each additional state law enforcement interest group decreases the hazard of adopting a MML by an estimated 5 %.

Figure 14. Coefficient Plot of Diffusion Variables, Controlling for Domestic Factors

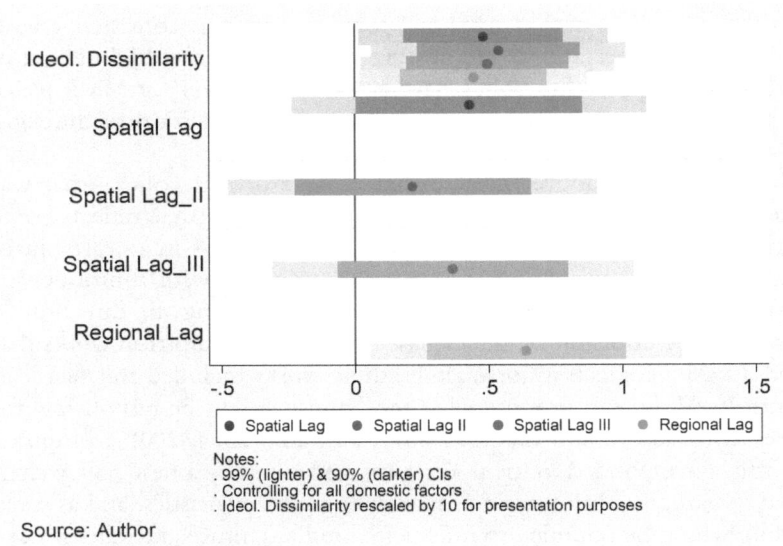

Turning to our key dependent variables, the coefficient for the ideological diffusion variable turned out highly significant and positive (p<0.01). Regardless of how bordering diffusion is controlled for (see A-Table 6

and Figure 14), if we exponentiate the coefficients for the ideological dissimilarity measure, we observe that a one-unit increase in this scale is significantly associated with a 5 % or 6 % increase in the hazard of enacting a medical marijuana policy in a given state.

We also note that, controlling for internal and external factors, a one additional adjacent state that enacts a medical marijuana law is significantly associated with a 53 % increase in the hazard adopting a similar policy in a given state; though the latter is marginally significant (alpha level 0.1); when one more neighbor within a given region experiences the event of interest, instead, the latter is highly correlated with an estimated 90 % increase in the hazard of enacting a MML (alpha level 0.01; see Figure 14 and A-Table 6).

In the model that incorporates all covariates, the rest of the variables did not reach traditional levels of statistical significance.

5.2.5 Discussion

The case of medical marijuana shows for the most part consistency with the theoretical expectations. We observe that more factors highlighted in the literature on morality policy have explanatory power for MML passages; however, an explanation of this policy without political or diffusion variables would be incomplete.

The results from above indicate that passage of this policy—that was included in this project as an example of legislation that reflects some but not all theoretical characteristics of morality policy—in a nearby jurisdiction j were positively and substantially associated with future events, as expected. I had formulated my expectation regarding the direction of the geographic diffusion influence based on previous empirical works that found a positive effect; unfortunately, these works included this factor as a control and did not propose what mechanism might be responsible for the result (Bradford and Bradford 2016; Ferraiolo 2004, 200). I proposed that officials responded to the uncertainty generated by a new policy alternative by gathering information through cognitive heuristics, and as such, learning would be bounded to units with similar culture and values. Even though the exact content of the information retrieved from this group of homophilous jurisdictions cannot be revealed with the present research design, the moral nature of the policy makes me believe that one of the main lessons learned from morally-aligned MML adopters is that the political risk of enacting a medical marijuana law in units with a similar moral profile was not high, i.e. a public with similar moral views did not respond to legislators' support for MML with electoral retaliation. These results contrast sharply with other analyses of MML that did not find discernible geographical diffusion effects, although this discrepancy might lie in the different sizes of the data sets (Crawford 2013, 40; Hannah and Mallinson 2017; Kim 2016).

On the other hand, the significant coefficient for the spatial lag could be capturing the effect of cross-unit opposition and/or advocacy that I described in previous sections: that a MML enacted in unit i entered the radar of lawmakers from unit j can also be explained by the proposition that opposition to policies with moral content is less likely to remain local (Hollander and Patapan 2016). As I mentioned before, given that moral values are non-negotiable and that legislation that targets such first principles will more often than not give rise to counter responses seeking not only to contain, but to eradicate a given morality law altogether wherever it appears (Hollander and Patapan 2016, 2), people from unit i are less likely to put up with the existence of a MML that, in spite of being adopted in unit j, casts doubt on the validity of their first principles.

When we shift our attention to a specific attribute, namely, ideology of previous adopters, we observe that legislators responded to the uncertainty generated by this policy not only by looking at the aftermath of adopting MML in states with similar values and culture, but also in jurisdictions with different ideologies, as indicated by the positive and statistically significant coefficient for adoptions by ideologically dissimilar states. It has been suggested that when lawmakers cannot easily situate a new policy in a liberal-conservative continuum, the likelihood that legislators look to the ideological patterns of those who have previously adopted the policy is higher (Grossback 2004, 523). Assuming that MML cannot be easily identified as a liberal/conservative measure, it is plausible that ideological information is a relevant factor for future MML adoptions, even if the information comes from ideologically dissimilar jurisdictions, which runs contrary to my expectations and previous works that although did not focus on MML, did find the hypothesized negative association in subnational US analyses, e.g., criminal justice reforms (Boushey 2016), academic bankruptcy laws and state lotteries (Grossback 2004). Another possibility is that ideologically dissimilar states experienced appealing benefits after they adopted a MML, which motivated legislators to follow through[33].

---

33 Testing the latter would require to test the consequences MML, which goes beyond the goals of this project.

In that case, looking at the ideologies of former adopters would provide more information than what the literature had suggested so far. Previous research has registered that legislators' decision to support the enactment of tax incentive policies and to expand Medicaid were also significantly influenced by decisions from units with which they are least ideologically aligned (Leiser 2015; Sylvester 2016, 31). Further research is needed to shed light on this pattern.

Contrary to previous studies that found out that citizen liberalism was a significant predictor of medical marijuana (Bradford and Bradford 2016; Hannah and Mallinson 2017; Kim 2016), controlling for internal and external factors, I did not find evidence that states with more liberal citizens were more likely to pass medical marijuana laws, just as previous studies about MML (Ferraiolo 2004, 201) or a policy with higher moral content, i.e., pre Roe v. Wade abortion (Mooney and Lee 1995).

Although MML was selected to represent policies with moderate level of moral content, I presented evidence that a specific religious group also played a central role in its adoption process. Previous research had reported that the level of evangelical adherence was a negative predictor of MML (Bradford and Bradford 2016; Hannah and Mallinson 2017); I focused on the influence of a narrower group, religious fundamentalists, and found out that adherents to these specific religious doctrines were significantly and negatively associated with passage of MML, as suggested by previous marijuana related analyses (Kim 2016; Meier 1994), and a myriad of studies that have identified the same pattern in analyses of policies with more or less moral content, e.g., general-fund and education lotteries (Berry and Berry 1990; Pierce and Miller 2000) and gay-related legislation (Haider-Markel 2001a; Haider-Markel and Meier 1996).

In line with the literature that emphasizes the role of political factors in morality policy, MML exhibited entrepreneurial politics. As expected, I found out that when electoral competition intensifies, enacting an otherwise politically-risky issue such as decriminalizing medical marijuana becomes more likely. Legislators who support MML are taking a major political risk because opponents may label them as "soft on drugs", however, when they perceive that they have a real chance of becoming the majority party (or of losing majority party status), legislators might be more likely to incur in such a risk, because in that situation the possible benefits of such action greatly outweigh the costs (Meier 1994, 107). Nonetheless, such claim needs consideration of the general opinion towards MML. Although I did not locate state data on attitudes towards medical marijuana, we can follow the strategy of previous works and resort to national public opinion figures to proxy for this (Butz, Fix, and Mitchell 2015; Jensen 2003; Kim 2016, 17; Mooney and Lee 2000). As previously mentioned, a survey from 2011 documents that a clear majority of the respondents agree that marijuana has legitimate medical uses: 77 % to 16 % (Pew Research Center 2011); three previous national polls recorded in 2003, 2005, and 2010, that a clear majority of the population had positive opinion regarding legal medical uses of cannabis: 78 %, 75 % and 70 %, correspondingly (Mendes 2010). We could cautiously interpret this as evidence that during the analysis period, MML featured characteristics of consensus morality policy[34], i.e., MML is an instance of a morality preferred by the majorities[35]. In such case, a positive and significant coefficient for electoral competition can be interpreted instead as evidence that candidates and parties cater to the preferences of the majorities by enacting popular policies (Lewis 2011; Smith and Fridkin 2008).

The latter would also help understand why I found evidence that law-enforcement and the medical community exerted substantial opposition to and support for MML, correspondingly, as previously suggested by previous analyses and anecdotal evidence (Ferraiolo 2004; Meier 1992; 1994), i.e., the argument that policies that elicit conflict over basic moral values, but that are supported by a clear majority, offer the opportunity for activists to affect the timing and extent of reform (Mooney and Lee 2000, 230); nonetheless, that account also predicts that not only organized interest, but the ideology of the elite will be central in the enactment stage of morality policies, which neither my results nor as a previous work on the matter support (Kim 2016).

Although many works do not control for party influences (Bradford and Bradford 2016; Hannah and Mallinson 2017; Kim 2016), I found evidence that another political factor was central in the policy making of medical marijuana. My results support the argument that law enforcement approa-

---

34 The picture for general use of marijuana is markedly different, though. Based in national polls, in 2011 50 % of a surveyed population opposed whereas 45 % opposed legalizing marijuana Pew Research Center (2011, 17), which would make it a contentious morality policy; however, for most of the past decades, marijuana legalization was a consensus morality policy, where clear majorities (81 % to 16 % and 63 % to 31 % in 1990 and 2000, correspondingly) opposed it Pew Research Center (2011, 17).

35 However, the picture was different at the beginning of the analysis period: in 1997 only a smaller majority (58 %) agreed that marijuana had legitimate medical uses, and only 34 % said the contrary Pew Research Center (2011), which would indicate that in the late 1990s, this issue could have been a contentious one.

ches to drug abuse (which contrasts with medical marijuana legislation) are generally more characteristic of Republicans, who are more conservative in general (Haider-Markel 2001a, 14; Lewis 2011, 374) and have generally advocated for treatment rather than law enforcement approach to drugs in particular (Meier 1994, 107). However, I did not identify discernible effects of unified Democratic governments, contrary to previous works (Crawford 2013, 40; Meier 1992).

The state context seems to have been at the margin in the political process of MML. In line with previous works that did not find discernible evidence that population that suffer the diseases that would make them eligible to access MML (Hannah and Mallinson 2017; Kim 2016), I did not find evidence that the incidence rate of cancer was a significant predictor of MML. Last, demographic factors (population nor states' education attainment) did not exert explanatory power, as previously documented (Bradford and Bradford 2016; Ferraiolo 2004, 201). I also presented evidence that during the period of analysis, the data did not present duration dependency issues, similar to a project that opted to use Cox regressions (Kim 2016), but contrary to projects that controlled for time dependency but failed to provide the rigorous tests of duration dependency that made me opt not to control for it; this difference, however, might be due to different data-set sizes (Bradford and Bradford 2016; Hannah and Mallinson 2017).

5.3 Anti-Obesity Legislation

5.3.1 Dependent Variable

One crucial aspect of data sets with policies with multiple components is how to determine the number of components and how to categorize each legislative piece within those components for a given policy area. In the literature, it is suggested to rely on previous analytic efforts from policymakers, policy experts, research groups or advocacy organizations, who at times explicitly divide policies into multiple components in order to conduct comparisons across jurisdictions (Boehmke 2009, 232–33).

Researchers from the National Center for Chronic Disease Prevention and Health Promotion and from the Centers for Disease Control and Prevention (Lankford et al. 2013, 115) compiled, to the best of my knowledge, the most comprehensive state policy efforts to control obesity in the USA.

Moreover, they systematically grouped individual policies of this policy area into four discrete categories:

> "State obesity legislation was collected from 2 sources: the Division of Nutrition, Physical Activity, and Obesity database and each state legislature's Web site. Both sources were searched with the key word "obesity" for the years 2001–2010. The 714 bills that were identified were then grouped according to the bill's action or setting (eg, school physical education, setting up a taskforce). For bills that overlapped categories (eg, school taskforce), the bills were placed in the setting where the bill would be actionable (eg, schools) A total of 103 bills were excluded because they were not focused on preventing obesity. Of these, 90 focused on protecting the food industry from liable suits and 13 did not feature obesity as a central focus." (Lankford et al. 2013, 115)

In that project, full text of the enacted bills was read and coded into "categories" by one single reviewer (to keep consistency) as follows. Enacted legislation supporting the creation of commissions, councils, committees, or with the purpose of carrying out studies were labeled as—assigned to the policy component—"Taskforce". Laws relating to strategies in schools were assigned to the category "School". Bills that either targeted, would benefit the community "in general", and that did not apply to a specific context were labeled as "Community". Last, legislation relating to the provision of insurance, medical care, or provider-based programs were grouped in the category "Healthcare" (Lankford et al. 2013, 115).

In order to provide a more comprehensive picture of legislative activity targeting obesity, I complemented the data of the former project[36] (93 policies, i.e., around 89% of the final dependent variable) with 12 policies that two previous works[37] recorded between 1998–2000 (see A-Table 3 for further details), so as to end up with a variable that spans the years 1998 – 2010. I followed the coding criteria of Lankford et al. (2013, 115) as closely as possible, in order to categorize the policies retrieved from the other

---

36 Personal correspondence with Tina Lankford. A previous project Marlow (2013) used the same data to analyze the determinants of adoption of AO legislation; however, the period of analysis was narrower, in that only the years 2001–2010 (90 policies) were analyzed.

37 These two projects tracked legislative activity during a smaller time span, i.e., four—1999 – 2003 (Wellever, Reichard, and Velasco, 2004, 7)–and six years— 1998 – 2005 (Boehmke 2009).

projects (which represent around 11 % of the final dependent variable) into the above mentioned policy categories.

The final structure of the dependent variable can be seen in the following table. In general, the data set records 105 enactments. Individual policies were assigned to only one of the four possible policy areas/components, i.e., policies could not address multiple areas at once. The area that experienced the highest level of activity during the period of analysis was AO legislation targeting schools, with 42 enactments, followed by "taskforce" (33 adoptions), "healthcare" with 21 occurrences and last, "community", with 9 enactments (see Table 8 and Figure 15).

Table 7. Enacted State Obesity Legislation by Component, 1998–2010

State	Bill Name	Year	Task-force	School	Community	Healthcare
Louisiana	HCR 11	1998	1			
Alabama	Ala. Acts, Act #98/ SJR27	1999	1			
Florida	SR 2734	1999				1
Louisiana	Chap 46 2611	1999	1			
New Jersey	NJ Stat. Ann. 26:1A-37.6	1999	1			
New Mexico	NM Stat. Ann 6–4–10	1999		1		
South Carolina	SCR252	1999	1			
California	AB 2038	2000	1			
Indiana	HR 35	2000		1		
Indiana	IC 27–8–14–1	2000				1
Iowa	EO 16	2000	1			
Mississippi	HB 199	2000		1		
California	SB19	2001		1		
Louisiana	HB1349	2001	1			
Maryland	HB675/SB522	2001				1
Maryland	SB522/HB675	2001				1
Mississippi	HB1053/SB2373	2001	1			
New York	A07199	2001	1			
Oklahoma	SB708	2001	1			
Oklahoma	HB1115	2001	1			
Tennessee	SB687	2001	1			
Tennessee	HB367	2001	1			

State	Bill Name	Year	Task-force	School	Community	Healthcare
						Policy Components/Areas
Mississippi	SB2249/HB1605	2002		1		
Arkansas	HB1583	2003		1		
California	SB677	2003		1		
California	SB875	2003			1	
Illinois	SB1589	2003	1			
Maine	LD471	2003	1			
Mississippi	HB989	2003	1			
Mississippi	SB2339/HB920	2003		1		
New Jersey	A3534	2003	1			
New York	S02045	2003	1			
North Carolina	SB34	2003	1			
Rhode Island	SB1201	2003	1			
Texas	SB474/HB1093	2003		1		
Texas	SB1357	2003		1		
Virginia	SB1081	2003				1
Colorado	SB103	2004		1		
Florida	S2372/HO935	2004			1	
Idaho	H0696	2004				1
Illinois	SB2940	2004		1		
Kentucky	SB179	2004	1			
Louisiana	SB871	2004		1		
Maryland	HB1410	2004				1
Maryland	SB868	2004				1
Mississippi	HB1046	2004	1			
New Hamp-shire	HB1352	2004		1		
South Carolina	SB1235	2004				1
Tennessee	SB2743	2004		1		
Washington	SB5436	2004		1		
California	SB12	2005		1		
Colorado	SB81	2005		1		
Colorado	HB1066	2005				1
Indiana	SB360	2005				1
Kansas	SB154	2005		1		

5. Analysis

State	Bill Name	Year	Task-force	School	Community	Healthcare
Louisiana	SB146	2005		1		
Maryland	SB473	2005		1		
Maryland	SB333/HB462	2005	1			
Nevada	SB197	2005	1			
North Carolina	HB855	2005		1		
North Carolina	SB961	2005		1		
Rhode Island	SB565	2005		1		
Rhode Island	HB5563	2005		1		
Tennessee	HB445	2005		1		
West Virginia	HB2816/SB416	2005		1		
Colorado	SB127	2006		1		
Delaware	SB289	2006	1			
Florida	SB1324	2006			1	
Iowa	HSB583	2006			1	
Iowa	SF2124	2006			1	
Oklahoma	SB1459	2006		1		
West Virginia	SB785	2006		1		
Mississippi	SB2369	2007		1		
New York	A04308	2007		1		
Rhode Island	H5900	2007			1	
Texas	SB556	2007	1			
Vermont	H887	2007				1
Virginia	HB2214	2007		1		
Virginia	SB974	2007		1		
California	SB564	2008		1		
California	SB1420	2008			1	
Kansas	HB2672	2008				1
Maryland	HB1176	2008	1			
New Hampshire	HB1422	2008	1			
New Hampshire	SB312	2008				1
North Carolina	HB2437	2008	1			
California	AB513	2009				1
Illinois	H3767	2009	1			

State	Bill Name	Year	Policy Components/Areas			
			Task-force	School	Community	Healthcare
Maine	H983	2009		1		
Maryland	H1264	2009		1		
Maryland	S879	2009		1		
Massachusetts	H4568	2009			1	
Mississippi	H1530	2009				1
North Carolina	S287	2009				1
North Carolina	S1151/H1775	2009			1	
North Carolina	H1726	2009		1		
North Carolina	H1775/S1296	2009		1		
North Carolina	S1152/H1777	2009	1			
Texas	S870	2009	1			
Vermont	S88	2009				1
Florida	SB140	2010		1		
Maryland	S1031	2010				1
Maryland	S700	2010				1
Maryland	H1017	2010				1
Massachusetts	H4459	2010		1		

Source: Author, with data from (Wellever, Reichard, and Velasco, 2004) and (Boehmke 2009) for the period 1998 – 2000, and (Lankford et al. 2013) for 2001 – 2010. Coding into (four) policy areas/components from {Lankford 2013 #212

Table 7 shows that in the period of analysis some jurisdictions enacted more than one law in each policy area, hence, some components have been passed more than 50 times (as can be seen in last column called "States", which indicates the number of jurisdictions that enacted each policy component during all the period of analysis; and in the line "States by year", which records the number of states that enacted any AO policy each year). The column titled "Total" indicates the number of components enacted during the whole period of observation. The line "Total by year" shows the number of components adopted each year. In years 2005, 2003, 2009 and 2004, a total of 15, 14, 14 and 13 policies, correspondingly (across all components) were adopted, which are the periods with the highest activity. On the other end, years 1998, 2000 and 2010 experienced the lowest activity, with only 1, 5 and 5 adoptions, correspondingly (across all components). The analyses, however, do not take into consideration events that occurred more than once within the same year, due to the binary nature of the response variable and the fact that it is recorded annually (i.e., "state-year" data)[38]. In such cases (N=13) of multiple events within the same year, the dependent variable is coded as one. In this vein, the last column ("DV") reflects the actual number of events considered in the analyses.

Table 8. Adoption of Anti-Obesity Legislation Components by Year

		Year													To-tal	Sta-tes	DV
		98	99	00	01	02	03	04	05	06	07	08	09	10			
		Adoptions by Year															
Policy Subject Area / Components	Community	0	0	0	0	0	1	1	0	3	1	1	2	0	9	6	8
	Healthcare	0	1	1	2	0	1	4	2	0	1	2	4	3	21	13	17
	School	0	1	2	1	1	5	6	11	3	4	1	5	2	42	23	36
	Taskforce	1	4	2	7	0	7	2	2	1	1	3	3	0	33	20	31
															105	62	92
	Total by year	1	6	5	10	1	14	13	15	7	7	7	14	5	105		
	States by year	1	6	11	17	17	25	35	43	46	51	54	60	62		62	

Source: Author, with data from (Lankford et al. 2013), (Wellever, Reichard, and Velasco, 2004) and (Boehmke 2009)

Figure 15 shows that by the end of 2010, the states that introduced the highest number of legislation to control obesity were Maryland, North Carolina, Mississippi and California, (12, 9, & 8 bills adopted in total, correspondingly). On the other side of the spectrum, eight states (the bottom of Figure 15) enacted only one policy, and 18 states didn't pass any of the four policy components of AO legislation (omitted from Figure 5; see A-Table 5 for the corresponding table).

---

38 For instance, in 2006 IA enacted two community-related bills; the (binary) outcome variable of that component cannot reflect the existence of more than one event in the same year in that unit. In other words, 13 events occurred more than once (twice, to be precise; only in one occasion, the number of multiple events within the same year was 3) in the same state. Refer to
for a full list.

Figure 15. Total AO Legislation by State & Component by 2010

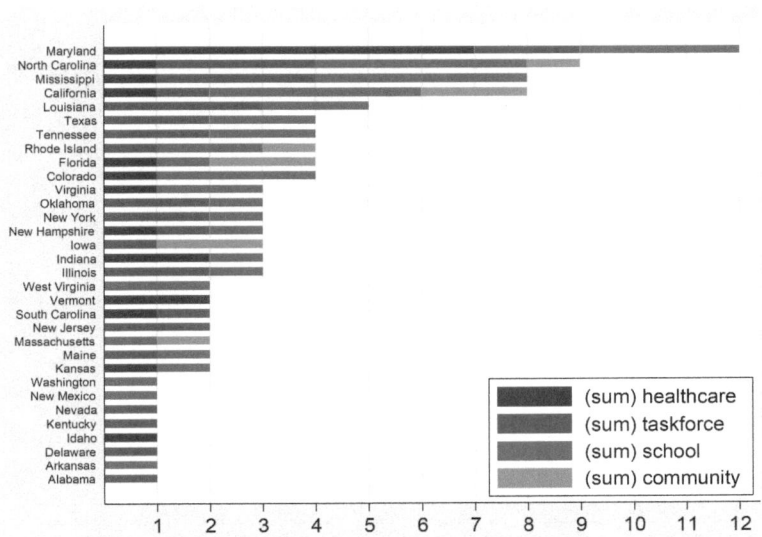

Source: author

If we plot a histogram of the (pooled) dependent variable considering the states that enacted at least one component of AO legislation (N=32; with 11.63 % of the response variable occurring in Maryland), we observe that by 2010, 1–3 % of the outcome variable occurred in 21 units (65.63 % of the 32 adopters), 3–5 % in 5 units (15.63 %), and the remaining 18.75 % is distributed in 6 states, as we can see in Figure 16 (see A-Table 10 for the corresponding table)

117

Figure 16. Histograms of the Percentage of All AO Legislation amongst Adopter States

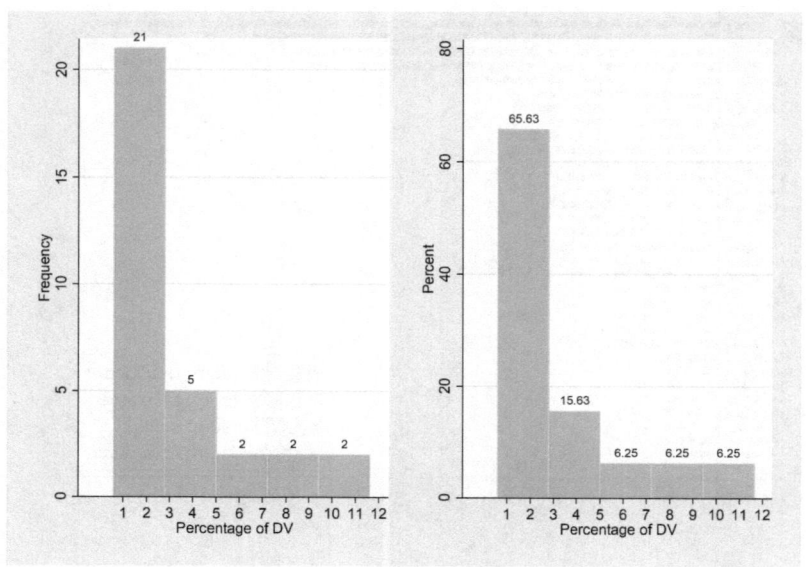

Figure 17. Cumulative Adoptions of Anti-Obesity Policies, by Component

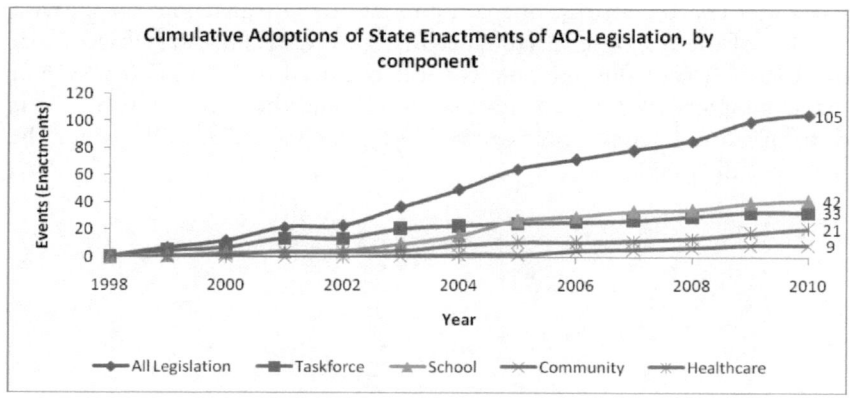

Source: author

To have a better sense of the dependent variable, the table below (divided in four sub tables, each corresponding to a policy component) lists the states that experienced what I refer to in this dissertation as multiple events, i.e., that enacted more any of the policy components of AO more than once. Columns with the suffix "_Nr_Repeated_Events" show the number of events that each polity experienced (refer to A-Table 10 and footnote 38 for a list of the only 13 states that experienced multiple events in the same year).

Table 9. States that Enacted more than one Component and Number thereof by 2010

state	school_Nr_Repeated_Events		state	taskforce_Nr_Repeated_Events
California	4		Illinois	2
Colorado	3		Louisiana	3
Louisiana	2		Maryland	2
Maryland	3		Mississippi	3
Mississippi	4		New Jersey	2
North Carolina	4		New York	2
Rhode Island	2		North Carolina	3
Tennessee	2		Oklahoma	2
Texas	2		Tennessee	2
Virginia	2		Texas	2
West Virginia	2			

state	healthcare_Nr_Repeated_Events		state	community_Nr_Repeated_Events
Indiana	2		California	2
Maryland	7		Florida	2
Vermont	2		Iowa	2

5.3.2 Descriptive Statistics

The table below presents the number of observations, mean, standard deviation, minimum and maximum values for all variables for the analysis period.

Table 10. Descriptive Statistics Anti-Obesity Legislation

Variable	N	Mean	SD	Min	Max
AO Adoption	2600	0.04	0.18	0.00	1.00
Electoral Competition	2600	38.81	11.04	12.05	63.10
Unified D. Government	2600	0.21	0.41	0.00	1.00
Unified R. Government	2600	0.23	0.42	0.00	1.00
Government Ideology	2600	48.51	23.15	4.05	91.03
Citizen Ideology	2600	51.85	15.73	8.45	95.97
Opponents	2600	4.44	6.55	0.00	37.39
Relig. Fundamentalists	2600	13.77	12.14	1.46	67.60
Problem Severity	2600	23.35	4.20	12.30	35.40
Population	2600	15.10	1.01	13.08	17.44
Education	2600	26.64	5.13	14.60	44.40
advocates	2600	19.25	16.01	2.16	94.69
Lagged Community	2600	0.03	0.18	0.00	1.00
Lagged Healthcare	2600	0.10	0.30	0.00	1.00
Lagged School	2600	0.19	0.40	0.00	1.00
Lagged Taskforce	2600	0.24	0.43	0.00	1.00
Time control	2600	6.00	3.74	0.00	12.00
Time control 2	2600	50.00	46.59	0.00	144.00
Time control 3	2600	468.00	547.03	0.00	1728.00
Ideol. Dissimilarity	2600	17.30	16.15	0.00	79.09
Spatial Lag	2600	0.62	1.02	0.00	6.00
Spatial Lag_II	2600	0.60	1.01	0.00	6.00
Spatial Lag_III	2600	0.61	1.01	0.00	6.00
Regional Lag	2600	0.67	0.99	0.00	5.00

Source: Author

Let us focus on the variable from which the ideological distance is calculated. In Figure 18, I plot the average of the ideology of the governments of non and adopter states (bottom panel) and the average ideology of all governments during analysis time (upper panel). In the bottom panel, we observe that in average, governments of states that adopted any anti-obesity measure had governments with liberal ideology, compared to non-adopters. In fact, amongst AO adopter states, we see few polities with ideologically conservative governments (FL, ID, SC and TX), as shown in the upper panel of Figure 18.

Figure 18. Government Ideology by (Non- & Adopter of all AO laws) State

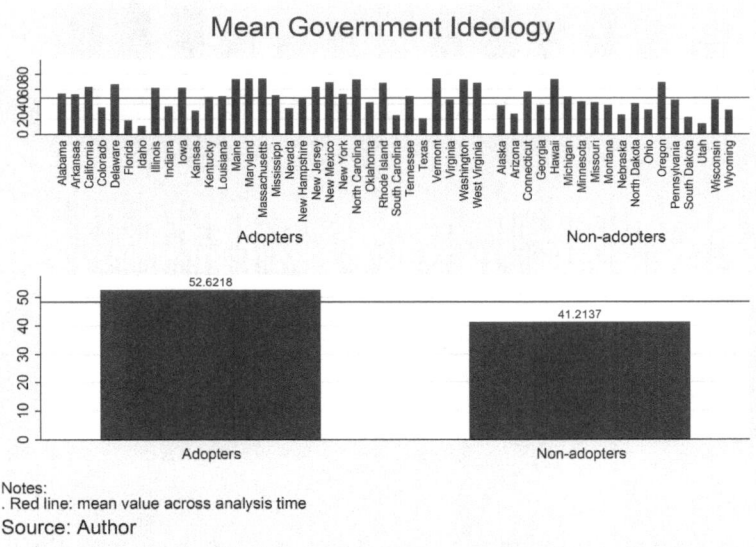

Notes:
. Red line: mean value across analysis time
Source: Author

In Figure 19, I plot the ideology of the governments measured at the year of enactment of any anti-obesity measure (bottom panel). Given that several states enacted AO policies in the same year, I also show the average government ideology by year (upper panel). In the bottom panel, we see that few governments of AO adopters exhibited conservative ideologies. However, if we consider the annual average government ideology, the upper panel of Figure 19 shows that only in year 2004 were the governments of adopter states (on average) slightly conservative: in that year, the government ideology of AO-laws adopters Colorado, Florida, Idaho, New Hampshire and South Carolina contrasts with the liberal ideology of the rest of states that enacted any anti-obesity law. In years 1998, 1999, 2005–2007 adopters of AO legislation were (on average) slightly above/below the mean value of government ideology. In the rest of the years (2000–2003; 2008–2010), governments of AO-adopter states were liberal.

Figure 19. Government Ideology by Adopter State of All AO laws

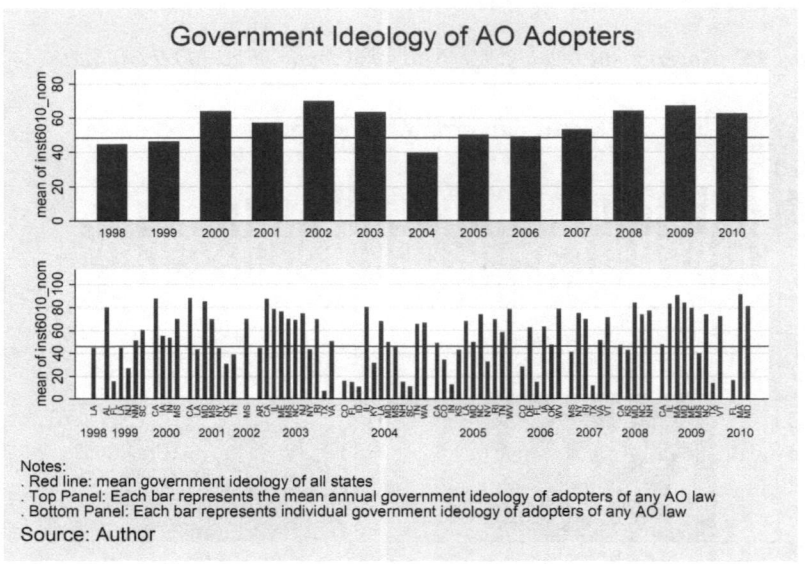

Let us explore the diffusion variables. Below, I show maps with the values of two diffusion measures by policy area for 2005 and 2010. For the ideological dissimilarity variable, hexagons with darker colors have larger ideological distances regarding jurisdictions that enacted the component in question in previous years. For instance, in year 2010, Hawaii, New Hampshire, the other seven states with the same color were very ideologically similar to the jurisdictions that between 1998 – 2009 enacted AO community legislation (see Table 7. Enacted State Obesity Legislation by Component, 1998-2010). For the geographical measure, I used the specification that uses the states of the "Pacific region"—WA, OR & CA (U.S. Census Bureau)—to define the neighbors of the two non-continental states, AK and HI (Imhof, 2006, 69; Kim 2016; King, Zeckhauser, and Kim 2004, 15–16); darker colors indicate a higher number of adoptions by neighbors in *t-1*.

Figure 20. Maps of Diffusion of Community Anti-Obesity Legislation in years 2005 & 2010.

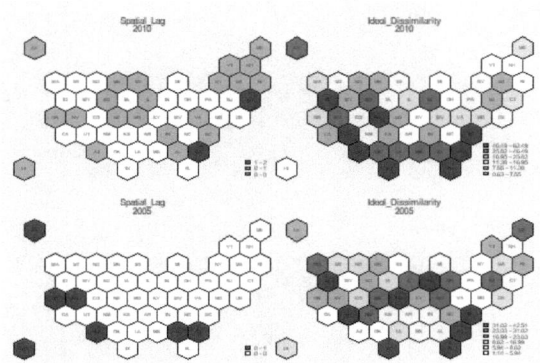

Source: Author

Figure 21. Maps of Diffusion of Taskforce Anti-Obesity Legislation in years 2005 & 2010.

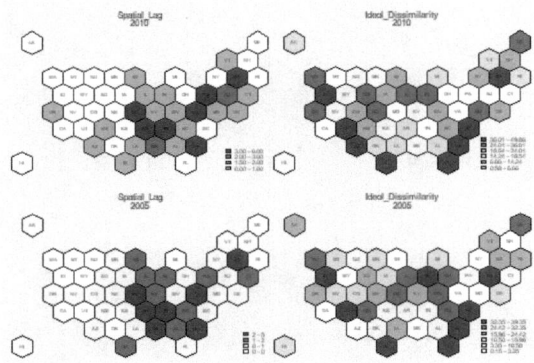

Source: Author

123

*Figure 22. Maps of Diffusion of Healthcare Anti-Obesity Legislation in years
2005 & 2010.*

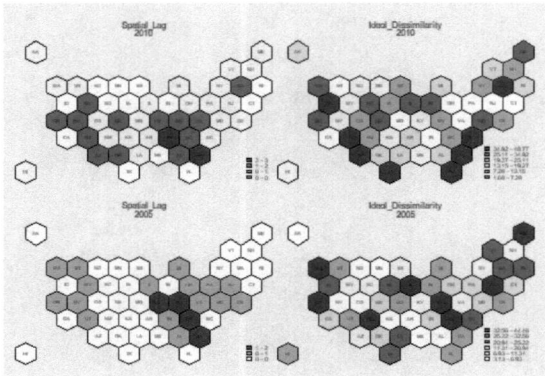

Source: Author

*Figure 23. Maps of Diffusion of School Anti-Obesity Legislation in years 2005
& 2010.*

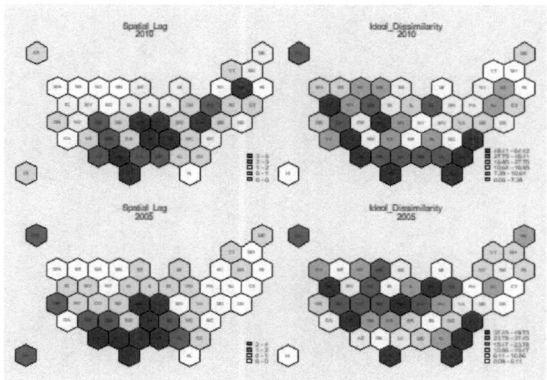

Source: Author

5.3.3 Model Selection

I will guide the reader through the model building process, as described in
section Model Selection.

The first step in selecting a final model consists of checking for multicolinearity. I found no evidence of multicolinearity amongst the variables (see A-Table 4), i.e., pairwise correlation coefficients did not show that any pair of variables were correlated above the traditional 0.75 level (Nelson 2007). The two diffusion variables that code AK & HI differently are highly correlated with the one that assigns no neighbors to those two non-continental jurisdictions (<0.9). This is obvious, since they are similar versions of themselves, and represents no problem, since none of these covariates will be included in the same model. Time controls (cubed time) are also highly correlated, which is also expected and represents no problem for estimation (Allison 2014; Box-Steffensmeier and Jones 2004).

The next step consists in identifying if the data exhibits duration dependency and how to account for it (Box-Steffensmeier and Jones 2004; Buckley and Westerland 2004; Carter and Signorino 2010; Beck, Katz, and Tucker 1998; Wong and Langevin 2007, 454–55). To test for different specifications of duration dependency, I estimated several models and tested the fit against a null model where no duration dependency was assumed, namely, I estimated models with internal and external determinants[39] with six functional forms for the baseline duration dependence, specifically linear, logarithmic, quadratic, cubic, splines and locally weighed regression (lowess). To evaluate which of these characterizations of duration dependency best fit the data, I computed the Wald test against the null model (Chen et al. 2003; Wong and Langevin 2007). If more than one functional form of time provides superior fit to the data than when compared to the null model, one would prefer the model that the largest chi square from the Wald tests (Box-Steffensmeier and Jones 2004). The cubic transformation of time provides a better fit for the AO community models, quadratic transformation for the taskforce model and lowess for the school model, as can be seen in A-Table 7. I will proceed with the model adjudication routine by including such best fitting transformations of time (except for the healthcare model, for which none of the six functional forms improved its fit).

---

39 As previously mentioned, the spatial and regional lag variables are highly correlated; hence, which geographical diffusion variable is included in the duration dependency analyses is inconsequential. Hence, the external determinants included in the all duration dependency analysis are the ideological diffusion variable and the geographical measure that includes AK and HI by coding the states that belong to the Pacific states region as their neighboring states (Washington, Oregon, and California) as Imhof (2006, 69) and King, Zeckhauser, and Kim (2004, 15–16)

Finally, one needs to compare the AIC and BIC statistics of nested models with internal and external determinants that differ in the characterization of geographical diffusion; I include these statistics at the bottom of A-Table 23, A-Table 24, A-Table 25 and A-Table 26 (see A-Table 21 for a summary of AIC & BIC), which present coefficients from the best fitting cloglog models. These statistics indicate that the model with regional lag is preferred for community and school components, while for taskforce and healthcare, the models with spatial lag should be preferred.

However, analyzing the components separately might not yield the most informative comparison, given that fluctuations in coefficients could emerge somewhat randomly, and such strategy ignores any commonality or cross-component influences. (Boehmke 2009). For that reason, I also present results of pooled models, where the unit of observation change from state-year to state-year-component. To account for different baseline hazards across events, I include an indicator for whether a jurisdiction has previously enacted legislation for the component in question (Boehmke 2009; Kreitzer 2015b). This will yield evidence of event (in)dependence, in the sense that states that have already adopted a component might (not) be (significantly) more (less) likely to adopt more legislation on that component.

Once again, one needs to compare the AIC and BIC statistics of nested models with internal and external determinants that differ in the characterization of geographical diffusion; I include these statistics at the bottom of A-Table 27 (see A-Table 17 for a table with all the coefficients; see A-Table 22 for a summary of AIC & BIC), which presents coefficients from the best fitting cloglog models. For the model that considers repeated enactments of all anti-obesity laws, both statistics indicate that the model with regional lag (last column) is preferred, followed by the model in column two. However, the coefficient estimates of internal and external determinants amongst these two preferred models differ minimally.

5.3.4 Results

This section is divided in four parts. In sections **Reduced Models by Component** and **Reduced Pooled Models** I will provide a brief description of results of models that include different vectors of variables according to the conceptual categories of the Unified Model (columns 1–4 of **Table 11, Table 12** and **Table 13**, and columns 1–5 of **Table 14**). In sections **Final Models by Component** and **Final Pooled Models**, I will describe results of the models that include all covariates, (included in columns 5 of the above mentioned tables, and column six of **Table 14**). The Community component did not have enough activity to generate meaningful statistical results (8 enactments only, see Table 7), hence, it is therefore not analyzed on its own.

All models report repeated-events estimations[40], control for serial auto-correlation in the unobserved relationships among state-year observations by clustering observations on each subject (state) (Buckley and Westerland 2004; Wong and Langevin 2007, 18) and control for time dependency according to the best fitting specification of time above selected (see A-Table 7). To avoid the assumption that the coefficients for each of the 4 components are the same across the separate models, in the last column of **Table 14**, I include four indicators[41] for whether a jurisdiction has enacted each of the other provisions (results of models that do not control for past community AO enactments differ minimally, see A-Table 15). Such indicators allow one to examine patterns of adoption across components by testing whether states that have passed, for instance, community AO legislation, are less likely to enact other components.

Table 11. Reduced Models of School Anti-Obesity Policies

	School1	School2	School3	School4	School5
Electoral Competition	0.98		0.99	1.00	1.00
	(0.02)		(0.02)	(0.02)	(0.02)
Unified D. Government	3.36		2.97	2.86	2.74
	(1.83)**		(1.62)**	(1.72)*	(1.91)
Unified R. Government	0.54		0.70	0.68	0.62
	(0.31)		(0.41)	(0.42)	(0.41)
Government Ideology	1.00		1.00	1.00	1.00

40 Results of single-event estimations differ minimally (see A-Table 12, A-Table 13, A-Table 14, & A-Table 16), therefore, only results of repeated-event models will be discussed.

41 These indicators are only included in repeated events models. Moreover, I set the value of the indicators to zero for observations corresponding to the same component, the reason being that there exists already a variable for the presence of the current component.

	School1	School2	School3	School4	School5
	(0.01)		(0.02)	(0.02)	(0.02)
Citizen Ideology		1.00	0.99	0.99	0.99
		(0.01)	(0.01)	(0.01)	(0.01)
Opponents		0.92	0.91	0.89	0.89
		(0.07)	(0.06)	(0.08)	(0.09)
Advocates		0.96	0.96	0.97	0.97
		(0.02)**	(0.02)**	(0.03)	(0.03)
Relig. Fundamen-talists		1.00	0.99	0.99	0.99
		(0.02)	(0.02)	(0.02)	(0.02)
Problem Severity				1.06	1.04
				(0.06)	(0.08)
Population				1.13	1.14
				(0.38)	(0.39)
Education				1.03	1.02
				(0.04)	(0.04)
Regional Lag					1.08
					(0.30)
Ideol. Dissimilarity					1.00
					(0.02)
Chi2	20.43	14.04	36.48	32.61	37.97
Df_M	5	5	9	12	14
P	0.00	0.02	0.00	0.00	0.00
Ll	-124.74	-125.05	-118.43	-117.62	-117.55
N	650	650	650	650	650

* $p<0.1$; ** $p<0.05$; *** $p<0.01$
Notes:
Hazard Ratios from cloglog models with robust standard errors clustered on state.
Models control for time dependency with a lowess term (not shown).
All significance tests are two-tailed.

Table 12. Reduced Models of Healthcare Anti-Obesity Policies

	Healthcare1	Healthcare2	Healthcare3	Healthcare4	Healthcare5
Electoral Competition	0.99		0.98	0.98	0.98
	(0.02)		(0.02)	(0.02)	(0.02)
Unified D. Government	1.21		1.61	1.03	0.98
	(1.03)		(1.06)	(0.60)	(0.73)
Unified R. Government	1.08		1.04	1.05	0.97
	(0.78)		(0.72)	(0.78)	(0.72)
Government Ideology	1.00		0.99	0.99	0.99
	(0.02)		(0.01)	(0.01)	(0.02)
Citizen Ideology		1.00	1.00	0.97	0.97
		(0.02)	(0.02)	$(0.01)^*$	$(0.01)^*$
Opponents		1.05	1.06	1.08	1.07
		$(0.03)^{**}$	$(0.03)^{**}$	$(0.03)^{**}$	$(0.03)^{**}$
Advocates		0.99	0.99	1.01	1.02
		(0.01)	(0.01)	(0.02)	(0.02)
Relig. Fundamentalists		0.99	0.98	0.99	0.99
		(0.02)	(0.03)	(0.03)	(0.03)
Problem Severity				1.08	1.07
				(0.07)	(0.08)
Population				1.48	1.49
				(0.45)	(0.44)
Education				1.17	1.16
				$(0.09)^{**}$	$(0.08)^{**}$
Regional Lag					1.12
					(0.26)
Ideol. Dissimilarity					1.00
					(0.02)
Chi2	0.40	5.98	12.69	31.92	37.19
Df_M	4	4	8	11	13
P	0.98	0.20	0.12	0.00	0.00
Ll	-78.57	-77.23	-76.53	-71.41	-71.29
N	650	650	650	650	650

* $p<0.1$; ** $p<0.05$; *** $p<0.01$
Notes:
Hazard Ratios from cloglog models with robust standard errors clustered on state.
Wald tests indicated no time dependency.
All significance tests are two-tailed.

Table 13. Reduced Models of Taskforce Anti-Obesity Policies

	Taskforce1	Taskforce2	Taskforce3	Taskforce4	Taskforce5
Electoral Competition	0.97		0.98	0.98	0.98
	(0.02)		(0.02)	(0.02)	(0.02)
Unified D. Government	1.91		1.60	1.39	0.66
	(0.92)		(0.84)	(0.77)	(0.37)
Unified R. Government	0.46		0.52	0.59	0.28
	(0.42)		(0.51)	(0.57)	(0.27)
Government Ideology	1.00		1.00	1.01	1.01
	(0.01)		(0.02)	(0.02)	(0.01)
Citizen Ideology		1.01	1.01	1.01	1.01
		(0.02)	(0.02)	(0.02)	(0.02)
Opponents		1.02	1.02	1.03	1.02
		(0.05)	(0.04)	(0.06)	(0.06)
Advocates		0.95	0.95	0.97	0.97
		(0.02)***	(0.02)**	(0.03)	(0.03)
Relig. Fundamentalists		1.02	1.02	1.02	1.01
		(0.02)	(0.02)	(0.02)	(0.02)
Problem Severity				1.16	1.18
				(0.12)	(0.12)
Population				1.24	1.20
				(0.29)	(0.28)
Education				1.04	1.03
				(0.06)	(0.06)
Regional Lag					1.08
					(0.25)
Ideol. Dissimilarity					1.04
					(0.01)***
Chi2	8.94	24.15	28.85	32.95	62.00
Df_M	6	6	10	13	15
P	0.18	0.00	0.00	0.00	0.00
Ll	-118.17	-117.75	-114.68	-113.22	-110.28
N	650	650	650	650	650

* $p<0.1$; ** $p<0.05$; *** $p<0.01$
Notes:
Hazard Ratios from cloglog models with robust standard errors clustered on state.
Models control for time dependency with squared time (not shown).
All significance tests are two-tailed.

5.3.4.1 Reduced Models by Component

If we ignore diffusion effects, demographic and morality policy factors, the models with only political representation variables (columns 1 of **Table 11**, **Table 12** and **Table 13**) indicate that for the school component of anti-obesity legislation, only unified Democratic Governments exert a positive ($p<0.05$) effect on the hazard of enacting school-related anti-obesity laws: states with unified Democratic governments face a hazard 3.36 times larger than polities whose government branches are not controlled by the Democratic party.

If we focus only on factors pointed out in the morality policy literature (columns 2), we identify three seemingly contradictory results, i.e., the coefficient for advocates is significantly associated with passing school and taskforce components of AO in a negative direction: a 1-unit increase in the latter is correlated with an estimated 4 % and 5 % decrease in the hazard of adopting school ($p<0.05$) and taskforce AO laws, whereas opponent interest groups are significantly associated with adoptions of healthcare component of AO in a positive direction: one additional interest group increases the hazard of enacting healthcare-related anti-obesity legislation by an estimated 5 % ($p<0.05$).

When we combine morality policy and political representation covariates in a model (columns three), but still ignore demographic and diffusion factors, we see the same patterns of the reduced modes, the only remarkable difference is that states with unified Democratic governments now face a hazard of enacting school-related anti-obesity laws 2.97 times larger than polities whose government branches are not controlled by the Democratic party ($p<0.05$).

If we add demographic factors to the equation, we observe in columns four that the confidence interval of the hazard ratios for the population, education attainment, and the percentage of obese population include 1 in models of school and taskforce components. However, education attainment is (positively) associated with the hazard of enacting healthcare-related anti-obesity laws ($p<0.05$), in addition to that, the coefficient for citizen ideology now (barely) reaches statistical significance: a 1-unit increase in the citizen ideology measure decreases the hazard of enacting healthcare-related anti-obesity legislation by an estimated 3 % ($p<0.1$); for this policy area, the coefficient for opponents behaves similar as in previous reduced models; the hazard ratios of the rest of the variables now include 1. In models of school- related AO legislation that include demographic factors, the hazard ratio for unified Democratic governments behaves similarly as in previous reduced models, and is the only predictor that reaches traditional levels of statistical significance. The hazard ratios of all variables in models of taskforce-AO laws that control for demographics now include one.

Interestingly, in none of the reduced models did I find evidence that neither governments controlled by the Republican Party, government ideology, nor religious fundamentalists were substantially associated with the hazard of passing components of anti-obesity legislation.

5.3.4.2 Reduced Pooled Models

If we ignore diffusion effects, demographic and morality policy factors, the model with only political representation variables (column 1 of Table **14**) indicates that when we pooled all components of anti-obesity legislation, only unified Democratic Governments exert a positive (p<0.05) effect on the hazard of enacting any anti-obesity law: states with unified Democratic governments face a hazard 1.99 times larger than polities whose government branches are not controlled by the Democratic party. If only the first passage of all AO components is considered, no political representation variable reaches traditional levels of statistical significance, as can be seen in A-Table 16.

Table 14. Reduced Models of All Anti-Obesity Policies

	1	2	3	4	5	6
Electoral Competition	0.98		0.98	0.98	0.99	0.99
	(0.01)		(0.01)*	(0.01)	(0.01)	(0.01)
Unified D. Government	1.99		1.78	1.66	1.37	1.17
	(0.68)**		(0.61)*	(0.61)	(0.54)	(0.42)
Unified R. Government	0.79		0.97	0.93	0.72	0.81
	(0.36)		(0.45)	(0.44)	(0.34)	(0.35)
Government Ideology	1.00		1.01	1.01	1.01	1.01
	(0.01)		(0.01)	(0.01)	(0.01)	(0.01)
Citizen Ideology		1.01	0.99	0.99	0.99	0.99
		(0.01)	(0.01)	(0.01)	(0.01)	(0.01)
Opponents		1.01	1.01	1.03	1.03	1.02

	1	2	3	4	5	6
		(0.02)	(0.02)	(0.03)	(0.03)	(0.03)
Advocates		0.96	0.96	0.98	0.98	0.98
		(0.01)***	(0.01)**	(0.02)	(0.02)	(0.01)
Relig. Fundamentalists		1.00	0.99	1.00	1.00	1.00
		(0.02)	(0.02)	(0.02)	(0.02)	(0.01)
Problem Severity				1.10	1.08	1.07
				(0.10)	(0.10)	(0.09)
Population				1.28	1.32	1.13
				(0.29)	(0.30)	(0.18)
Education				1.06	1.05	1.06
				(0.04)	(0.04)	(0.03)*
Regional Lag				1.29	1.34	
					(0.14)**	(0.14)***
Ideol. Dissimilarity					1.01	1.01
					(0.01)*	(0.01)**
Lagged Community						1.99
						(0.78)*
Lagged Healthcare						0.98
						(0.33)
Lagged School						1.83
						(0.62)*
Lagged Taskforce						1.44
						(0.34)
Chi2	25.70	22.45	51.31	57.02	87.22	140.31
Df_M	7	7	11	14	16	20
P	0.00	0.00	0.00	0.00	0.00	0.00
Ll	-381.90	-382.96	-375.61	-371.77	-368.06	-362.57
N	2,600	2,600	2,600	2,600	2,600	2,600

* $p<0.1$; ** $p<0.05$; *** $p<0.01$
Hazard Ratios from cloglog models with robust standard errors clustered on state.
Models control for time dependency with cubed time (not shown).
All significance tests are two-tailed.

If we focus only on factors pointed out in the morality policy literature (column 2), we note that only one coefficient of that conceptual category is significantly associated with passing any anti-obesity measure: a 1-unit increase in my measure for AO supportive interest groups is correlated with an estimated 4 % decrease in the hazard of adopting any AO law in repeated occasions and for the first time (p<0.01). The rest of the hazard ratios for variables from morality policy literature contained one.

When we combine morality policy and political representation covariates in a model, but still ignore demographic and diffusion factors (column three), we see a similar pattern of previous reduced modes, the only remarkable difference is that states with higher levels of electoral competition now face a lower hazard of enacting any anti-obesity law in repeated occasions, although marginally significant, i.e., a one-unit increase in the scale of electoral competition is associated with a 4 % decrease in the hazard of enacting any anti-obesity law (p<0.1) in repeated occasions only.

If we add demographic factors to the equation, we observe in column four that none of the hazard ratios for the included predictors reaches traditional levels of statistical significance.

Interestingly, in none of the reduced models did I find evidence that neither governments controlled by the Republican party, government nor citizen ideology, opposing AO interest groups nor religious fundamentalists were substantially associated with the hazard of passing any anti-obesity policy.

5.3.4.3 Final Models by Component

Full models of the healthcare component of AO indicate that states with conservative ideology, with more AO-opposing interest groups and with higher education attainment records are more likely to enact healthcare-related anti-obesity legislation: a one-unit increase in the citizen ideology measure decreases the hazard of enacting legislation in this policy area by an estimated 3 % (confidence level 90 %), whereas an analogue increase in the opponents and education attainment variables is associated with estimated 7 % and 16 % increases in the hazard of passing healthcare-related AO laws (confidence level 95 %). The confidence interval of the rest of the coefficients—including diffusion variables—includes zero.

When I estimate full models of the school component of anti-obesity legislation, none of the coefficients for controls, political nor morality policy categories reached statistical significance. We see a similar pattern in full models of AO-taskforce component; the only difference is that the only significant predictor is the measure for ideological dissimilarity (see Figure 24): controlling for internal determinants and bordering diffusion, a one-unit increase in the ideological dissimilarity scale is associated with an estimated 4 % increase in the hazard of passing AO-taskforce component laws. The confidence interval of the rest of the coefficients—including diffusion variables—includes zero.

Figure 24. Coefficient Plot of Diffusion Variables of Taskforce-AO, Controlling for Domestic Factors

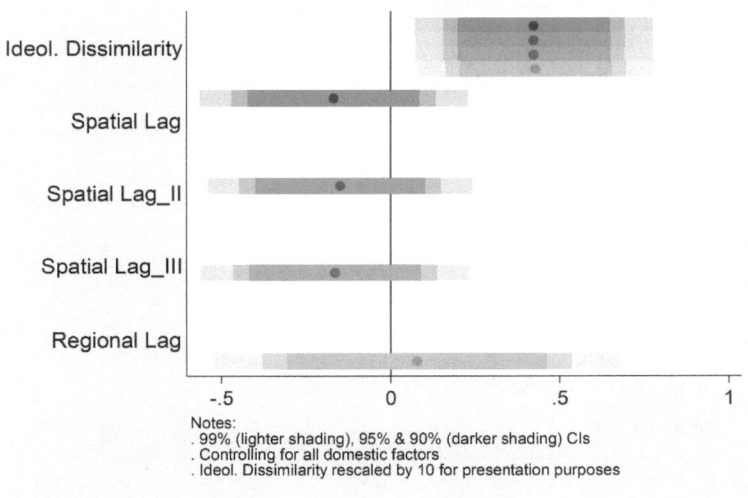

Source: Author

5.3.4.4 Final Pooled Models

When we add diffusion effects to the equation, we observe in column 6 of **Table 14** a remarkably different vector of factors that turned out statistically significant, compared to reduced models: based on results presented in column 6 we can conclude that, in average (because this model pools the information of all policy areas), legislators did not draw information about anti-obesity legislation from ideologically similar states, as captured by the "Ideological Diffusion" covariate (p<0.05), whose direction implies that, controlling for geographical diffusion effects and internal factors, states enacted AO legislation even though they were not ideologically close to previous adopters. This result does not vary when I model the first enactment of all components of anti-obesity legislation (90 % confidence level, though), shown in column five of A-Table 16 and in Figure 25, nor when I exclude indicators of enactments of the individual components of AO legislation (column 5 of **Table 14**). When I exponentiate regression coefficients[42], we observe that one unit increase in the ideological distance actually increases the odds of enacting any anti-obesity policy by an estimated 1 % (2 % in the first-events model), controlling for internal and external determinants.

Figure 25. Coefficient Plot of Diffusion Variables of All AO Laws, Controlling for Domestic Factors

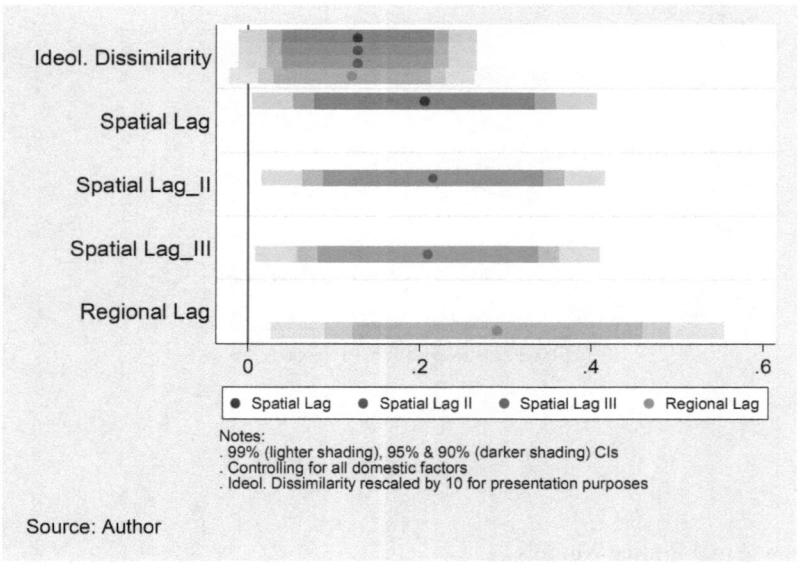

Source: Author

---

42 Exponentiated coefficient are "hazard ratios" (which are interpreted similarly to odds ratios), i.e., hazard ratios greater (less) than one indicate that a unit increase in the covariate corresponds to an increase (decrease) in the hazard of experiencing the event (enacting the corresponding legislation), all else equal (Cleves 2010).

The general measure of similarity ("regional lag") also reached traditional levels of statistical significance (see Figure 25), i.e., one additional co-regional state that enacted an AO is associated with an estimated 34 % increase in the hazard of passing any anti-obesity measure (99 % confidence level), controlling for domestic factors, ideological diffusion and AO component activity (when the latter indicators are omitted, the estimated increase is instead 29 %, same alpha level; if we model the first event only, the estimated increase is 30 %, 95 % alpha level, as can be seen in in column five of A-Table 16).

In the model that controls for internal and external factors, we also note that two of the indicators of past enactments of AO components turned out statistically significant: states that passed community-related AO laws face a 1.99 greater hazard of enacting any anti-obesity law, whereas jurisdictions that passed school-related AO laws face a hazard 1.83 times greater of enacting any anti-obesity law, although the latter results barely reached statistical significance. When we omit the indicator for past community-AO enactments, the main difference is that the indicator for past adoptions of taskforce-AO laws turns out positive, although also marginally significant (see A-Table 15).

Interestingly, in the full model, none of the internal determinants proposed in political representation and morality policy literatures are significant predictors of repeated (nor single) passages of anti-obesity legislation.

5.3.5 Discussion

At first glance, the case of anti-obesity legislation seems to show remarkable results, in that none of the predictors emphasized by neither the literature on morality policy nor on political representation had explanatory power for these laws. However, this pattern of little to no influence of predictive power of political and moral-related factors has been documented in the literature before (Marlow 2013; Rodriguez 2010). In fact, the only domestic factors that are substantially associated with the (pooled) outcome variable are past enactments of AO-community laws, AO-school laws and the level of education attainment. The diffusion variables, however, were the only factors that exerted substantial influence. This result highlights the relevance of accounting for interdependence in apparently little-politicized areas (Oliver and Lee 2005, 939).

The results from above indicate that passage of anti-obesity policies in general in *t-1*—that was included in this project as an example of legislation that reflects minimal to no characteristics of morality policy—in a nearby jurisdiction j were substantially associated with events in $t+1$. This goes in line with my hypothesis that this diffusion effect might be due to officials' responding to the uncertainty generated by the emergence of new policy alternatives by looking for information about them, and that such learning occurred to some extent through cognitive heuristics. For this reason, learning was bounded to units in the geographic vicinity, which in the USA share similar demographic profiles, culture and values. Even though the exact content of the information retrieved from this group of homophilous jurisdictions cannot be revealed with the present research design, the little political attention that these laws seem to have generated during the analysis period (Oliver and Lee 2005, 939) and their higher level of technical complexity makes me believe that the lessons drawn from neighboring jurisdictions could have been more related with the actual effectiveness of previous enactments.

Contrary to my expectations, information about these policies seems to have been additionally drawn from ideologically different states, based on the direction and confidence interval of the ideological dissimilarity measure in the pooled models. One plausible explanation for this could be that these policies actually managed to ameliorate obesity rates in the adopting polities. For that reason, policymakers from jurisdictions without such policies decided to follow the example, even though the latter were ideologically different from the former. In the same vein, when one looks at the politics of individual policy areas of anti-obesity legislation, we observe a similar pattern only in one component. Learning about task-force-related anti-obesity laws also diffused from ideologically dissimilar jurisdictions; however, contrary to when we analyzed all obesity-related laws, past passages of taskforce-related AO laws in neither bordering nor co-regional polities had a substantial effect on the hazard of adopting this component of obesity laws, i.e., lawmakers were positively influenced by enactments of taskforce-AO legislation in jurisdictions beyond their geographic surrounding. Previous works also reported that information drawn from ideologically different states was positively associated with the odds of policy enactment, in particular, passage of research and development tax credits (Leiser 2015) and state expansions of Medicaid (Sylvester 2016, 31). Further research is needed to shed light on this pattern.

The other two components (school and healthcare) were not explained by the state-external characteristics that I considered. This does not imply that diffusion of these policy components did not occur, though. Diffusion might have occurred through other channels, which my measures failed to capture.

Similar to when one focuses on all anti-obesity laws, domestic factors highlighted in political representation and morality policy literature did not predict enactment of taskforce nor school components of AO laws. The only domestic factors that are substantially associated with the (pooled) outcome variable are past enactments of community, school components and the level of education attainment. As previously mentioned, this confirms previous works on the matter (Marlow 2013; Rodriguez 2010).

Jurisdictions with a specific combination of internal characteristics derived from morality policy literature are indeed more prone to enact healthcare-related anti-obesity laws: states with more conservative citizens, higher education attainment levels, and more opponents to AO. The latter is actually surprising, as it is intuitive that more opponents of anti-obesity legislation would be associated with less AO laws. While this may seem like a counter-intuitive finding, states with more healthcare-related AO laws may need less opposition by interest groups, unlike states that have no AO laws at all. Indeed, previous works have found the same apparently counter-intuitive negative effect of interest groups on the odds of passing legislation that they actually oppose. These works have interpreted the result as evidence that certain interest groups might be less interested to lobby against a policy that they are opposed to in states that have passed a given amount of such law or attributed the result to improper model specification. Specifically, a pro-Assisted Reproductive Technologies interest group was found positively associated with enactments of restrictive ART laws and negatively related to adoptions of permissive ART legislation (Heidt-Forsythe 2017, 6), and a pro-gun interest groups decreased the odds of passing stand-your-ground laws (Butz, Fix, and Mitchell 2015, 366).

5.4 Cross-Policy Comparison

I turn now to compare the diffusion of policies that differ in the degree to which they feature the characteristics of morality policy. I will do so by comparing single-spell models of SSM, MML and all anti-obesity laws (pooled AO). The main goal is to compare the diffusion effects across models. Then I describe results, discuss them, and conclude.

As mentioned before, in order to test the variation in the explanatory variables across different policies I follow the literature (Philander and

Abarbanel 2014; Taylor et al. 2012, 81) and implement a two stage seemingly unrelated estimation (SUE) procedure (Weesie 1999, 34) and compare the magnitude of exponentiated beta coefficients (Buis 2017, 11). In order to make the cross-case comparison more feasible, in this section I drop the policy-specific variables from the final models presented in previous chapters and model single adoptions of all anti-obesity laws (results change minimally when repeated-events models of AO are modelled and policy-specific variables are kept, or when geographical diffusion is modelled differently, see A-Table 28 and A-Table 20[43]). Results are shown in Table 15. Models control for geographic diffusion with the best fitting specifications of the geographical diffusion variable, as discussed in the corresponding previous sections. Models that exhibit duration dependency control for it with the best fitting specification thereof, as explained in previous chapters (time controls not displayed to save space).

Table 15. *Full AO, MML, & SSM Models*

	SSM	MML	AO
Spatial Lag	0.70**	1.90***	1.33**
	(0.11)	(0.36)	(0.17)
Ideol. Dissimilarity	1.00	1.04**	1.02***
	(0.02)	(0.02)	(0.01)
Electoral Competition	1.05**	1.06**	0.99
	(0.02)	(0.03)	(0.01)
Unified D. Government	0.86	0.55	1.17
	(0.63)	(0.42)	(0.55)
Unified R. Government	5.96**	0.21*	0.80
	(4.34)	(0.17)	(0.37)
Government Ideology	1.02	0.98	1.02
	(0.02)	(0.02)	(0.01)
Citizen Ideology	0.98	1.01	0.99
	(0.02)	(0.02)	(0.01)
Fundamentalists	1.10***	0.87***	1.00
	(0.03)	(0.05)	(0.02)
lPopulation	1.16	0.88	1.40*
	(0.21)	(0.28)	(0.25)

43 Although policy-specific variables appear in the same rows of A-Table 20, please bear in mind that they differ substantially across the models.

	SSM	MML	AO
Education	0.96	0.95	1.02
	(0.06)	(0.05)	(0.03)
Constant	0.00***	0.11	0.00***
	(0.00)	(0.63)	(0.00)
Chi2	74.66	34.2	36.65
Df_M	13	10	13
P	1.10e-10	.0001708	.0004703
Ll	-88.37	-58.53	-265
N	316	673	2234

* p<0.1; ** p<0.05; *** p<0.01

Hazard Ratios from simultaneously estimated cloglog models. Simultaneously estimated robust standard errors, clustered on state (in parentheses). MML did not exhibit time dependence; AO and SSM control for time dependency with cubed time and splines, correspondingly (not shown). All significance tests are two-tailed.

Table 16. P-values from Wald chi2 Tests of (Selected) Coefficients' Equality Across Equations

Variables	p-value
[MML]Spatial Lag = [AO]Spatial Lag	0.14
[MML]Spatial Lag = [SSM]Spatial Lag	0.00
[AO]Spatial Lag = [SSM]Spatial Lag	0.00
[MML]Ideol. Dissimilarity = [AO]Ideol. Dissimilarity	0. 17
[MML]Electoral Competition = [SSM]Electoral Competition	0. 74
[MML]Unified R. Government = [SSM]Unified R. Government	0.00
[MML]Fundamentalists = [SSM]Fundamentalists	0.00

Source: Author

5.4.1 Internal Determinants Results

Regarding domestic variables, we observe consistency in the results of both SSM and MML, and a marked difference compared to the domestic politics of AO, i.e., the coefficients for religious fundamentalists, unified Republican governments and electoral competition turned out statistically significant for medical marijuana laws and same-sex marriage bans, as can be seen in Figure 26, that plots the corresponding coefficients of these three covariates for SSM and MML models, controlling for external factors.

Figure 26. Coefficient plots of Selected Domestic Factors of MML and SSM

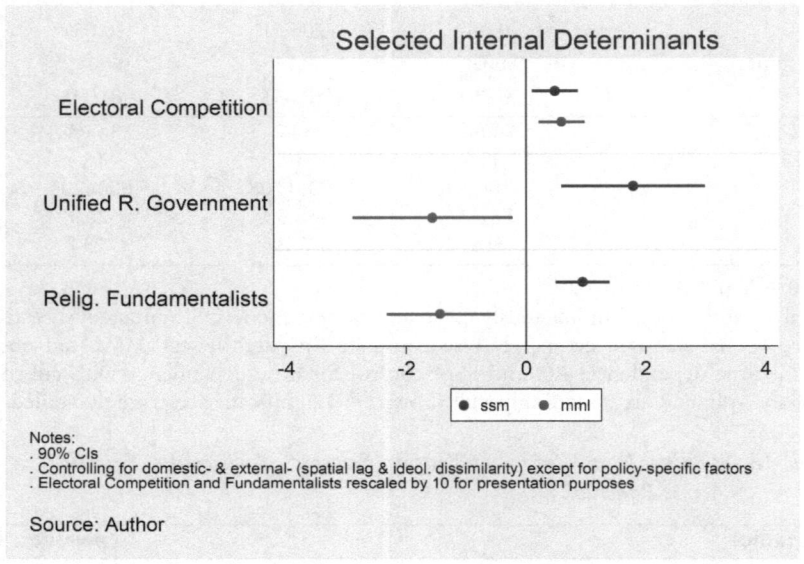

Notes:
. 90% CIs
. Controlling for domestic- & external- (spatial lag & ideol. dissimilarity) except for policy-specific factors
. Electoral Competition and Fundamentalists rescaled by 10 for presentation purposes

Source: Author

States whose three branches of government were controlled by the Republicans were less likely to enact a medical marijuana policy (p<0.1) and more likely to adopt a policy barring recognition of same-sex marriage (p<0.05); if one exponentiates the coefficients, we observe that the estimated hazard of enacting a SSM ban for those jurisdictions with unified Republican governments is 5.96 times the hazard of passing the same law for jurisdictions without unified Republican governments, whereas unified Republican governments decreases the hazard of passing a medical marijuana law by an estimated 79 %. Hence, controlling for external and other internal determinants, Republican governments were negatively associated with the odds of passing two policies with considerable morality content, and the chi-square tests conducted after implementing the two stage seemingly unrelated estimation procedure (Table 16) indicated that the magnitude of such association was substantially higher for the policy on the most conservative side of the spectrum (p<0.1). On the contrary, governments controlled by Republicans were not significantly associated with enactments of our example of legislation that hardly displays the characteristics of morality policy.

States with higher percentages of adherents to fundamentalist doctrines were significantly less likely to enact a medical marijuana policy and more likely to outlaw recognition of same-sex marriage (p<0.01), and unrelated to anti-obesity policy. If we obtain hazard ratios from the coefficient estimates, we observe that each additional adherent to a fundamentalist religion increases the hazard of passing laws prohibiting recognition of SSM and decreases the hazard of enacting a MML by estimated 10 % and 13 %, correspondingly; the two stage seemingly unrelated estimation procedure (Table 16) indicated that these estimated effects are substantially different (p<0.01).

The level of electoral competition increased the odds of both banning recognition of same-sex marriage SSM and of passing medical marijuana laws (p<.05), whereas it did not reach traditional levels of statistical significance for anti-obesity laws. If we obtain hazard ratios, we observe that each 1-point increase in the electoral competition variable increases the hazard of adopt a policy barring recognition of SSM and of enacting a MML by estimated 5 % and 6 %, correspondingly. The two stage seemingly unrelated estimation procedure indicated, however, that these estimated effects are not significantly different (Table 16).

5.4.2 Diffusion Results

We observe for the most part consistency in the measures of geographical diffusion across the policies in Table 15. On the one hand, controlling for domestic determinants and ideological diffusion, the coefficient for the measure that captures the number of events that occurred in the past year in the geographic vicinity (spatial lag), turned out statistically significant and signed as expected, namely, more neighbors with same-sex marriage bans is negatively associated with the hazard of enacting an SSM ban (p<0.05), whereas states with more neighbors that adopted a medical marijuana law or any anti-obesity measure in the past year were more likely to enact a MML (p<0.01) and any AO (p<.05), correspondingly (graphically summarized in Figure 27). The exponentiated coefficients indicate that, controlling for internal factors and ideological distance, one additional neighbor with a SSM ban is associated with a 30 % decrease in the hazard of banning homosexual marriages, whereas the same increase in the spatial lag variables of medical marijuana and anti-obesity laws is associated with estimated 90 % and 33 % increments in the hazard of enacting MML and AO, correspondingly.

Figure 27. Coefficient Plot of Diffusion Variables.

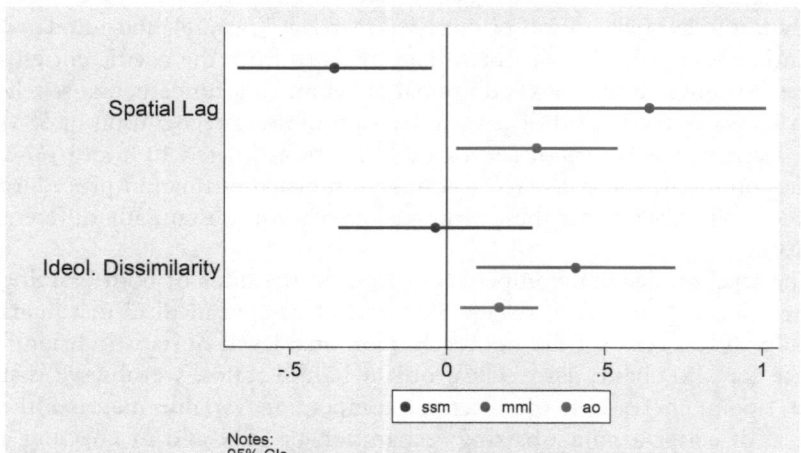

Notes:
95% CIs
. Controlling for domestic-, except for policy-specific factors
. Ideol. Dissimilarity rescaled by 10 for presentation purposes

Source: Author

The chi-square tests of equality conducted after implementing the two stage seemingly unrelated estimation procedure (contained in Table 16) indicated that the estimated magnitude of the effect of the spatial lag is substantially smaller for same-sex marriage bans compared to both medical marijuana policy ($p<0.01$) and to anti-obesity laws ($p<0.01$). In other words, the estimated effect of the geographic diffusion variable on the hazards of enacting the policy with all the theoretical characteristics of morality policy is significantly smaller than its effect on the hazard of adopting policies with less characteristics of this type of legislation. Interestingly, if one only focuses on exponentiated coefficients, the case in the middle of the spectrum experienced the highest estimated impact of bounded-learning from morally similar jurisdictions. Table 16, however, showed that the geographic diffusion effect on the hazard of adopting AO is not significantly larger compared to MML, hence, this result has to be interpreted with caution.

The coefficient for the specific diffusion measure (ideological dissimilarity) turned out statistically significant for MML ($p<0.05$) and AO ($p<0.01$), unlike for same-sex marriage bans (see Figure 27). The direction of the effect of ideological distance, however, runs contrary to my expectations, i.e., these coefficients were positively signed. Focusing on exponentiated coefficients only, we observe that the estimated effect of this measure is quite similar for a policy with a moderate level of moral content (MML) and for the policy on the most liberal side of the continuum, namely a one-unit increase in the scale of ideological dissimilarity increases the hazard of adopting a medical marijuana policy and of enacting any anti-obesity policy by estimated 4 % and 2 %, correspondingly. These apparently similar magnitudes, however, have to be interpreted with caution, too, given that the chi-square test conducted after implementing the two stage seemingly unrelated estimation procedure indicated that the estimated effect of this covariate on the hazard of enacting medical marijuana and anti-obesity laws are not statistically different (Table 16); in other words, we cannot conclude whether the latter is larger/smaller as the former.

5.4.3 Discussion

Before I discuss the main results, I provide a few comments regarding the domestic factors.

5.4.3.1 Internal Determinants

Although I limited my comparative theoretical expectations to diffusion, the cross-policy comparisons revealed a few interesting associations worth mentioning. The interpretation of the ensuing comparisons of internal determinants has an exploratory nature. Briefly, when we omit policy-specific factors (problem severity, advocates and opponents), we observed a striking similarity in the domestic politics of two policies whose level of morality policy characteristics varies, whereas neither political representation factors nor predictors from the literature on morality policy were associated with the policy with minimal morality policy attributes. To sum up, Republican controlled governments and rates of adherence to fundamentalist religions were significantly associated with enactments of medical marijuana policy and same-sex marriage bans (negatively for the former and positively for the latter, as expected); electoral competition is substantially and positively associated with both policies on the left side of the continuum, and as the we move to the right on the continuum, the effect of the Republican party diminishes significantly. Let me elaborate.

First, the domestic politics of the AO contrasts sharply with the internal determinants of legislation with higher levels of moral content, in support of works that suggest that the "politics" of non- and morality policy differ (Lee 1996; Lowi 1988; Mooney and Schuldt 2008). This absence of explanatory power of factors pointed out in the literatures of political representation and morality policy for AO is not all too surprising. Although there are only a handful studies that analyzed state anti-obesity legislation in the USA from a political perspective, the few existing analyses have also pointed towards the little association of traditional political variables and obesity-related measures (Marlow 2013; Rodriguez 2010). This supports the claim that anti-obesity legislation has attracted little political attention during the analysis period (Oliver and Lee 2005); in more recent years, however, this situation might be changing (Kam 2017).

Controlling for diffusion effects and a vector of theoretically relevant domestic factors, adherence to fundamentalist religions exerted significant effects on the hazard of policy adoption: negative when it came to a relatively liberal policy (MML), similar to previous works (Hannah and Mallinson 2017; Kim 2016)—who, however, operationalized the strength of this group with a broader definition; and positive for a conservative measure (SSM), in line similar to previous works (Haider-Markel 2001a; Lewis 2011; Taylor et al. 2012)—some of which, nonetheless, measured this factor with the rate of evangelical adherents. The effect of this variable did vary significantly across legislation; interestingly, though, the estimated size of this effect on the hazard of event occurrence was bigger for the policy in the middle of the continuum than for the illustrative case of classic morality policy (SSM). One might expect that the influence of this religion-based conservative group were larger on the odds of enacting a policy that involves the highest level of moral conflict. Most analyses of MML have even omitted the inclusion of religious activists (Bradford and Bradford 2016; Crawford 2013; Ferraiolo 2004; Meier 1992). However, although most religions oppose drugs, and it is suggested that explanations of drug-related policy making should control for religious opposition (Meier 1994), my measurement of religious opposition might not be the most adequate to capture religious-based activism against a policy with moderate level of moral content. Nonetheless, the comparative task at hand required to strive for comparability across policies, as mentioned earlier.

Second, the level of electoral competition did turn out statistically significant for the policies on the left of the spectrum, similar to previous research that found a discernible, positive effect of this covariate on the odds of enacting same-sex related laws (Lewis 2011; Taylor et al. 2012) and marijuana-related laws (Meier 1994), but different to works that found no effect on SSM bans (Haider-Markel 2001a). Based on the national public opinion figures on these two policies, I argued earlier that these policies played out as consensus morality policies, where law makers and parties do not hesitate to express their support, particularly in jurisdictions with high levels of electoral completion, where the electoral security is weaker, which ultimately increases the policy's chances of serious consideration (Mooney and Lee 1995, p. 617–p. 618). By the same token, the sign and significance of my partisanship variables support the claim that the Republican party benefits from opposing (supporting) liberal (conservative) morality policies, like MML and SSM in that these situations enables the Republican party to mobilize conservative voters, whereas the Democratic party cannot capitalize from such events (Engeli, Green-Pedersen, and Larsen 2012, 168; Lewis 2011; Tatalovich and Daynes 2011). Moreover, we observed that the effect of unified Republican governments decreases significantly as one moves from the most conservative side of the continuum to the middle thereof, and it dissipates for the case on the liberal side of the continuum.

5.4.3.2 Diffusion

To sum up, the results indicate that the motivation to learn about the consequences of previous morality-policy enactments in jurisdictions that share similar values and culture increases as legislation presents less characteristics of morality policy. As a result, the magnitude of the diffusion effect on the likelihood of policy adoption increases as the law in question becomes technically complex and less salient. Nonetheless, as the levels of morality-policy characteristics decrease, policies diffuse not only as a result of learning exclusively from similar jurisdictions, in addition to that, information about less salient, more technically complex legislation is also drawn from ideologically dissimilar units. Let me elaborate.

Taking into consideration the non- and geographic diffusion measures together, one could say that, controlling for theoretically relevant internal determinants, learning about the implications of enacting the policy that was selected as an instance of classic morality policies (SSM) was bounded to the experiences of jurisdictions with similar moral attributes, given that the ideological dissimilarity and spatial lag variables turned out statistically in- and significant, correspondingly; learning about policies distinctly situated in a morality policy continuum was to some extent bounded to the experiences of jurisdictions with similar moral attributes, as indicated by the significant coefficient for geographic diffusion in MML and AO[44] models. Furthermore, in addition to having learned from similar states, information from dissimilar jurisdictions played a substantial role for policies with less moral content, as illustrated with the insignificance of this predictor for SSM, and its significance for the cases on the middle and liberal sides of the spectrum (MML and AO).

Second, variation in the level of moral content does affect the extent to which information retrieved from jurisdictions with similar moral profiles is drawn, as shown by the fact that the post seemingly unrelated estimation tests indicated that the estimated effect of the geographic diffusion covariate was substantially smaller for the case on the left side of the morality policy continuum (SSM) compared to the cases that featured less characteristics of morality policy (MML and AO), i.e., learning from similar jurisdictions increased significantly as we moved towards the liberal side of the morality continuum. However, based on post seemingly unrelated estimation tests, we cannot conclude that more information about AO was drawn from—neither non- nor homophilous—other jurisdictions than about MML.

But why does the effect of diffusion driven by learning from homophilous units decrease as we move along a morality policy continuum, in a way that the bounded-learning effect was significantly smaller for the illustrative case of policy with all the characteristics of morality policy compared to the illustrative cases of policies situated in the middle and on the liberal end of the continuum? We can rely on the claim that policy attributes affect the diffusion and learning patterns of policies (Boushey 2010; 2016, 200; Hays and Glick 1997; Makse and Volden 2011; Mallinson 2016; Mooney and Lee 1999b; Mooney and Schuldt 2008; Nicholson-Crotty 2009).

---

44 One cautionary note is granted. Bear in mind that AO has very few characteristics of morality policy. Moreover, we noted that none of the domestic factors that explained SSM and MML—legislation about which we did find evidence to assume that they can be located in a continuum as I did in this project—had explanatory power for AO. Hence, it might be that the geographical diffusion measure is not capturing moral interdependence of AO, but, e.g., economic/competitive interdependence. In other words, the diffusion mechanism for AO needs not be learning bounded to jurisdictions with similar moral profiles. However, as previously mentioned, the goal of the project required to strive for comparability and measured diffusion in an analogous manner for all the policies analyzed.

This small but growing line of work has documented that across policy types, two attributes seem to exert substantial effects on one particular type of policy diffusion, namely, learning-driven diffusion. Although the methods and data used by these works differ substantially from those utilized in this project—and they have not tested their claims on morality policy—we have a common interest of exploring variation in policies' attributes and its implication for their diffusion. As mentioned in previous sections, these works proved that technical simplicity of a given policy decreases the likelihood that legislators react—to the uncertainty that emerges from the situation where they have to decide whether to support or reject a given policy innovation—by gathering lesser amounts of information from—i.e., learning less about—past experiences, which in turn determines the speed at which policies diffuse. When policies diffuse as a result of legislators learning from past enactments, I claimed in previous sections that if policy makers react to the latter scenario by learning less about past experiences, one empirical implication should be that not only the speed of diffusion, but also the size of the diffusion effect should decrease, i.e., the influence of the enactment of technically simple policy Y in unit j on the odds of enacting the same non-complex policy Y in unit i in $t+1$ should be smaller, compared to the effect of the enactment of technically complex policy Z in unit j on the odds of passing the same complex policy Z in unit i in $t+1$, the reason—mechanism of diffusion—being that legislators are tempted to learn less about simple policies than about complex policies (Boushey 2010; 2016, 200; Hays and Glick 1997; Makse and Volden 2011; Mallinson 2016; Mooney and Lee 1999b; Nicholson-Crotty 2009).

Another consistent finding from this literature is that the salience of a given law has a similar effect. The more salient a given policy is, the less a given legislator is tempted to learn from past experiences, and the policy will be enacted less as a result of learning from previous adoptions. In other words, the enactment of salient policies might be influenced to some extent by what legislators might have learned from external sources, but such learning effect on the odds passing a salient policy will be smaller compared to the influence of learning on the likelihood of adopting a less salient policy, due in part to the fact that demand pressures from citizens should be smaller in the latter scenario (Mooney and Lee 2000; Nicholson-Crotty 2009, 195–96).

These findings help refine the traditional question that motivated earlier scholarship on morality policy, which focused on whether domestic factors of this type of policy differed when compared to the internal politics of policies with no moral content (Lowi 1988). Whereas the domestic politics of morality policies do differ, I claim that morality policies have in common with non-morality policies that their learning-driven diffusion patterns vary in similar ways. In other words, morality policies with high salience and low levels of technical details diffuse in a similar way as technically simple and highly salient non-morality policies. This had been suggested earlier in an analysis that found that a policy with high scores in all the characteristics of morality policy—pre-Roe permissive abortion reforms in the USA—actually diffused in a similar way as non-morality laws (Mooney and Lee 1995). That project, however, focused on one policy only.

This finding goes contrary to the claim that legislators draw equal amounts of information about morality policies from other states because such laws are equally fraught with uncertainty (Hollander and Patapan 2016, 18). Morality policies do involve uncertainty; however, we saw that the less simplicity and salience a policy entailed, the higher the influence of diffusion on the odds of policy enactment.

Nevertheless, why was information about MML and AO additionally retrieved from ideologically dissimilar units? One plausible explanation is that uncertainty about what consequences would follow passage of more technically-complex policies forced/motivated politicians not to limit their searches for information to homophilous polities, but to look for information in dissimilar units. Moreover, it is also plausible that the uncertainty stemming from these laws—that involve more technical details—was less of an electoral nature, for which substantial information—e.g., policy effectiveness—could have been more or equally relevant than political information. In this case, drawing policy-information from jurisdictions that do not share similar ideological attributes seems plausible. The fact that the ideological dissimilarity variable did not impact the hazard of enacting our illustrative policy with more moral content (SSM) is in line with such an account, i.e., given that it is more likely that the information that legislators might have looked for regarding a less technically-complex policy is of political nature, it is plausible that information had not been retrieved from ideologically dissimilar units.

By the same token, I find mixed results regarding the proposition that government officials are interested in gauging the ideological position of legislation when a given policy cannot be easily situated on a scale (e.g., a liberal-conservative ideological one), and that for that purpose, policy makers look to the ideological patterns of those who have already adopted these policies (Grossback 2004, 523). On the one hand, the significant effect of the variable that would test such proposition (ideological dissimilarity) on the odds of adoption of SSM (and insignificance on the hazard of adoption of MML and AO) would support the argument. Contrary to the latter proposition, though, we observed that officials relied to a larger extent not on the experiences of their ideologically similar peers, rather, information from ideologically dissimilar states was indeed influential on future policy choices. In other words, states passed MML and AO even though these policies were not closer to the potential adopters' ideal point in an ideological dimension. However, an alternative interpretation for the direction of the effect of ideological dissimilarity on MML and AO is that the public reaction to or consequences from enacting Y in ideologically dissimilar unit j could have been desirable from the standpoint of legislators from i, in spite of the fact that Y might not match the ideology of i.

However, my results might also indicate that the proposition that public support for morality policies affects their politics has empirical implications for learning about and diffusion of morality policies. If we focus on the cases on the extremes of the morality continuum—about which the post-SUE Wald test revealed that there existed a substantially different effect of learning from homophilous units—tight variations in public sentiment in favor of anti-obesity legislation might have concerned electorally motivated policy makers far more than the rather wider variations in favor of SSM bans. In other words, given that there existed no clear majority in support of/opposition to AO, policymakers had only "mixed signals" about the public preferences, and as such, they might have been specially interested in retrieving more information regarding the more contentious anti-obesity laws, hence, they had a particular incentive to monitor the aftermath of enactment of AO in similar jurisdictions, more so than about SSM. An empirical implication of such interpretation would be that the effect of learning from homophilous units on AO should be significantly larger than the effect on MML—about which national figures indicate that, just as SSM, it constitutes a consensus morality policy. We did not see that pattern, however.

6. Conclusions

At the beginning of this dissertation, I asked what was the role of bounded-learning in the diffusion of morality policies. Based on the findings from individual analyses of Same-Sex Marriage bans (SSM), Medical Marijuana Laws (MML), and Anti-Obesity Legislation (AO) enacted in the USA at the state level between 1995 – 2011, included in the **Analysis** section, I provided theoretical and empirical evidence that bounded-learning is one driving force behind the diffusion of these policies. One plausible explanation for their diffusion is that lawmakers react to the uncertainty—of what political and policy consequences the enactment of these policies would bring about—by searching for information, i.e., by learning. Learning about consequences of SSM ban enactments was bounded to the experiences of polities with similar culture and values, and the information drawn from these sources discouraged future enactments. One plausible explanation for this negative effect is that the electoral consequences observed in SSM-ban adopters were not politically appealing. Learning about MML and AO was also bounded to similar states, but in addition to that, and presumably, due to the lower levels of technical simplicity and salience, these policies also diffused as a consequence of learning from ideologically contrasting units. All in all, MML and AO enactments increased the odds of future enactments thereof. One plausible explanation for this pattern is that in these more complex, less salient policies, not only electoral information but also substantial information about policy effectiveness could have encouraged future passages. In these analyses I found that (supporting and opposing) interest groups were significantly (positively and negatively, correspondingly) associated with passage of MML only.

Based on the above mentioned findings, I proceeded to explore the second research question, i.e., how the learning-driven diffusion of policies varied as their degree of "morality" differed. Based on the findings contained in the section called **Cross-Policy Comparison**, I conclude that the size of the diffusion impact on the odds of policy adoption increases as the policy in question reflects less characteristics of morality policy, namely, diffusion increases as legislation becomes less salient and less technically simple. In other words, the incentive to learn about the consequences of previous enactments of morality policies in jurisdictions that share similar values and culture grows as laws present less attributes of morality policy.

Results also show that as the levels of morality-policy attributes decrease, policies diffuse not only driven by learning from similar jurisdictions. In addition to that, information about less salient, more technically complex morality policies is also retrieved from ideologically dissimilar units. In these comparative analyses, I also found out that, excluding policy-specific factors, Republican controlled governments and rates of adherence to fundamentalist religions were substantially correlated with passage of medical marijuana laws and same-sex marriage bans (negatively for the former, positively for the latter, as expected). Another relevant domestic factor for policies on the left side of the continuum is electoral competition, which turned out significantly and positively associated with enactments of SSM bans and MML. Last, the effect of unified Republican government decreases significantly as policies reflect less characteristics of morality legislation.

As mentioned in section **Contribution and Research Questions**, I contribute to the literature with the first cross-policy comparative analysis of legislation that reflects different levels of morality policy characteristics. I focused specifically on their diffusion—another understudied area. I answered my questions in three steps, as explained in section **Research Design**. First, in the **Theory** section, I proposed bounded-learning as mechanism for the diffusion of morality policies. Then, I analyzed the selected policies individually through Event History Analysis. Third, in order to increase comparability, I dropped the policy-specific variables (opponents, advocates and problem severity) and used Seemingly Unrelated Estimations (SUE), in order to compare the size of the diffusion effect across my cases.

6.1 Limitations and Avenues for further Research

Let me revise some limitations of my project and propose avenues for further research.

The literature on policy diffusion argues that several mechanisms can come into play in diffusion processes, that no single method is able to test all possible mechanisms for diffusion at once, and that researchers are to be especially clear about what can and cannot be inferred from the study (Gilardi 2004; 2015; Karch 2007b; Maggetti and Gilardi 2015; Sponsler 2010). In this vein, I do not claim that the mechanism proposed in this work is the only cause for diffusion. Further mechanisms might come into play, for instance, competition for economic resources gathered from sales of medical marijuana, or competition about the location of food-producing companies. Moreover, as discussed in the text, my measures of diffusion cannot reveal exactly the information that officials from polity j retrieved from unit i. This can be explored in several ways in future projects. On the one hand, one can look for data that reflects how effective policies were and weigh the influence of neighbors based on this, for instance, by allowing neighbors to influence the dependent variable only if they reach a given theoretically defined threshold. This would yield evidence that the information retrieved during the learning process is less political and more substantive. Alternatively, one could switch the unit of observation from state-year to state dyad-year and estimate accordingly. This would allow to test, for instance, whether "imitation" is the mechanism behind diffusion. Another interesting avenue would be to use alternative connectivity matrices.

Second, one could actually quantify the extent to which policies feature characteristics of morality policy. One way to start would be to code with binary or ordinal indicators how policies score in the identified characteristics of morality policy, similar to what authors did for criminal justice reforms (Boushey 2016; Makse and Volden 2011).

Moreover, there is no consensus in the statistical literature whether coefficient estimates of dependent variables with different N are actually comparable (Allison 1999; Buis 2017; Mood 2010). The strategy of implementing a two stage seemingly unrelated estimation procedure (Weesie 1999, 34) could be alternated in future works with other alternatives pointed out in the literature (Buis 2017, 8; Mood 2010), e.g., by using average marginal effects, implementing linear probability models using standardized regression coefficients, or estimating the degree of heterogeneity and controlling for it.

I mentioned that diffusion will certainly occur amongst citizens, too, who in turn demand action from their representatives. In this project, I focused only on diffusion derived from officials learning from other jurisdictions. One alternative would be to use public opinion data on each policy, and construct a public-opinion spatial lag, which would represent the average public opinion in neighboring states in the previous year and test whether this influences passage in $t+1$ or $t+2$. This would require, of course, to either find state-level, issue-specific public opinion, which is unlikely for certain policies. However, recent developments suggest that one could estimate state public opinion based on national polls through multilevel regression, imputation, and poststratification (Pacheco 2011).

6.2 Generalizability

These conclusions, however, are based on a carefully selected, purposive small sample composed of three policies, about which we assumed that they varied significantly in the extent to which they presented attributes of morality policy. This strategy follows closely the methodological suggestions in the field (Mooney and Schuldt 2008) and was previously implemented (Hollander and Patapan 2016). However, I believe that my key finding—learning-driven diffusion increases as policies show less morality policy characteristics—will have some explanatory power in analyses of other units, more so than my findings regarding internal determinants. Let me elaborate.

Although legislation that generates moral conflicts is introduced all around the world, the level of conflict generated will certainly depend on what basic moral values are pervasive in the unit of analysis and how they are distributed amongst the population. In other words, the conflicts over values, identity and culture that routinely spill into the political realm need not be the same in all countries (Doan 2014). Polities with less religious attendance and less religious diversity will certainly experience lesser levels of moral conflict stemming from policies that in the USA did constitute examples of morality policy. By the same token, lower church attendance rates, smaller adherence rates of religions that in the USA are of considerable size (or inexistence of some of these) and/or presence of different religious groups, will affect the strength of religious advocacy, who—as we saw in the results of medical marijuana and same-sex marriage bans—played a central role in the enactment of these policies.

In general, the quality of democracy in other countries will affect how morality policies play out. Particularly, public involvement and their capacity to react to controversial legislation will be conditioned by this. Official interest groups play no minor role in the policy making process in the USA (Nice 1994); their role will probably differ in countries with different lobbying regulations. Parties in other countries with close ties to religions with conservative doctrines will probably oppose liberal moral policies, as the Republican Party in the USA does; by the same token, liberal parties might assume less passive roles than the Democratic Party in the USA when it comes to morality policies (Tatalovich and Daynes 2011). Moreover, several countries have not only more than two parties, but also have different rates of electoral competition. The latter will have implications for legislators' motivation to play active roles in morally controversial issues.

Regarding the generalizability to other countries of my diffusion findings, there are at least two caveats. On the one hand, subnational units from other countries might have lesser policy autonomy—and their politicians will probably exhibit more party discipline, too—than in the USA, which will unquestionably hinder inter-state learning-driven diffusion of morality policies, which might instead be decided at the national level. Another aspect that will very likely differ in analyses of other countries is the geographical location of the sources from where legislators draw information. The geographic and demographic composition of the USA is structured in such a way that physically adjacent units are be similar in terms of culture, values and certain demographic characteristics; moreover, the constant mixing of population and media has given rise to a historical pattern of looking at geographically proximate units to retrieve information (Foster 1978; Gray 1994; Karch 2007b; Lutz 1987; Mintrom 1997; Mooney 2001a; Mooney and Lee 1995; Seljan and Weller 2011, 353; Stream 1999). Units with similar moral profiles need not be adjacent in other countries.

However, I believe that the inferences that I drew regarding the key argument will have decent explanatory power in other settings. Although morality policies will be constituted by different issues in other countries, democratically elected legislators will experience similar levels of uncertainty whenever their citizens demand action regarding a given morality issue. Under such circumstances, I believe that policy makers will respond as risk-averse, electorally-minded actors, and as such, will have an incentive to look for information about the consequences of previous passages in other jurisdictions before they decide to support or reject a given morality policy. Under such circumstances, I believe that learning will probably be conditioned by cognitive heuristics and bounded—to different extents, though—to units that share similar moral profiles. More important, as the levels of technical simplicity and salience of a morality policy decrease, I believe that elected public officials from other countries will react similarly, i.e., by learning more about previous morality policy (rejections) enactments, and as a result, the impact of previous morality policy (non) adoptions on the law maker's policy choice will be higher.

Appendix

A-Figure 1. Method of Adoption of MML During the Analysis Period

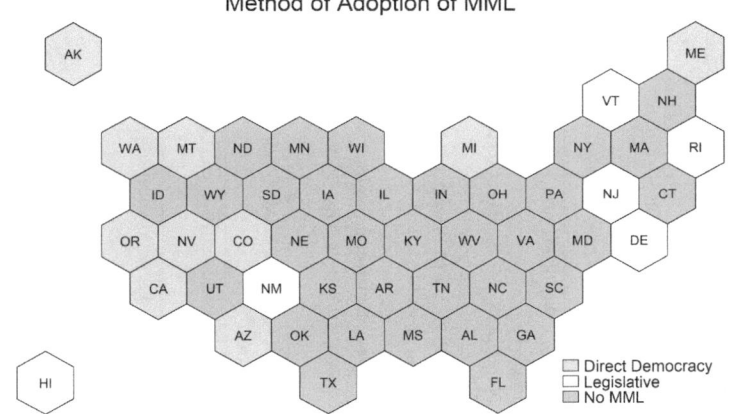

Source: Author

A-Table 1: *Variables Description*

Variable/H	Type	Measurement	Source
Outcome: Enactment of MM Enactment of SSM ban Enactment of AO	Dichotomous	0 = no adoption; 1 = adoption (except for AO, see chapter thereof)	(Marijuana Policy Project 2013) (Lewis 2011) (Lankford et al. 2013)
Diffusion	Continuous	1. "Spatial Lag": Neighbors, AK & HI set to border western states, as (Imhof, 69) 2. "Spatial Lag_II": Neighbors, AK & HI set to 0, as (Berry and Berry 1990) 3. "Spatial Lag_III": AK & HI set to border western states, as (Chamberlain and Haider-Markel 2005, 454) 4. "Regional Lag": neighbors within 9 Regions 5. Ideological: Most recent adoption with heavier weight	Author
Terminally ill	Continuous	age-adjusted cancer death rates per 100,000 population*	(United States Census Bureau Various Years)
Citizen Ideology	Continuous	liberal-to-conservative ideological position of the citizenry	(Berry et al. 2010)
Government Ideology	Continuous	liberal-to-conservative ideological position of government	(Berry et al. 2010)
LGBT interest groups	Continuous (years 1990, 1997 & 2007)	number of LGBT interest groups per 1 million people living in the state	(Gray and Lowery 2001, 266–67; Lowery et al. 2013, 582–83).

Variable/H	Type	Measurement	Source
Education	Continuous	Percentage of state residents over 25 who hold a bachelor's degree or above	American Community Surveys
(log)Population	Continuous	Log number of residents in each state	(United States Census Bureau Various years)
Unified Democrat Government	Dichotomous	1 = Democrat control of state executive & legislative branches; 0 = non Democrat control	NCSL & NGA several years
Religious Fundamentalists	Continuous t-invariant	Percentage of a state's population adhering to fundamentalist protestant groups in year 2000	(Jones et al. 2002)
Law-enforcement interest groups	Continuous (years 1990, 1997 & 2007)	number of state police & sheriff interest groups per 1 million people living in the state	(Gray and Lowery 2001, 266–67; Lowery et al. 2013, 582–83).
Medical interest groups	Continuous, (years 1990, 1997 & 2007)	number of medical doctors', health professionals' and physicians' state interest groups per 1 million people living in the state	(Gray and Lowery 2001, 266–67; Lowery et al. 2013, 582–83).
Obese Population	Continuous	proportion of population with a body mass index higher than 30	(Centers for Disease Control and Prevention)
Political Competition	Continuous	State legislative district-level index of party competition	(Holbrook and van Dunk 1993)
Unified Republican Government	Dichotomous	1 = Republican control of state executive & legislative branches; 0 = non republican control	NCSL & NGA several years

All variables are annually varying covariates, unless indicated otherwise in "Type" column.

Source: Author

A-Table 2. *Correlation Coefficients for SSM*

		(1)	(2)	(3)	(4)	(5)	(6)	(7)	(8)	(9)	(10)	(11)	(12)	(13)	(14)	(15)	(16)	(17)	(18)	(19)
(1)	censor_SSM	1.00																		
(2)	Electoral Competition	0.04	1.00																	
(3)	Unified D. Government	-0.04	-0.08	1.00																
(4)	Unified R. Government	0.17	0.22	-0.23	1.00															
(5)	Government Ideology	-0.14	-0.10	0.61	-0.68	1.00														
(6)	Citizen Ideology	-0.16	-0.00	0.03	-0.23	0.46	1.00													
(7)	Opponents	-0.01	-0.05	-0.07	-0.11	0.04	0.10	1.00												
(8)	Relig. Fundamentalists	0.18	-0.35	0.14	0.00	-0.16	-0.60	-0.14	1.00											
(9)	Problem Severity	-0.06	-0.16	-0.08	-0.16	0.15	0.42	0.25	-0.36	1.00										
(10)	Population	-0.01	-0.08	-0.02	-0.07	-0.05	0.09	-0.14	-0.07	0.19	1.00									
(11)	Education	-0.03	0.06	-0.07	-0.05	0.14	0.53	0.18	-0.51	0.63	0.18	1.00								
(12)	spline1	0.05	-0.20	-0.10	-0.05	0.03	0.36	0.26	-0.27	0.82	0.06	0.61	1.00							
(13)	spline2	-0.01	-0.21	-0.05	-0.09	0.09	0.34	0.19	-0.23	0.80	0.06	0.54	0.94	1.00						
(14)	spline3	-0.01	-0.21	-0.04	-0.10	0.10	0.33	0.17	-0.22	0.77	0.05	0.51	0.91	1.00	1.00					
(15)	Ideol. Dissimilarity	0.11	-0.06	0.26	-0.12	0.30	0.28	0.03	-0.14	0.25	-0.07	0.35	0.37	0.24	0.21	1.00				
(16)	Spatial Lag	0.06	-0.15	-0.07	0.11	-0.19	-0.03	0.19	-0.04	0.47	0.01	0.26	0.70	0.59	0.55	0.24	1.00			
(17)	Spatial Lag_II	0.06	-0.15	-0.07	0.11	-0.19	-0.03	0.19	-0.04	0.47	0.01	0.26	0.70	0.59	0.55	0.24	1.00	1.00		
(18)	Spatial Lag_III	0.06	-0.15	-0.07	0.11	-0.19	-0.03	0.19	-0.04	0.47	0.01	0.26	0.70	0.59	0.55	0.24	1.00	1.00	1.00	
(19)	Regional Lag	0.07	-0.16	-0.01	0.01	-0.03	0.11	0.24	-0.12	0.51	-0.09	0.33	0.71	0.59	0.55	0.29	0.85	0.85	0.85	1.00

Source: Author

A-Table 3. Correlation Coefficients for MML

		(1)	(2)	(3)	(4)	(5)	(6)	(7)	(8)	(9)	(10)	(11)	(12)	(13)	(14)	(15)	(16)	(17)
(1)	adoptmml	1.00																
(2)	Electoral Competition	0.13	1.00															
(3)	Unified D. Government	0.00	-0.04	1.00														
(4)	Unified R. Government	-0.04	0.12	-0.31	1.00													
(5)	Government Ideology	0.04	0.03	0.64	-0.73	1.00												
(6)	Citizen Ideology	0.09	0.16	0.21	-0.28	0.50	1.00											
(7)	Opponents	0.03	0.19	-0.02	0.10	-0.03	-0.01	1.00										
(8)	Relig. Fundamentalists	-0.10	-0.29	-0.04	0.14	-0.28	-0.61	-0.11	1.00									
(9)	Problem Severity	-0.06	-0.25	0.09	-0.15	0.14	0.03	-0.04	-0.01	1.00								
(10)	Population	-0.06	-0.26	0.03	-0.11	-0.01	0.11	-0.59	-0.03	0.14	1.00							
(11)	Education	0.07	0.18	0.07	-0.03	0.18	0.45	-0.06	-0.32	0.04	0.16	1.00						
(12)	advocates	0.08	0.24	-0.04	0.24	-0.07	0.04	0.62	-0.12	-0.09	-0.63	0.02	1.00					
(13)	Ideol. Dissimilarity	0.06	-0.06	0.17	0.41	-0.23	-0.03	0.05	0.13	0.03	0.01	0.12	0.06	1.00				
(14)	Spatial Lag	0.07	0.03	-0.02	0.17	-0.13	-0.15	0.10	0.15	-0.06	-0.18	0.23	0.14	0.27	1.00			
(15)	Spatial Lag_II	0.03	0.02	-0.04	0.18	-0.16	-0.17	0.12	0.16	-0.03	-0.16	0.23	0.15	0.25	0.98	1.00		
(16)	Spatial Lag_III	0.06	0.03	-0.01	0.17	-0.13	-0.14	0.10	0.15	-0.05	-0.18	0.23	0.14	0.27	1.00	0.98	1.00	
(17)	Regional Lag	0.13	-0.00	0.04	0.06	-0.00	0.01	0.19	0.11	-0.05	-0.24	0.25	0.12	0.19	0.80	0.76	0.79	1.00

Source: Author

A-Table 4. Correlation Coefficients for AO

		(1)	(2)	(3)	(4)	(5)	(6)	(7)	(8)	(9)	(10)	(11)	(12)	(13)	(14)	(15)	(16)	(17)	(18)	(19)	(20)	(21)	(22)	(23)	(24)
(1)	Adopts Provision	1.00																							
(2)	Electoral Competition	-0.05	1.00																						
(3)	Unified D. Government	0.08	0.04	1.00																					
(4)	Unified R. Government	-0.04	0.04	-0.28	1.00																				
(5)	Government Ideology	0.06	0.09	0.65	-0.71	1.00																			
(6)	Citizen Ideology	0.02	0.20	0.21	-0.26	0.53	1.00																		
(7)	Opponents	-0.02	0.24	0.10	-0.15	0.23	0.33	1.00																	
(8)	Relig. Fundamentalists	0.00	-0.32	-0.06	0.20	-0.31	-0.61	-0.18	1.00																
(9)	Problem Severity	0.05	-0.16	0.13	-0.07	0.04	-0.13	0.07	0.23	1.00															
(10)	Population	0.08	-0.22	0.07	-0.07	-0.01	0.01	-0.37	-0.01	0.15	1.00														
(11)	Education	0.03	0.24	0.09	-0.07	0.21	0.46	0.16	-0.36	-0.19	0.14	1.00													
(12)	advocates	-0.07	0.23	-0.10	0.20	-0.06	0.09	0.35	-0.12	-0.16	-0.64	0.00	1.00												
(13)	Lagged Community	0.04	-0.03	0.03	0.02	0.02	0.09	0.01	-0.10	0.08	0.20	0.11	-0.07	1.00											
(14)	Lagged Healthcare	0.03	-0.13	-0.02	0.12	-0.13	-0.02	0.04	-0.02	0.15	0.13	0.20	-0.05	0.17	1.00										
(15)	Lagged School	0.09	-0.15	0.29	-0.19	0.21	0.04	0.04	0.02	0.39	0.17	0.08	-0.12	0.14	0.23	1.00									
(16)	Lagged Taskforce	0.09	-0.12	0.21	-0.20	0.21	0.03	0.01	0.12	0.41	0.20	-0.01	-0.19	0.20	0.01	0.31	1.00								

		(1)	(2)	(3)	(4)	(5)	(6)	(7)	(8)	(9)	(10)	(11)	(12)	(13)	(14)	(15)	(16)	(17)	(18)	(19)	(20)	(21)	(22)	(23)	(24)
(17)	Time	0.03	-0.00	0.13	-0.07	0.12	0.16	0.29	-0.00	0.74	0.04	0.31	-0.01	0.20	0.25	0.40	0.32	1.00							
(18)	Time2	0.02	0.01	0.15	-0.07	0.13	0.14	0.32	0.00	0.70	0.04	0.30	0.00	0.21	0.25	0.39	0.29	0.96	1.00						
(19)	Time3	0.01	0.02	0.15	-0.07	0.13	0.11	0.32	0.00	0.65	0.03	0.28	0.00	0.21	0.25	0.37	0.27	0.91	0.99	1.00					
(20)	Ideol. Dissimilarity	0.05	-0.04	0.12	0.31	-0.19	-0.05	0.03	0.10	0.22	0.05	0.12	-0.02	0.04	0.16	0.09	0.06	0.33	0.26	0.22	1.00				
(21)	Spatial Lag	0.05	-0.18	0.08	-0.08	0.05	-0.01	0.03	0.16	0.43	0.12	0.05	-0.10	-0.04	0.05	0.20	0.14	0.45	0.43	0.41	0.15	1.00			
(22)	Spatial Lag_II	0.06	-0.19	0.09	-0.08	0.04	-0.03	0.01	0.17	0.44	0.16	0.05	-0.11	-0.03	0.06	0.22	0.15	0.43	0.42	0.40	0.15	0.98	1.00		
(23)	Spatial Lag_III	0.06	-0.19	0.08	-0.09	0.05	-0.01	0.02	0.16	0.43	0.14	0.05	-0.11	-0.04	0.05	0.21	0.15	0.44	0.43	0.40	0.15	1.00	0.99	1.00	
(24)	Regional Lag	0.07	-0.14	0.10	0.02	0.04	0.08	0.14	0.08	0.44	0.03	0.11	-0.04	0.10	0.24	0.17	0.14	0.51	0.50	0.48	0.22	0.64	0.62	0.63	1.00

Source: Author

A-Table 5. *Diffusion Models of SSM bans (Hazard Ratios)*

Event History Analyses of Same-Sex Marriage Bans
1995 – 2006

	SSM	SSM	SSM	SSM
Electoral Competition	1.05	1.05	1.05	1.05
	(0.02)**	(0.02)**	(0.02)**	(0.02)**
Unified D. Government	0.96	0.96	0.96	0.73
	(0.74)	(0.74)	(0.74)	(0.55)
Unified R. Government	6.15	6.15	6.15	5.87
	(4.40)**	(4.40)**	(4.40)**	(4.19)**
Government Ideology	1.02	1.02	1.02	1.02
	(0.02)	(0.02)	(0.02)	(0.02)
Citizen Ideology	0.98	0.98	0.98	0.99
	(0.02)	(0.02)	(0.02)	(0.02)
Opponents	0.98	0.98	0.98	1.02
	(0.09)	(0.09)	(0.09)	(0.10)
Relig. Fundamentalists	1.10	1.10	1.10	1.11
	(0.03)***	(0.03)***	(0.03)***	(0.04)***
Problem Severity	5.54	5.54	5.54	12.61
	(9.66)	(9.66)	(9.66)	(23.30)
Population	1.11	1.11	1.11	1.14
	(0.21)	(0.21)	(0.21)	(0.25)
Education	0.95	0.95	0.95	0.98
	(0.06)	(0.06)	(0.06)	(0.05)
spline1	270.87	270.87	270.87	148.41
	(249.35)***	(249.35)***	(249.35)***	(110.45)***
spline2	0.00	0.00	0.00	0.00
	(0.00)***	(0.00)***	(0.00)***	(0.00)***
spline3	7.57e+28	7.57e+28	7.57e+28	6.47e+28
	(9.78e+29)***	(9.78e+29)***	(9.78e+29)***	(7.85e+29)***
Ideol. Dissimilarity	0.99	0.99	0.99	1.00

	SSM	SSM	SSM	SSM
	(0.02)	(0.02)	(0.02)	(0.02)
Spatial Lag	0.72			
	(0.11)**			
Spatial Lag_II		0.72		
		(0.11)**		
Spatial Lag_III			0.72	
			(0.11)**	
Regional Lag				1.04
				(0.16)
Constant	0.00	0.00	0.00	0.00
	(0.00)***	(0.00)***	(0.00)***	(0.00)***
Chi2	80.86	80.86	80.86	80.15
Df_M	15	15	15	15
P	0.00	0.00	0.00	0.00
Ll	-87.97	-87.97	-87.97	-89.85
N	316	316	316	316
AIC	207.9455	207.9455	207.9455	211.7054
BIC	236.1247	236.1247	236.1247	239.8846

* $p<0.1$; ** $p<0.05$; *** $p<0.01$
Notes:
Hazard Ratios from cloglog models with robust standard errors clustered on state.
A- & BIC calculated based on 43 events.
All significance tests are two-tailed.

A-Table 6. Diffusion Models of MML (Hazard Ratios)

Event History Analyses of Medical Marijuana Laws
1996 – 2011

	MML	MML	MML	MML
Electoral Competition	1.06	1.06	1.06	1.07
	(0.03)**	(0.03)**	(0.03)**	(0.03)**
Unified D. Government	0.60	0.68	0.61	0.61
	(0.48)	(0.58)	(0.50)	(0.46)
Unified R. Government	0.11	0.10	0.11	0.10
	(0.10)**	(0.09)**	(0.10)**	(0.11)**
Government Ideology	0.98	0.97	0.97	0.98
	(0.02)	(0.02)	(0.02)	(0.02)
Citizen Ideology	1.01	1.02	1.01	1.01

	MML	MML	MML	MML
	(0.02)	(0.02)	(0.02)	(0.02)
Opponents	0.95	0.94	0.95	0.95
	(0.03)*	(0.03)**	(0.03)*	(0.03)*
Relig. Fundamentalists	0.87	0.89	0.88	0.84
	(0.05)**	(0.05)**	(0.05)**	(0.06)**
Problem Severity	0.99	0.99	0.99	0.99
	(0.01)	(0.01)	(0.01)	(0.01)
Population	0.86	0.81	0.84	0.99
	(0.33)	(0.30)	(0.32)	(0.41)
Education	1.00	1.01	1.01	0.97
	(0.06)	(0.06)	(0.06)	(0.06)
advocates	1.04	1.04	1.04	1.05
	(0.02)*	(0.02)**	(0.02)*	(0.03)*
Ideol. Dissimilarity	1.05	1.06	1.05	1.05
	(0.02)***	(0.02)***	(0.02)***	(0.02)***
Spatial Lag	1.53			
	(0.39)*			
Spatial Lag_II		1.24		
		(0.33)		
Spatial Lag_III			1.44	
			(0.38)	
Regional Lag				1.90
				(0.43)***
Constant	0.16	0.31	0.21	0.07
	(0.95)	(1.82)	(1.30)	(0.49)
Chi2	61.70	38.91	50.74	122.09
Df_M	13	13	13	13
P	0.00	0.00	0.00	0.00
Ll	-58.44	-59.38	-58.78	-55.74
N	673	673	673	673
AIC	144.8870	146.7583	145.5535	139.4837
BIC	155.7033	157.5745	156.3698	150.2999

* $p<0.1$; ** $p<0.05$; *** $p<0.01$
Notes:
Hazard ratios from cloglog models with robust standard errors clustered on state.
A- & BIC calculated based on 16 events.
All significance tests are two-tailed.

A-Table 7. Wald Tests of Duration Dependence for PEHA & AO-component models

	PEHA	Community	Healthcare	School	Taskforce
Test 1	(1) [comp_adopt]duration_ = 0 chi2(1) = 4.65 Prob > chi2 = 0.0310	(1) [comp_adopt]duration_ = 0 chi2(1) = 2.69 Prob > chi2 = 0.1010	(1) [comp_adopt]duration_ = 0 chi2(1) = 1.30 Prob > chi2 = 0.2541	(1) [comp_adopt]duration_ = 0 chi2(1) = 0.00 Prob > chi2 = 0.9943	(1) [comp_adopt]duration_ = 0 chi2(1) = 4.36 Prob > chi2 = 0.0368
Test 2	(1) [comp_adopt]dur = 0 chi2(1) = 1.82 Prob > chi2 = 0.1778	(1) [comp_adopt]dur = 0 chi2(1) = 6.22 Prob > chi2 = 0.0126	(1) [comp_adopt]dur = 0 chi2(1) = 1.01 Prob > chi2 = 0.3148	(1) [comp_adopt]dur = 0 chi2(1) = 1.73 Prob > chi2 = 0.1890	(1) [comp_adopt]dur = 0 chi2(1) = 1.42 Prob > chi2 = 0.2327
Test 3	(1) [comp_adopt]lowesst = 0 chi2(1) = 4.15 Prob > chi2 = 0.0417	(1) [comp_adopt]lowesst = 0 chi2(1) = 10.99 Prob > chi2 = 0.0009	(1) [comp_adopt]lowesst = 0 chi2(1) = 2.61 Prob > chi2 = 0.1060	(1) **[comp_adopt]lowesst = 0** **chi2(1) = 11.45** **Prob > chi2 = 0.0007**	(1) [comp_adopt]lowesst = 0 chi2(1) = 2.58 Prob > chi2 = 0.1082
Test 4	(1) [comp_adopt]duration_ = 0 (2) [comp_adopt]dur2 = 0 chi2(2) = 13.64 Prob > chi2 = 0.0011	(1) [comp_adopt]duration_ = 0 (2) [comp_adopt]dur2 = 0 chi2(2) = 11.59 Prob > chi2 = 0.0030	(1) [comp_adopt]duration_ = 0 (2) [comp_adopt]dur2 = 0 chi2(2) = 3.58 Prob > chi2 = 0.1666	(1) [comp_adopt]duration_ = 0 (2) [comp_adopt]dur2 = 0 chi2(2) = 8.19 Prob > chi2 = 0.0167	(1) **[comp_adopt]duration_ = 0** (2) **[comp_adopt]dur2 = 0** **chi2(2) = 4.94** **Prob > chi2 = 0.0847**
Test 5	(1) **[comp_adopt]duration_ = 0** (2) **[comp_adopt]dur2 = 0** (3) **[comp_adopt]dur3 = 0** **chi2(3) = 14.33** **Prob > chi2 = 0.0025**	(1) **[comp_adopt]duration_ = 0** (2) **[comp_adopt]dur2 = 0** (3) **[comp_adopt]dur3 = 0** **chi2(3) = 11.90** **Prob > chi2 = 0.0077**	(1) [comp_adopt]duration_ = 0 (2) [comp_adopt]dur2 = 0 (3) [comp_adopt]dur3 = 0 chi2(3) = 5.38 Prob > chi2 = 0.1461	(1) [comp_adopt]duration_ = 0 (2) [comp_adopt]dur2 = 0 (3) [comp_adopt]dur3 = 0 chi2(3) = 7.70 Prob > chi2 = 0.0526	(1) [comp_adopt]duration_ = 0 (2) [comp_adopt]dur2 = 0 (3) [comp_adopt]dur3 = 0 chi2(3) = 5.32 Prob > chi2 = 0.1499
Test 6	(1) [comp_adopt]spline1 = 0 (2) [comp_adopt]spline2 = 0 (3) [comp_adopt]spline3 = 0 chi2(3) = 14.03 Prob > chi2 = 0.0029	(1) [comp_adopt]spline1 = 0 (2) [comp_adopt]spline2 = 0 (3) [comp_adopt]spline3 = 0 chi2(3) = 7.69 Prob > chi2 = 0.0528	(1) [comp_adopt]spline1 = 0 (2) [comp_adopt]spline2 = 0 (3) [comp_adopt]spline3 = 0 chi2(3) = 4.10 Prob > chi2 = 0.2513	(1) [comp_adopt]spline1 = 0 (2) [comp_adopt]spline2 = 0 (3) [comp_adopt]spline3 = 0 chi2(3) = 9.23 Prob > chi2 = 0.0263	(1) [comp_adopt]spline1 = 0 (2) [comp_adopt]spline2 = 0 (3) [comp_adopt]spline3 = 0 chi2(3) = 5.60 Prob > chi2 = 0.1327

Source: Author

A-Table 8. Wald Tests of Duration Dependence for MML & SSM Models

MML	SSM
(1) [adoptmml]duration_ = 0	(1) [censor_SSM]duration_ = 0
chi2(1) = 0.13 Prob > chi2 = 0.7228	chi2(1) = 11.14 Prob > chi2 = 0.0008
(1) [adoptmml]ldur = 0	(1) [censor_SSM]ldur = 0
chi2(1) = 0.21 Prob > chi2 = 0.6430	chi2(1) = 21.88 Prob > chi2 = 0.0000
(1) [adoptmml]lowesst = 0	(1) [censor_SSM]lowesst = 0
chi2(1) = 0.03 Prob > chi2 = 0.8606	chi2(1) = 32.42 Prob > chi2 = 0.0000
(1) [adoptmml]duration_ = 0 (2) [adoptmml]dur2 = 0	(1) [censor_SSM]duration_ = 0 (2) [censor_SSM]dur2 = 0
chi2(2) = 0.18 Prob > chi2 = 0.9125	chi2(2) = 20.35 Prob > chi2 = 0.0000
(1) [adoptmml]duration_ = 0 (2) [adoptmml]dur2 = 0 (3) [adoptmml]dur3 = 0	(1) [censor_SSM]duration_ = 0 (2) [censor_SSM]dur2 = 0 (3) [censor_SSM]dur3 = 0
chi2(3) = 0.75 Prob > chi2 = 0.8621	chi2(3) = 35.44 Prob > chi2 = 0.0000
(1) [adoptmml]spline1 = 0 (2) [adoptmml]spline2 = 0 (3) [adoptmml]spline3 = 0	**(1) [censor_SSM]spline1 = 0** **(2) [censor_SSM]spline2 = 0** **(3) [censor_SSM]spline3 = 0**
chi2(3) = 0.93 Prob > chi2 = 0.8194	**chi2(3) = 39.53** **Prob > chi2 = 0.0000**

Source: Author

A-Table 9. Enacted State Obesity Legislation by Component, 1998–2001

Year	State	Bill name, by Author		Bill Content
		(Wellever, Reichard, and Velasco 2004)	(Boehmke 2009)	
1998	LA		HCR 11	The resolution directs the Department of Health and Hospitals to study the effect of obesity in both adults and children; to make recommendations for improvement in awareness of the problem of obesity and suggested treatment; and to report the findings of this study and recommendations to the Legislature prior to the 1999 Regular Session.
1999	SC	SCR252	S 252	Requests that the Department of Health and Environmental Control study the effect of obesity in adults and children.
1999	NM	NM Stat. Ann 6–4–10		Allows money from the tobacco settlement fund to be appropriated for public school programs including extracurricular and after-school programs designed to involve students in athletic activities.
1999	AL	SJR27	Ala. Acts, Act #98	Requests that the state Department of Health conduct studies to create public awareness of and control morbid obesity.
1999	FL		SR 2734	This resolution requires comprehensive coverage of diabetic treatment, supplies and self-management training in all federal and federally regulated insurance programs
1999	LA	Chap 46 2611		Establishes the Council on Obesity Prevention and Management.
1999	NJ	NJ Stat. Ann. 26:1A-37.6		Establishes New Jersey Council for Physical Fitness and Sports, which will assist the Department of Education to develop health, physical fitness and wellness programs for students.
2000	IN	HR35	HR 35	The resolution encourages the Indiana department of education and local school boards to provide regular fitness programs for all students.
2000	IA		EO 16	Creates the Iowa Food Policy Council.
2000	CA		AB 2038	Enacts the Inclusion of Women and Minorities in Clinical Research Act to ensure the inclusion of women and minorities in research trials and studies of diseases, disorders, and conditions of particular concern to these populations – including obesity
2000	MS		HB 199 & SB 2861	Amends the Nurse Intervention Program, available to all public school districts in the state, to include specific preventive services, i.e., nutrition education and counseling to prevent obesity and/or other eating disorders which may lead to life-threatening conditions
2000	IN	IC 27–8–14–1		Requires insurers to cover non-experimental surgical treatments for morbid obesity.

Source: Author, with data from (Wellever, Reichard, and Velasco, 2004) and (Boehmke 2009)

A-Table 10.   States with Multiple Events in Same Year, by Component

Healthcare			School		
State	year	NrRepeated_healthcare	state	year	NrRepeated_school
Maryland	2001	2	Maryland	2009	2
Maryland	2004	2	North Carolina	2005	2
Maryland	2010	3	North Carolina	2009	2
			Rhode Island	2005	2
			Texas	2003	2
			Virginia	2007	2
Taskforce			Community		
state	year	NrRepeated_taskforce	state	year	NrRepeated_community
Oklahoma	2001	2	Iowa	2006	2
Tennessee	2001	2			

Source: Author.
Note: Columns entitled "NrRepeated_" record the number of events that occurred in a given state in the same year and that were not considered for the analysis for the reasons mentioned in the text (the total number of events not considered sums to 13: 4 for healthcare, 2 for taskforce, 6 for school and 1 for community AO legislation.)

A-Table 11.   Enacted State Obesity Legislation by Component, 1998–2001

state	healthcare	taskforce	school	community	total	Percentage DV	rank
Maryland	7	2	3	0	12	11.42857	1
North Carolina	1	3	4	1	9	8.571428	2
California	1	1	4	2	8	7.619048	3.5
Mississippi	1	3	4	0	8	7.619048	3.5
Louisiana	0	3	2	0	5	4.761905	5
Texas	0	2	2	0	4	3.809524	8
Florida	1	0	1	2	4	3.809524	8
Colorado	1	0	3	0	4	3.809524	8
Tennessee	0	2	2	0	4	3.809524	8
Rhode Island	0	1	2	1	4	3.809524	8
Iowa	0	1	0	2	3	2.857143	14
New Hampshire	1	1	1	0	3	2.857143	14
Indiana	2	0	1	0	3	2.857143	14
Oklahoma	0	2	1	0	3	2.857143	14
Virginia	1	0	2	0	3	2.857143	14

state	healthcare	taskforce	school	community	total	Percentage DV	rank
New York	0	2	1	0	3	2.857143	14
Illinois	0	2	1	0	3	2.857143	14
South Carolina	1	1	0	0	2	1.904762	21
New Jersey	0	2	0	0	2	1.904762	21
West Virginia	0	0	2	0	2	1.904762	21
Maine	0	1	1	0	2	1.904762	21
Kansas	1	0	1	0	2	1.904762	21
Vermont	2	0	0	0	2	1.904762	21
Massachusetts	0	0	1	1	2	1.904762	21
Arkansas	0	0	1	0	1	0.952381	28.5
Idaho	1	0	0	0	1	0.952381	28.5
Kentucky	0	1	0	0	1	0.952381	28.5
Delaware	0	1	0	0	1	0.952381	28.5
Alabama	0	1	0	0	1	0.952381	28.5
New Mexico	0	0	1	0	1	0.952381	28.5
Washington	0	0	1	0	1	0.952381	28.5
Nevada	0	1	0	0	1	0.952381	28.5

Source: Author

Appendix

A-Table 12. Reduced Models of School Component of Anti-Obesity Policy (1st Event)

	School1	School2	School3	School4	School5
Electoral Competition	0.96		0.97	0.97	0.97
	(0.02)**		(0.02)*	(0.02)	(0.02)
Unified D. Government	3.78		3.16	2.88	2.25
	(2.43)**		(2.12)*	(2.05)	(1.89)
Unified R. Government	1.33		1.82	1.79	1.40
	(0.95)		(1.33)	(1.30)	(0.95)
Government Ideology	1.01		1.02	1.02	1.03
	(0.02)		(0.02)	(0.02)	(0.03)
Citizen Ideology		1.00	0.98	0.98	0.98
		(0.02)	(0.02)	(0.02)	(0.02)
Opponents		0.94	0.95	0.94	0.93
		(0.07)	(0.06)	(0.10)	(0.11)
Advocates		0.97	0.98	0.99	0.99
		(0.02)*	(0.02)	(0.03)	(0.03)
Relig. Fundamentalists		0.99	0.97	0.97	0.97
		(0.02)	(0.03)	(0.03)	(0.03)
Problem Severity				1.09	1.08
				(0.08)	(0.09)
Population				1.21	1.23
				(0.38)	(0.40)
Education				1.02	1.01
				(0.06)	(0.07)
Regional Lag					1.04
					(0.29)
Ideol. Dissim.(1st event)					1.02
					(0.02)
Chi2	22.72	8.66	29.00	27.58	26.57
Df_M	5	5	9	12	14
P	0.00	0.12	0.00	0.01	0.02
Ll	-82.78	-86.79	-80.83	-79.86	-79.47
N	524	524	524	524	524

* $p<0.1$; ** $p<0.05$; *** $p<0.01$

Notes:

Hazard Ratios from cloglog models with robust standard errors clustered on state.

Models control for time dependency with a lowess term (not shown).

All significance tests are two-tailed.

A-Table 13. Reduced Models of Healthcare Component of Anti-Obesity Policy (1st Event)

	Healthcare1	Healthcare2	Healthcare3	Healthcare4	Healthcare5
Electoral Competition	0.99		0.98	0.98	0.99
	(0.03)		(0.02)	(0.02)	(0.02)
Unified D. Government	1.71		1.89	1.12	0.93
	(1.47)		(1.60)	(1.05)	(1.06)
Unified R. Government	0.80		0.96	1.06	0.92
	(0.68)		(0.83)	(0.98)	(0.88)
Government Ideology	0.99		0.98	1.00	1.00
	(0.02)		(0.02)	(0.02)	(0.02)
Citizen Ideology		0.99	0.99	0.96	0.95
		(0.02)	(0.02)	(0.02)**	(0.02)**
Opponents		1.05	1.06	1.09	1.08
		(0.03)*	(0.03)*	(0.04)**	(0.04)**
Advocates		0.99	0.99	1.02	1.02
		(0.02)	(0.02)	(0.03)	(0.03)
Relig. Fundamentalists		0.99	0.99	1.00	1.00
		(0.02)	(0.03)	(0.02)	(0.02)
Problem Severity				1.05	1.02
				(0.09)	(0.11)
Population				1.78	1.85
				(0.71)	(0.76)
Education				1.20	1.19
				(0.10)**	(0.11)*
Regional Lag					1.21
					(0.39)
Ideol. Dissim.(1st event)					1.00
					(0.02)
Chi2	1.07	4.57	6.94	23.97	25.70
Df_M	4	4	8	11	13
P	0.90	0.33	0.54	0.01	0.02
Ll	-61.99	-61.27	-60.78	-56.49	-56.22
N	586	586	586	586	586

* $p<0.1$; ** $p<0.05$; *** $p<0.01$
Notes:
Hazard Ratios from cloglog models with robust standard errors clustered on state.
Wald tests indicated no time dependency.
All significance tests are two-tailed.

A-Table 14. Reduced Models of Taskforce Component of Anti-Obesity Policy (1st Event)

	Taskforce1	Taskforce2	Taskforce3	Taskforce4	Taskforce5
Electoral Competition	0.99		1.00	1.00	0.99
	(0.02)		(0.02)	(0.02)	(0.02)
Unified D. Government	2.14		1.60	1.38	0.60
	(1.51)		(1.32)	(1.20)	(0.69)
Unified R. Government	0.35		0.34	0.39	0.23
	(0.33)		(0.40)	(0.44)	(0.27)
Government Ideology	1.00		1.00	1.00	1.01
	(0.02)		(0.02)	(0.02)	(0.02)
Citizen Ideology		1.02	1.01	1.02	1.01
		(0.02)	(0.02)	(0.02)	(0.02)
Opponents		1.08	1.06	1.07	1.06
		(0.04)*	(0.04)	(0.06)	(0.06)
Advocates		0.93	0.94	0.95	0.95
		(0.03)**	(0.03)**	(0.03)	(0.03)
Relig. Fundamentalists		1.03	1.03	1.04	1.03
		(0.02)	(0.02)	(0.02)	(0.02)
Problem Severity				1.13	1.18
				(0.18)	(0.19)
Population				1.12	1.04
				(0.40)	(0.35)
Education				1.03	1.02
				(0.08)	(0.08)
Regional Lag					0.94
					(0.38)
Ideol. Dissim.(1st event)					1.04
					(0.03)
Chi2	8.39	16.41	18.57	17.74	20.31
Df_M	6	6	10	13	15
P	0.21	0.01	0.05	0.17	0.16
Ll	-77.75	-75.96	-73.85	-73.22	-71.56
N	496	496	496	496	496

* $p<0.1$; ** $p<0.05$; *** $p<0.01$

Notes:

Hazard Ratios from cloglog models with robust standard errors clustered on state.

Models control for time dependency with squared time (not shown).

All significance tests are two-tailed.

*A-Table 15. PEHA Models not- and Controlling for Past Adoptions of Commu-
nity Component of AO*

	1	2
Lagged Community	0.69	
	(0.39)*	
Lagged Healthcare	-0.02	0.01
	(0.34)	(0.35)
Lagged School	0.60	0.63
	(0.34)*	(0.35)*
Lagged Taskforce	0.36	0.42
	(0.24)	(0.24)*
Time	0.28	0.31
	(0.29)	(0.29)
Time2	-0.05	-0.05
	(0.05)	(0.05)
Time3	0.00	0.00
	(0.00)	(0.00)
Problem Severity	0.06	0.04
	(0.08)	(0.07)
Population	0.12	0.18
	(0.16)	(0.18)
Education	0.06	0.05
	(0.03)*	(0.03)
Electoral Competition	-0.01	-0.01
	(0.01)	(0.01)
Unified D. Government	0.16	0.12
	(0.36)	(0.35)
Unified R. Government	-0.21	-0.20
	(0.43)	(0.42)
Government Ideology	0.01	0.01
	(0.01)	(0.01)
Citizen Ideology	-0.01	-0.01
	(0.01)	(0.01)
Opponents	0.02	0.03
	(0.02)	(0.02)
Advocates	-0.02	-0.02
	(0.01)	(0.01)
Relig. Fundamentalists	-0.00	-0.01

	1	2
	(0.01)	(0.02)
Regional Lag	0.29	0.29
	(0.10)***	(0.10)***
Ideol. Dissimilarity	0.01	0.01
	(0.01)**	(0.01)*
Constant	-8.17	-8.36
	(3.85)**	(3.88)**
Chi2	140.31	147.85
Df_M	20	19
P	0.00	0.00
Ll	-362.57	-363.57
N	2,600	2,600

* $p<0.1$; ** $p<0.05$; *** $p<0.01$
Notes:
Coefficients from cloglog models with robust standard errors clustered on state.
Models control for time dependency with cubed time (not shown).
All significance tests are two-tailed.

A-Table 16. Reduced Models of All Anti-Obesity Policies (1st Event)

	1	2	3	4	5
Electoral Competition	0.98		0.98	0.98	0.98
	(0.01)		(0.01)*	(0.01)	(0.01)
Unified D. Government	1.87		1.68	1.58	1.18
	(0.76)		(0.70)	(0.68)	(0.54)
Unified R. Government	0.98		1.26	1.23	0.90
	(0.47)		(0.62)	(0.61)	(0.45)
Government Ideology	1.01		1.01	1.01	1.02
	(0.01)		(0.01)	(0.01)	(0.01)
Citizen Ideology		1.00	0.99	0.99	0.99
		(0.01)	(0.01)	(0.01)	(0.01)
Opponents		1.02	1.02	1.04	1.04
		(0.02)	(0.02)	(0.02)	(0.02)
Advocates		0.96	0.97	0.97	0.98
		(0.01)***	(0.01)***	(0.01)*	(0.01)*
Relig. Fundamentalists		1.00	0.99	0.99	0.99
		(0.02)	(0.02)	(0.02)	(0.02)

	1	2	3	4	5
Problem Severity				1.05	1.05
				(0.08)	(0.09)
Population				1.19	1.22
				(0.28)	(0.27)
Education				1.05	1.05
				(0.05)	(0.05)
Regional Lag					1.30
					(0.17)*
Ideol. Dissim.(1st event)					1.02
					(0.01)**
Chi2	23.60	17.88	39.37	40.20	59.61
Df_M	7	7	11	14	16
P	0.00	0.01	0.00	0.00	0.00
Ll	-273.03	-273.86	-268.81	-267.00	-263.24
N	2,234	2,234	2,234	2,234	2,234

* $p<0.1$; ** $p<0.05$; *** $p<0.01$
Hazard Ratios from cloglog models with robust standard errors clustered on state.
Models control for time dependency with cubed time (not shown).
All significance tests are two-tailed

A-Table 17. *PEHA Diffusion Models Plus Time & Lagged Enactments of Other Components*

	AO	AO	AO	AO
Electoral Competition	-0.01	-0.01	-0.01	-0.01
	(0.01)	(0.01)	(0.01)	(0.01)
Unified D. Government	0.21	0.21	0.21	0.16
	(0.37)	(0.37)	(0.37)	(0.36)
Unified R. Government	-0.11	-0.09	-0.10	-0.21
	(0.41)	(0.41)	(0.41)	(0.43)
Government Ideology	0.01	0.01	0.01	0.01
	(0.01)	(0.01)	(0.01)	(0.01)
Citizen Ideology	-0.01	-0.01	-0.01	-0.01
	(0.01)	(0.01)	(0.01)	(0.01)
Opponents	0.03	0.03	0.03	0.02

	AO	AO	AO	AO
	(0.03)	(0.03)	(0.03)	(0.02)
Relig. Fundamentalists	-0.00	-0.00	-0.00	-0.00
	(0.01)	(0.01)	(0.01)	(0.01)
Problem Severity	0.08	0.08	0.08	0.06
	(0.08)	(0.08)	(0.08)	(0.08)
Population	0.08	0.08	0.08	0.12
	(0.17)	(0.17)	(0.17)	(0.16)
Education	0.06	0.06	0.06	0.06
	(0.03)*	(0.03)*	(0.03)*	(0.03)*
Advocates	-0.02	-0.02	-0.02	-0.02
	(0.02)	(0.02)	(0.02)	(0.01)
Lagged Community	0.84	0.85	0.85	0.69
	(0.42)**	(0.42)**	(0.42)**	(0.39)*
Lagged Healthcare	0.21	0.21	0.21	-0.02
	(0.35)	(0.35)	(0.35)	(0.34)
Lagged School	0.54	0.54	0.54	0.60
	(0.34)	(0.34)	(0.34)	(0.34)*
Lagged Taskforce	0.36	0.36	0.36	0.36
	(0.25)	(0.25)	(0.25)	(0.24)
Time	0.26	0.26	0.26	0.28
	(0.29)	(0.29)	(0.29)	(0.29)
Time2	-0.04	-0.04	-0.04	-0.05
	(0.05)	(0.05)	(0.05)	(0.05)
Time3	0.00	0.00	0.00	0.00
	(0.00)	(0.00)	(0.00)	(0.00)
Ideol. Dissimilarity	0.01	0.01	0.01	0.01
	(0.01)**	(0.01)**	(0.01)**	(0.01)**
Spatial Lag	0.21			
	(0.08)***			
Spatial Lag_II		0.22		
		(0.08)***		
Spatial Lag_III			0.21	
			(0.08)***	
Regional Lag				0.29
				(0.10)***

	AO	AO	AO	AO
Constant	-8.07	-7.92	-8.01	-8.17
	(3.90)**	(3.92)**	(3.91)**	(3.85)**
Chi2	168.23	168.67	168.09	140.31
Df_M	20	20	20	20
P	0.00	0.00	0.00	0.00
Ll	-364.07	-363.87	-364.00	-362.57
N	2,600	2,600	2,600	2,600
AIC	770.1496	769.7498	769.9964	767.1496
BIC	823.1071	822.7074	822.9540	820.1071

* $p<0.1$; ** $p<0.05$; *** $p<0.01$
Notes:
Coefficients from cloglog models with robust standard errors clustered on state.
A- & BIC calculated based on 92 events.
All significance tests are two-tailed.

A-Table 18. MML Diffusion Models

Event History Analyses of Medical Marijuana Laws
1996 – 2011

	MML	MML	MML	MML
Electoral Competition	0.06	0.06	0.06	0.06
	(0.03)**	(0.03)**	(0.03)**	(0.03)**
Unified D. Government	-0.51	-0.39	-0.49	-0.50
	(0.80)	(0.85)	(0.81)	(0.75)
Unified R. Government	-2.20	-2.29	-2.24	-2.30
	(0.95)**	(0.94)**	(0.95)**	(1.06)**
Government Ideology	-0.02	-0.03	-0.03	-0.02
	(0.02)	(0.02)	(0.02)	(0.02)
Citizen Ideology	0.01	0.02	0.01	0.01
	(0.02)	(0.02)	(0.02)	(0.02)
Opponents	-0.05	-0.06	-0.05	-0.05
	(0.03)*	(0.03)**	(0.03)*	(0.03)*
Relig. Fundamentalists	-0.14	-0.12	-0.13	-0.17
	(0.06)**	(0.05)**	(0.06)**	(0.07)**
Problem Severity	-0.01	-0.01	-0.01	-0.01
	(0.01)	(0.01)	(0.01)	(0.01)

	MML	MML	MML	MML
Population	-0.16	-0.21	-0.18	-0.01
	(0.38)	(0.38)	(0.39)	(0.41)
Education	0.00	0.01	0.01	-0.03
	(0.06)	(0.06)	(0.06)	(0.07)
advocates	0.04	0.04	0.04	0.05
	(0.02)*	(0.02)**	(0.02)*	(0.02)*
Ideol. Dissimilarity	0.05	0.05	0.05	0.04
	(0.02)***	(0.02)***	(0.02)***	(0.02)***
Spatial Lag	0.43			
	(0.26)*			
Spatial Lag_II		0.22		
		(0.27)		
Spatial Lag_III			0.37	
			(0.26)	
Regional Lag				0.64
				(0.23)***
Constant	-1.86	-1.18	-1.56	-2.62
	(6.09)	(5.92)	(6.18)	(6.70)
Chi2	61.70	38.91	50.74	122.09
Df_M	13	13	13	13
P	0.00	0.00	0.00	0.00
Ll	-58.44	-59.38	-58.78	-55.74
N	673	673	673	673
AIC	144.8870	146.7583	145.5535	139.4837
BIC	155.7033	157.5745	156.3698	150.2999

* $p<0.1$; ** $p<0.05$; *** $p<0.01$
Notes:
Coefficients from cloglog models with robust standard errors clustered on state.
A- & BIC calculated based on 16 events.
All significance tests are two-tailed.

A-Table 19. SSM Diffusion Models plus Time Controls

Event History Analyses of Same-Sex Marriage Bans
1995 – 2006

	SSM	SSM	SSM	SSM
Electoral Competition	0.05	0.05	0.05	0.05
	(0.02)**	(0.02)**	(0.02)**	(0.02)**
Unified D. Government	-0.04	-0.04	-0.04	-0.31
	(0.77)	(0.77)	(0.77)	(0.74)
Unified R. Government	1.82	1.82	1.82	1.77
	(0.71)**	(0.71)**	(0.71)**	(0.71)**
Government Ideology	0.02	0.02	0.02	0.02
	(0.02)	(0.02)	(0.02)	(0.02)
Citizen Ideology	-0.02	-0.02	-0.02	-0.01
	(0.02)	(0.02)	(0.02)	(0.02)
Opponents	-0.02	-0.02	-0.02	0.02
	(0.10)	(0.10)	(0.10)	(0.10)
Relig. Fundamentalists	0.10	0.10	0.10	0.10
	(0.03)***	(0.03)***	(0.03)***	(0.03)***
Problem Severity	1.71	1.71	1.71	2.53
	(1.74)	(1.74)	(1.74)	(1.85)
Population	0.11	0.11	0.11	0.13
	(0.19)	(0.19)	(0.19)	(0.22)
Education	-0.05	-0.05	-0.05	-0.02
	(0.06)	(0.06)	(0.06)	(0.05)
spline1	5.60	5.60	5.60	5.00
	(0.92)***	(0.92)***	(0.92)***	(0.74)***
spline2	-31.98	-31.98	-31.98	-31.37
	(5.98)***	(5.98)***	(5.98)***	(5.49)***
spline3	66.50	66.50	66.50	66.34
	(12.93)***	(12.93)***	(12.93)***	(12.13)***
Ideol. Dissimilarity	-0.01	-0.01	-0.01	-0.00
	(0.02)	(0.02)	(0.02)	(0.02)
Spatial Lag	-0.33			
	(0.16)**			
Spatial Lag_II		-0.33		

	SSM	SSM	SSM	SSM
	(0.16)**			
Spatial Lag_III			-0.33	
			(0.16)**	
Regional Lag				0.04
				(0.16)
Constant	-20.49	-20.49	-20.49	-20.45
	(4.72)***	(4.72)***	(4.72)***	(5.06)***
Chi2	80.86	80.86	80.86	80.15
Df_M	15	15	15	15
P	0.00	0.00	0.00	0.00
Ll	-87.97	-87.97	-87.97	-89.85
N	316	316	316	316
AIC	207.9455	207.9455	207.9455	211.7054
BIC	236.1247	236.1247	236.1247	239.8846

* $p<0.1$; ** $p<0.05$; *** $p<0.01$
Notes:
Coefficients from cloglog models with robust standard errors clustered on state.
A- & BIC calculated based on 43 events.
All significance tests are two-tailed.

A-Table 20. Full Models with Policy-Specific Variables (Hazard Ratios)

	SSM	MML	PEHA	Hlth	Schl	Tskf
Spatial Lag	0.72	1.53	1.23	0.62	0.99	0.85
	(0.11)**	(0.39)*	(0.10)***	(0.23)	(0.20)	(0.13)
Ideol. Dissimilarity	0.99	1.05	1.01	1.00	1.00	1.04
	(0.02)	(0.02)***	(0.01)**	(0.02)	(0.02)	(0.01)***
Electoral Competition	1.05	1.06	0.99	0.97	1.00	0.98
	(0.02)**	(0.03)**	(0.01)	(0.02)*	(0.02)	(0.02)
Unified D. Government	0.96	0.60	1.23	1.06	2.75	0.67
	(0.74)	(0.48)	(0.46)	(0.78)	(1.93)	(0.38)
Unified R. Government	6.15	0.11	0.90	0.99	0.65	0.26
	(4.40)**	(0.10)**	(0.37)	(0.68)	(0.41)	(0.27)
Government Ideology	1.02	0.98	1.01	1.00	1.00	1.01
	(0.02)	(0.02)	(0.01)	(0.01)	(0.02)	(0.01)
Citizen Ideology	0.98	1.01	0.99	0.97	0.99	1.01
	(0.02)	(0.02)	(0.01)	(0.01)**	(0.01)	(0.02)
Relig. Fundamentalists	1.10	0.87	1.00	0.99	0.99	1.02
	(0.03)***	(0.05)**	(0.01)	(0.04)	(0.02)	(0.02)

	SSM	MML	PEHA	Hlth	Schl	Tskf
Population	1.11	0.86	1.09	1.46	1.13	1.20
	(0.21)	(0.33)	(0.19)	(0.43)	(0.38)	(0.28)
Education	0.95	1.00	1.06	1.20	1.03	1.04
	(0.06)	(0.06)	(0.03)*	(0.10)**	(0.04)	(0.06)
Problem Severity	5.54	0.99	1.08	1.12	1.06	1.21
	(9.66)	(0.01)	(0.08)	(0.08)	(0.08)	(0.13)*
Opponents	0.98	0.95	1.03	1.09	0.89	1.02
	(0.09)	(0.03)*	(0.03)	(0.03)***	(0.09)	(0.06)
advocates		1.04	0.98	1.01	0.97	0.97
		(0.02)*	(0.01)	(0.02)	(0.03)	(0.03)
Chi2	80.86	61.70	168.23	36.50	32.76	60.57
Df_M	15	13	20	13	14	15
P	0.00	0.00	0.00	0.00	0.00	0.00
Ll	-87.97	-58.44	-364.07	-70.83	-117.61	-110.02
N	316	673	2,600	650	650	650

* $p<0.1$; ** $p<0.05$; *** $p<0.01$
Notes:
Hazard Ratios from cloglog models with robust standard errors clustered on state.
Wald tests of MML & AO-healthcare Models indicated no time dependency.
PEHA & AO-Community control for time dependency with cubed time, AO-Task-force with squared time, AO-School with lowess & SSM with splines (not shown)
PEHA model includes 4 indicator variables for whether a state has adopted each of the other components (not shown).
All significance tests are two-tailed.

A-Table 21. Akaike-, Bayes Statistics, Sign & p-values of Spatial Variables for All Selected Models

Policy	Sta-tistic	Coeffici-ent	Spatial Lag	Spatial Lag II	Spatial Lag III	Regional Lag
AO		**Coeffici-ent**	(+)***	(+)***	(+)***	(+)***
	AIC		770.1496	**769.7498**	769.9964	**767.1496**
	BIC		823.1071	**822.7074**	822.9540	**820.1071**
MML		**Coeffici-ent**	(+)*	(+)	(+)	(+)***
	AIC		**144.8870**	146.7583	145.5535	**139.4837**
	BIC		**155.7033**	157.5745	156.3698	**150.2999**
SSM		**Coeffici-ent**	(-)**	(-)**	(-)**	(-)
	AIC		**207.9455**	207.9455	207.9455	211.7054
	BIC		**236.1247**	236.1247	236.1247	239.8846

Source: Author

Notes:

1.(+) depicts positive- & (-) negative regression coefficients. Stars refer to statistical significance: *p<0.1; ** p<0.05; *** p<0.01

2.Cells in bold refer to models with smallest Akaike & Bayes statistics. For AO (PE-HA) & MML, models with the regional lag diffusion variable feature the smallest AIC & BIC values. However, the lowest AIC & BIC statistics for the (final) SSM model does not correspond to the model with the regional lag variable, but to any of the other three models. For that reason, I also highlight the lowest Bayes' & Akaike's statistics when only spatial lag variables are compared.

3.Sign & significance of ideological diffusion variables do not vary across models of the same policy with different spatial lag variables. For AO & MML: positive and statistically significant (p<0.01); for SSM: negative and statistically insignificant.

A-Table 22. Akaike-, Bayes Statistics, Sign & p-values of Diffusion Variables for AO policy components

Policy	Sta-tistic	Coeffi-cient	Spa-tial Lag .	Ideo l. Diss .	Spa-tial Lag II .	Ideo l. Diss .	Spa-tial Lag III .	Ideo l. Diss .	Re-gio-nal Lag	Ideo l. Diss .
Task-force	Coeffi-cient		(-)	(+)***	(-)	(+)***	(-)	(+)***	(+)	(+)***
	AIC		**252.0348**		252.1642		252.0670		252.5646	
	BIC		**275.9790**		276.1083		276.0111		276.5087	
Com-mun.	Coeffi-cient		(-)	(+)	(-)	(+)	(-)	(+)	(+)	(+)
	AIC		90.8943		90.9282		90.8978		**90.2877**	
	BIC		94.2471		94.2810		94.2507		**93.6405**	
School	Coeffi-cient		(-)	(+)	(+)	(+)	(-)	(+)	(+)	(+)
	AIC		265.2167		265.2095		265.2205		**265.0930**	
	BIC		291.2818		291.2745		291.2856		**291.1581**	
He-althca-re	Coeffi-cient		(-)	(+)	(-)	(+)	(-)	(+)	(+)	(+)
	AIC		**169.6583**		169.7209		169.6944		170.5850	
	BIC		**184.2816**		184.3442		184.3178		185.2083	

Source: Author

Notes:

(+) depicts positive- & (-) negative regression coefficients. Stars refer to statistical significance: *p<0.1; ** p<0.05; *** p<0.01

Cells in bold refer to models with smallest Akaike & Bayes statistics. For community and school components of AO policy, models with the regional lag diffusion variable feature the smallest AIC & BIC values; For taskforce and healthcare components, the spatial lag variables have feature the smallest AIC & BIC.

A-Table 23. Diffusion Models of Healthcare Component of AO Legislation

	healthcare	healthcare	healthcare	healthcare
Electoral Competition	-0.03	-0.03	-0.03	-0.02
	(0.02)*	(0.02)*	(0.02)*	(0.02)
Unified D. Government	0.06	0.06	0.06	-0.02
	(0.74)	(0.74)	(0.74)	(0.74)
Unified R. Government	-0.01	0.00	0.00	-0.03
	(0.69)	(0.68)	(0.68)	(0.74)
Government Ideology	-0.00	-0.00	-0.00	-0.01
	(0.02)	(0.02)	(0.02)	(0.02)
Citizen Ideology	-0.04	-0.04	-0.04	-0.03
	(0.02)**	(0.02)**	(0.02)**	(0.02)*
Relig. Fundamentalists	-0.01	-0.01	-0.01	-0.01
	(0.04)	(0.04)	(0.04)	(0.03)
Population	0.38	0.38	0.38	0.40
	(0.29)	(0.29)	(0.29)	(0.30)
Education	0.19	0.18	0.19	0.15
	(0.08)**	(0.08)**	(0.08)**	(0.07)**
Problem Severity	0.11	0.11	0.11	0.07
	(0.07)	(0.07)	(0.07)	(0.07)
Opponents	0.08	0.08	0.08	0.07
	(0.03)***	(0.03)***	(0.03)***	(0.03)**
Advocates	0.01	0.01	0.01	0.02
	(0.02)	(0.02)	(0.02)	(0.02)
Ideol. Dissimilarity	0.00	0.00	0.00	0.00
	(0.02)	(0.02)	(0.02)	(0.02)
Spatial Lag	-0.48			
	(0.37)			
Spatial Lag_II		-0.46		
		(0.37)		
Spatial Lag_III			-0.47	
			(0.37)	
Regional Lag				0.11
				(0.23)
Constant	-14.42	-14.45	-14.43	-13.85
	(6.52)**	(6.54)**	(6.54)**	(6.45)**
Chi2	36.50	36.44	36.48	37.19
Df_M	13	13	13	13
P	0.00	0.00	0.00	0.00

	healthcare	healthcare	healthcare	healthcare
Ll	-70.83	-70.86	-70.85	-71.29
N	650	650	650	650
AIC	169.6583	169.7209	169.6944	170.5850
BIC	184.2816	184.3442	184.3178	185.2083

* $p<0.1$; ** $p<0.05$; *** $p<0.01$
Notes:
Coefficients from cloglog models with robust standard errors clustered on state.
A- & BIC calculated based on 21 events.
Wald tests indicated no time dependency.
All significance tests are two-tailed.

A-Table 24. Diffusion Models of School Component of AO Legislation

	School	School	School	School
Electoral Competition	-0.00	-0.00	-0.00	-0.00
	(0.02)	(0.02)	(0.02)	(0.02)
Unified D. Government	1.01	1.01	1.01	1.01
	(0.70)	(0.69)	(0.70)	(0.70)
Unified R. Government	-0.43	-0.43	-0.43	-0.48
	(0.64)	(0.63)	(0.63)	(0.66)
Government Ideology	0.00	0.00	0.00	0.00
	(0.02)	(0.02)	(0.02)	(0.02)
Citizen Ideology	-0.01	-0.01	-0.01	-0.01
	(0.01)	(0.01)	(0.01)	(0.01)
Relig. Fundamentalists	-0.01	-0.01	-0.01	-0.01
	(0.02)	(0.02)	(0.02)	(0.02)
Population	0.12	0.12	0.12	0.13
	(0.34)	(0.34)	(0.34)	(0.34)
Education	0.03	0.03	0.03	0.02
	(0.04)	(0.04)	(0.04)	(0.04)
Problem Severity	0.06	0.05	0.06	0.04
	(0.08)	(0.08)	(0.08)	(0.08)
Opponents	-0.11	-0.11	-0.11	-0.12
	(0.10)	(0.10)	(0.10)	(0.10)
Advocates	-0.03	-0.03	-0.03	-0.03
	(0.03)	(0.03)	(0.03)	(0.03)
Ideol. Dissimilarity	0.00	0.00	0.00	0.00
	(0.02)	(0.02)	(0.02)	(0.02)
Spatial Lag	-0.01			

	School	School	School	School
	(0.21)			
Spatial Lag_II		0.02		
		(0.22)		
Spatial Lag_III			-0.00	
			(0.21)	
Regional Lag				0.08
				(0.28)
Constant	-7.31	-7.18	-7.28	-6.99
	(6.11)	(6.23)	(6.15)	(5.97)
Chi2	32.76	32.54	32.69	37.97
Df_M	14	14	14	14
P	0.00	0.00	0.00	0.00
Ll	-117.61	-117.60	-117.61	-117.55
N	650	650	650	650
AIC	265.2167	265.2095	265.2205	265.0930
BIC	291.2818	291.2745	291.2856	291.1581

* $p<0.1$; ** $p<0.05$; *** $p<0.01$
Notes:
Coefficients from cloglog models with robust standard errors clustered on state.
A- & BIC calculated based on 42 events.
All models control for time dependency with a lowess term.
All significance tests are two-tailed.

A-Table 25. Diffusion Models of Community Component of AO Legislation

	Community	Community	Community	Community
Electoral Competition	-0.04	-0.04	-0.04	-0.04
	(0.03)	(0.03)	(0.03)	(0.03)
Unified D. Government	-1.69	-1.70	-1.69	-1.90
	(1.22)	(1.23)	(1.22)	(1.01)*
Unified R. Government	4.75	4.75	4.74	4.65
	(1.53)***	(1.53)***	(1.52)***	(1.45)***
Government Ideology	0.12	0.12	0.12	0.12
	(0.03)***	(0.03)***	(0.03)***	(0.03)***
Citizen Ideology	-0.05	-0.05	-0.05	-0.06
	(0.05)	(0.05)	(0.05)	(0.06)
Relig. Fundamentalists	-0.02	-0.02	-0.02	-0.04
	(0.05)	(0.05)	(0.05)	(0.06)

	Community	Community	Community	Community
Population	1.46	1.48	1.46	1.76
	(0.92)	(0.89)*	(0.91)	(0.95)*
Education	-0.03	-0.03	-0.03	-0.06
	(0.11)	(0.11)	(0.11)	(0.09)
Problem Severity	-0.32	-0.32	-0.32	-0.38
	(0.20)	(0.20)	(0.20)	(0.19)**
Opponents	0.16	0.16	0.16	0.19
	(0.10)*	(0.10)*	(0.10)*	(0.09)**
Advocates	-0.07	-0.07	-0.07	-0.07
	(0.03)***	(0.02)***	(0.02)***	(0.03)**
Ideol. Dissimilarity	0.02	0.02	0.02	0.03
	(0.02)	(0.02)	(0.02)	(0.02)
Spatial Lag	-0.56			
	(0.97)			
Spatial Lag_II		-0.51		
		(0.96)		
Spatial Lag_III			-0.55	
			(0.97)	
Regional Lag				1.00
				(0.80)
Constant	-32.04	-32.35	-32.10	-33.95
	(21.55)	(21.01)	(21.42)	(20.80)
Chi2	182.66	176.00	180.02	104.54
Df_M	16	16	16	16
P	0.00	0.00	0.00	0.00
Ll	-28.45	-28.46	-28.45	-28.14
N	650	650	650	650
AIC	90.8943	90.9282	90.8978	90.2877
BIC	94.2471	94.2810	94.2507	93.6405

* $p<0.1$; ** $p<0.05$; *** $p<0.01$

Notes:

Coefficients from cloglog models with robust standard errors clustered on state.

A- & BIC calculated based on 9 events.

All models control for time dependency with cubed time.

All significance tests are two-tailed.

A-Table 26. Diffusion Models of Taskforce Component of AO Legislation

	Taskforce	Taskforce	Taskforce	Taskforce
Electoral Competition	-0.02	-0.02	-0.02	-0.02
	(0.02)	(0.02)	(0.02)	(0.02)
Unified D. Government	-0.39	-0.40	-0.39	-0.42
	(0.57)	(0.57)	(0.57)	(0.57)
Unified R. Government	-1.35	-1.34	-1.35	-1.27
	(1.03)	(1.02)	(1.03)	(0.98)
Government Ideology	0.01	0.01	0.01	0.01
	(0.01)	(0.01)	(0.01)	(0.01)
Citizen Ideology	0.01	0.01	0.01	0.01
	(0.02)	(0.02)	(0.02)	(0.02)
Relig. Fundamentalists	0.02	0.02	0.02	0.01
	(0.02)	(0.02)	(0.02)	(0.02)
Population	0.18	0.19	0.18	0.18
	(0.24)	(0.24)	(0.24)	(0.23)
Education	0.04	0.04	0.04	0.03
	(0.06)	(0.06)	(0.06)	(0.06)
Problem Severity	0.19	0.19	0.19	0.17
	(0.11)*	(0.11)*	(0.11)*	(0.10)
Opponents	0.02	0.02	0.02	0.02
	(0.06)	(0.06)	(0.06)	(0.06)
Advocates	-0.03	-0.03	-0.03	-0.03
	(0.03)	(0.03)	(0.03)	(0.03)
Ideol. Dissimilarity	0.04	0.04	0.04	0.04
	(0.01)***	(0.01)***	(0.01)***	(0.01)***
Spatial Lag	-0.17			
	(0.15)			
Spatial Lag_II		-0.15		
		(0.15)		
Spatial Lag_III			-0.16	
			(0.15)	
Regional Lag				0.08
				(0.23)
Constant	-10.94	-11.01	-10.96	-10.30
	(5.02)**	(5.06)**	(5.03)**	(5.04)**

	Taskforce	Taskforce	Taskforce	Taskforce
Chi2	60.57	60.32	60.55	62.00
Df_M	15	15	15	15
P	0.00	0.00	0.00	0.00
Ll	-110.02	-110.08	-110.03	-110.28
N	650	650	650	650
AIC	252.0348	252.1642	252.0670	252.5646
BIC	275.9790	276.1083	276.0111	276.5087

* $p<0.1$; ** $p<0.05$; *** $p<0.01$
Notes:
Coefficients from cloglog models with robust standard errors clustered on state.
A- & BIC calculated based on 33 events.
All models control for time dependency with squared time.
All significance tests are two-tailed.

A-Table 27. Diffusion Models of All AO Laws

	AO	AO	AO	AO
Electoral Competition	-0.01	-0.01	-0.01	-0.01
	(0.01)	(0.01)	(0.01)	(0.01)
Unified D. Government	0.21	0.21	0.21	0.16
	(0.37)	(0.37)	(0.37)	(0.36)
Unified R. Government	-0.11	-0.09	-0.10	-0.21
	(0.41)	(0.41)	(0.41)	(0.43)
Government Ideology	0.01	0.01	0.01	0.01
	(0.01)	(0.01)	(0.01)	(0.01)
Citizen Ideology	-0.01	-0.01	-0.01	-0.01
	(0.01)	(0.01)	(0.01)	(0.01)
Opponents	0.03	0.03	0.03	0.02
	(0.03)	(0.03)	(0.03)	(0.02)
Relig. Fundamentalists	-0.00	-0.00	-0.00	-0.00
	(0.01)	(0.01)	(0.01)	(0.01)
Problem Severity	0.08	0.08	0.08	0.06
	(0.08)	(0.08)	(0.08)	(0.08)
Population	0.08	0.08	0.08	0.12
	(0.17)	(0.17)	(0.17)	(0.16)

	AO	AO	AO	AO
Education	0.06	0.06	0.06	0.06
	(0.03)*	(0.03)*	(0.03)*	(0.03)*
Advocates	-0.02	-0.02	-0.02	-0.02
	(0.02)	(0.02)	(0.02)	(0.01)
Ideol. Dissimilarity	0.01	0.01	0.01	0.01
	(0.01)**	(0.01)**	(0.01)**	(0.01)**
Spatial Lag	0.21			
	(0.08)***			
Spatial Lag_II		0.22		
		(0.08)***		
Spatial Lag_III			0.21	
			(0.08)***	
Regional Lag				0.29
				(0.10)***
Constant	-8.07	-7.92	-8.01	-8.17
	(3.90)**	(3.92)**	(3.91)**	(3.85)**
Chi2	168.23	168.67	168.09	140.31
Df_M	20	20	20	20
P	0.00	0.00	0.00	0.00
Ll	-364.07	-363.87	-364.00	-362.57
N	2,600	2,600	2,600	2,600
AIC	770.1496	769.7498	769.9964	767.1496
BIC	823.1071	822.7074	822.9540	820.1071

* $p<0.1$; ** $p<0.05$; *** $p<0.01$
Notes:
Coefficients from cloglog models with robust standard errors clustered on state.
A- & BIC calculated based on 92 events.
All models control for time dependency with cubed time and past component activity (not shown).
All significance tests are two-tailed.

A-Table 28. EHAs of SSM, MML, (Repeated-Events) AO Components &
(Pooled) EHA of AO

	SSM	MML	PEHA	AO-Hlth	AO_Schl	AO-Tskf
Spatial Lag	0.70	1.90	1.37	1.00	1.06	0.90
	(0.11)**	(0.36)***	(0.14)***	(0.29)	(0.23)	(0.14)
Ideol. Dissimilarity	1.00	1.04	1.01	1.01	1.00	1.04
	(0.02)	(0.02)**	(0.01)**	(0.01)	(0.02)	(0.01)***
Electoral Competition	1.05	1.06	0.99	0.98	0.99	0.98
	(0.02)**	(0.03)**	(0.01)	(0.02)	(0.02)	(0.02)
Unified D. Government	0.86	0.55	1.16	1.10	2.45	0.73
	(0.63)	(0.42)	(0.40)	(0.90)	(1.70)	(0.39)
Unified R. Government	5.96	0.21	0.74	0.86	0.65	0.23
	(4.34)**	(0.17)*	(0.29)	(0.56)	(0.40)	(0.23)
Government Ideology	1.02	0.98	1.01	0.99	1.01	1.01
	(0.02)	(0.02)	(0.01)	(0.01)	(0.02)	(0.01)
Citizen Ideology	0.98	1.01	0.99	0.99	0.98	1.01
	(0.02)	(0.02)	(0.01)	(0.02)	(0.01)	(0.02)
Relig. Fundamentalists	1.10	0.87	1.00	0.99	1.00	1.03
	(0.03)***	(0.05)***	(0.02)	(0.03)	(0.02)	(0.02)
Population	1.16	0.88	1.31	0.97	1.66	1.62
	(0.21)	(0.28)	(0.16)**	(0.30)	(0.39)**	(0.31)**
Education	0.96	0.95	1.03	1.15	1.00	0.96
	(0.06)	(0.05)	(0.03)	(0.07)**	(0.05)	(0.04)
Chi2	77.47	106.37	147.51	12.88	35.70	48.58
Df_M	13	10	17	10	11	12
P	0.00	0.00	0.00	0.23	0.00	0.00
Ll	-88.37	-58.53	-364.60	-74.62	-120.82	-112.34
N	316	673	2,600	650	650	650

* $p<0.1$; ** $p<0.05$; *** $p<0.01$

Notes:

Hazard Ratios from cloglog models with robust standard errors clustered on state.

PEHA controls for time dependency with cubed time & SSM with splines (not shown); MML presented no time dependency

PEHA model includes 4 indicator variables for whether a state has adopted each of the other components (not shown).

All significance tests are two-tailed.

A-Table 29. EHAs of SSM, MML, (Repeated-Events) AO Components &
(Pooled) EHA of AO

	SSM	MML	PEHA	Hlth	Schl	Tskf
Spatial Lag	0.70	1.64	1.23	1.00	0.99	0.90
	(0.11)**	(0.37)**	(0.10)***	(0.29)	(0.16)	(0.14)
Ideol. Dissimilarity	1.00	1.04	1.01	1.01	1.00	1.04
	(0.02)	(0.02)**	(0.01)**	(0.01)	(0.02)	(0.01)***
Electoral Competition	1.05	1.06	0.99	0.98	0.99	0.98
	(0.02)**	(0.03)**	(0.01)	(0.02)	(0.02)	(0.02)
Unified D. Government	0.86	0.58	1.21	1.10	2.49	0.73
	(0.63)	(0.47)	(0.43)	(0.90)	(1.70)	(0.39)
Unified R. Government	5.96	0.20	0.81	0.86	0.66	0.23
	(4.34)**	(0.15)**	(0.31)	(0.56)	(0.41)	(0.23)
Government Ideology	1.02	0.98	1.01	0.99	1.01	1.01
	(0.02)	(0.02)	(0.01)	(0.01)	(0.02)	(0.01)
Citizen Ideology	0.98	1.02	1.00	0.99	0.98	1.01
	(0.02)	(0.02)	(0.01)	(0.02)	(0.01)	(0.02)
Relig. Fundamentalists	1.10	0.88	1.00	0.99	1.00	1.03
	(0.03)***	(0.05)**	(0.01)	(0.03)	(0.02)	(0.02)
Population	1.16	0.79	1.27	0.97	1.64	1.62
	(0.21)	(0.25)	(0.16)*	(0.30)	(0.37)**	(0.31)**
Education	0.96	0.98	1.03	1.15	1.00	0.96
	(0.06)	(0.05)	(0.03)	(0.07)**	(0.05)	(0.04)
Chi2	77.47	36.57	167.41	12.88	35.42	48.58
Df_M	13	10	17	10	11	12
P	0.00	0.00	0.00	0.23	0.00	0.00
Ll	-88.37	-60.89	-366.64	-74.62	-120.88	-112.34
N	316	673	2,600	650	650	650

* $p<0.1$; ** $p<0.05$; *** $p<0.01$

Notes:

Hazard Ratios from cloglog models with robust standard errors clustered on state.
Wald tests of MML & AO-healthcare Models indicated no time dependency.
PEHA & AO-Community control for time dependency with cubed time, AO-Task-force with squared time, AO-School with lowess & SSM with splines (not shown)
PEHA model includes 4 indicator variables for whether a state has adopted each of the other components (not shown).
All significance tests are two-tailed.

References

Agresti, Alan. 1990. *Categorical data analysis*.

Aldrich, J., and D. Rhode. 2001. "The Logic of Conditional Party Government: Revisiting the Electoral Connection." In *Congress reconsidered*. 7th ed., eds. Lawrence C. Dodd and Bruce I. Oppenheimer. Washington: Congressional Quarterly Press.

Allison, Paul D. 1999. "Comparing Logit and Probit Coefficients Across Groups." *Sociological Methods & Research* 28 (2): 186–208.

———. 2014. *Event history and survival analysis* [en]. Los Angeles: SAGE.

Barclay, Scott, and Shauna Fisher. 2003. "The States and the Differing Impetus for Divergent Paths on Same-Sex Marriage, 1990-2001." *Policy Studies Journal* 31 (3): 331–52.

Beer, Caroline and Cruz-Aceves, Victor. 2018 "Extending Rights to Marginalized Minorities: Same-Sex Relationship Recognition in Mexico and the United States", State Politics & Policy Quarterly, 18(1), pp. 3–26. doi: 10.1177/1532440017751421.

Berry, Frances S., and William D. Berry. 1990. "State Lottery Adoptions as Policy Innovations: An Event History Analysis." [en].

———, eds. 2007. *Innovation and Diffusion Models in Policy Research* [en]. Boulder, Colo: Westview Press.

———. 2014. "Innovation and Diffusion Models in Policy Research." [en]. In *Theories of the Policy Process* [en]. 3rd ed., eds. Paul A. Sabatier and Christopher M. Weible. New York: Westview Press, 307–59.

Berry, W. D., R. C. Fording, E. J. Ringquist, R. L. Hanson, and C. E. Klarner. 2010. "Measuring Citizen and Government Ideology in the U.S. States: A Re-appraisal." *State Politics & Policy Quarterly* 10 (2): 117–35.

Beck, Nathaniel, Katz, Jonathan N., and Tucker, Richard. 1998. "Taking Time Seriously: Time-Series-Cross-Section Analysis with a Binary Dependent Variable." [en].

Bewley-Taylor, David R. 2009. "The American Crusade: The Internationalization of Drug Prohibition." *Addiction Research & Theory* 11 (2): 71–81.

Boehmer, Tegan K., Douglas A. Luke, Debra L. Haire-Joshu, Hannalori S. Bates, and Ross C. Brownson. 2008. "Preventing childhood obesity through state policy. Predictors of bill enactment." [eng]. *American journal of preventive medicine* 34 (4): 333–40.

Boehmke, F. J. 2009. "Approaches to Modeling the Adoption and Diffusion of Policies with Multiple Components." [en]. *State Politics & Policy Quarterly* 9 (2): 229–52.

Boehmke, F. J., and R. P. Branton. 2014. "Sub-National Politics: A Methodological Perspective." In *The Oxford Handbook of State and Local Government*, ed. Donald P. Haider-Markel. Oxford University Press.

Boushey, Graeme. 2010. *Policy diffusion dynamics in America* [en]. New York: Cambridge University Press.

———. 2012. "Punctuated Equilibrium Theory and the Diffusion of Innovations." *Policy Studies Journal* 40 (1): 127–46.

———. 2016. "Targeted for Diffusion?: How the Use and Acceptance of Stereotypes Shape the Diffusion of Criminal Justice Policy Innovations in the American States." *American Political Science Review* 110 (01): 198–214.

Bowen Jr., William R. 2005. "Policy Innovation and Health Insurance Reform in the American States: An Event History Analysis of State Medical Savings Account Adoptions (1993-1996)." [en]. Doctoral Dissertation. Florida State University.

Box-Steffensmeier, Janet M., and Bradford S. Jones. 2004. *Event history modeling: A guide for social scientists* [da]. *Analytical methods for social research*. Cambridge, New York: Cambridge University Press.

Bradford, Ashley C., and David W. Bradford. 2016. "Factors driving the diffusion of medical marijuana legalisation in the United States." *Drugs: Education, Prevention and Policy* 24 (1): 75–84.

Buckley, Jack, and Chad Westerland. 2004. "Duration Dependence, Functional Form, and Corrected Standard Errors: Improving EHA Models of State Policy Diffusion." [en]. *State Politics and Policy Quarterly* 4 (1): 94–113.

Buis, Maarten. 2017. "Logistic regression: When can we do what we think we can do?" http://maartenbuis.nl/wp/oddsratio.html.

Butz, Adam M., Michael P. Fix, and Joshua L. Mitchell. 2015. "Policy Learning and the Diffusion of Stand-Your-Ground Laws." *Politics & Policy* 43 (3): 347–77.

Carley, Sanya, Sean Nicholson-Crotty, and Chris J. Miller. 2017. "Adoption, reinvention and amendment of renewable portfolio standards in the American states." *Journal of Public Policy* 37 (04): 431–58.

Carter, David B., and Curtis S. Signorino. 2010. "Back to the Future: Modeling Time Dependence in Binary Data." *Political Analysis* 18 (03): 271–92.

Cawley, John, and Feng Liu. 2008. "Correlates of state legislative action to prevent childhood obesity." [eng]. *Obesity (Silver Spring, Md.)* 16 (1): 162–67.

Centers for Disease Control and Prevention. "BRFSS Prevalence & Trends Data." Centers for Disease Control and Prevention, CDC. https://www.cdc.gov/brfss/br fssprevalence/ (2015).

Chamberlain, Robert, and Donald P. Haider-Markel. 2005. ""Lien On Me": State Policy Innovation in Response to Paper Terrorism." *Political Research Quarterly* 58 (3): 449–60.

Chen, X., P. Ender, M. Mitchell, and C. Wells. 2003 "Stata FAQ." http://stats.idre.u cla.edu/stata/faq/how-can-i-perform-the-likelihood-ratio-wald-and-lagrange-multi plier-score-test-in-stata/ (March 8, 2017).

Cleves, Mario A. 2010. *An introduction to survival analysis using Stata* [en]. 3rd ed. College Station Tex.: Stata Press.

Crawford, Seth S. 2013. "The political economy of medical marijuana." [en]. PhD dissertation. University of Oregon.

Cruz-Aceves,Victor and Mallinson, Daniel J. 2019. "Clarifying the Measurement of Relative Ideology in Policy Diffusion Research". State and Local Government Review. 51(3):179-186. doi:10.1177/0160323X20902818

Dennis, Christopher, and Marshall H. Medoff. 2011. "Public Preferences, Political Party Control, and Restrictive State Abortion Laws." *The American Review of Politics* 30: 307–31.

Doan, A. E., and D. R. McFarlane. 2012. "Saying No to Abstinence-Only Education: An Analysis of State Decision-Making." *Publius: The Journal of Federalism* 42 (4): 613–35.

Doan, Alesha E. 2014. "Morality Politics." In *The Oxford Handbook of State and Local Government*, ed. Donald P. Haider-Markel. Oxford University Press.

Dodson, Elizabeth A., Chris Fleming, Tegan K. Boehmer, Debra Haire-Joshu, Douglas A. Luke, and Ross C. Brownson. 2009. "Preventing childhood obesity through state policy: qualitative assessment of enablers and barriers." [eng]. *Journal of public health policy* 30 Suppl 1: S161-76.

Doyle, W. R. 2006. "Adoption of Merit-Based Student Grant Programs: An Event History Analysis." [en]. *Educational Evaluation and Policy Analysis* 28 (3): 259–85.

Dutton, Sarah, Jennifer de Pinto, Anthony Salvanto, and Fred Backus. 2014. "Majority of Americans now support legal pot, poll says." CBS News Poll Report. https://www.cbsnews.com/news/majority-of-americans-now-support-legal-pot-po ll-says/.

Eaton, Lisa J. 2013. "Policy Adoption By State Governments: An Event History Analysis Of Factors Influencing States To Enact Inpatient Health Care Transparency Laws."

Ekins, Emily, and Jonathan Haidt 2016. "Donald Trump supporters think about morality differently than other voters. Here's how." *Vox Media*. https://www.vox.com/2016/2/5/10918164/donald-trump-morality (Accessed March 5, 2018).

Elazar, Daniel J. 1994. *The American mosaic: The impact of space, time, and culture on American politics / Daniel J. Elazar*. Boulder, Colo, Oxford: Westview.

Engeli, Isabelle, Christoffer Green-Pedersen, and Lars T. Larsen, eds. 2012. *Morality politics in Western Europe: Parties, agendas and policy choices. Comparative studies of political agendas series*. Houndmills, Basingstoke, Hampshire: Palgrave Macmillan.

Fernandez, J. J., and M. Lutter. 2013. "Supranational cultural norms, domestic value orientations and the diffusion of same-sex union rights in Europe, 1988-2009." *International Sociology* 28 (1): 102–20.

Ferraiolo, Kathleen. 2004. "Popular 'Medicine': Policymaking by Direct Democracy and the Medical Marijuana Movement of the 1990s." [en]. PhD. University of Virginia.

—————. 2007. "From Killer Weed to Popular Medicine: The Evolution of American Drug Control Policy, 1937-2000." [en].

—————. 2009. "Marketing a Policy Idea: Elite Frame Selection and Development in Ballot Initiative Campaigns." [en]. *Politics & Policy* 37 (2): 337–68.

—————. 2014. "Morality Framing in U.S. Drug Control Policy: An Example From Marijuana Decriminalization." [en]. *World Medical & Health Policy* 6 (4): 347–74.

Foster, John L. 1978. "Regionalism and Innovation in the American States." *The Journal of Politics* 40 (1): 179–87.

Frum, D. 2012. "Bloomberg's visionary move against obesity." CNN.

Füglister, K., F. Gilardi, and S. Luyet. 2009. *Learning From Others The Diffusion of Hospital Financing Reforms in OECD Countries.*

Gardner, James A., and Jim Rossi, eds. 2010. *New Frontiers of State Constitutional Law.* Oxford University Press.

Garson, David. 2013. *Parametric Survival Analysis (Event History Analysis).*

Gibson, M. T. 2004. "Culture Wars in State Education Policy: A Look at the Relative Treatment of Evolutionary Theory in State Science Standards*." *Social Science Quarterly* 85 (5): 1129–49.

Gilardi, Fabrizio. 2004. "Delegation in the regulatory state. Origins and diffusion of independent regulatory agencies in Western Europe." [eng]. PhD. University of Lausanne.

—————. 2015. *Four Ways We Can Improve Policy Diffusion Research* [en].

Goertz, Gary. 2006. *Social science concepts: A user's guide.* Princeton: Princeton University Press.

Goldman, Gretchen, Christina Carlson, Deborah Bailin, Lindsey Fong, and Pallavi Phartiyal. 2014. "Appendix C: Lobbying and Political Contribution Analysis." In *Added Sugar, Subtracted Science: How Industry Obscures Science and Undermines Public Health Policy on Sugar.*

Gray, Virginia. 1973. "Innovation in the States: A Diffusion Study." [en]. *The American Political Science Review* 67 (4): 1174–85.

—————. 1994. "Competition, Emulation, and Policy Innovation." In *New perspectives on American politics*, eds. Lawrence C. Dodd and Calvin Jillson. Washington, DC: CQ Press.

Gray, Virginia, and David Lowery. 1996. *The Population Ecology of Interest Representation.* Ann Arbor, MI: University of Michigan Press.

—————. 2001. "The Institutionalization of State Communities of Organized Interests." *Political Research Quarterly* 54 (2): 265–84.

Grossback, L. J. 2004. "Ideology and Learning in Policy Diffusion." [en]. *American Politics Research* 32 (5): 521–45.

Haider-Markel, Donald P. 2001a. "Policy Diffusion as a Geographical Expansion of the Scope of Political Conflict: Same-Sex Marriage Bans in the 1990s." [en].

—————. 2001b. "Shopping for Favorable Venues in the States: Institutional Influences on Legislative Outcomes of Same-Sex Marriage Bills." *The American Review of Politics.*

————, ed. 2014. *The Oxford Handbook of State and Local Government*. Oxford University Press.

Haider-Markel, Donald P., and Matthew S. Kaufman. 2006. "Public Opinion and Policy Making in the Culture Wars: Is There a Connection Between Opinion and State Policy on Gay and Lesbian Issues?" [en]. In *Public opinion in state politics* [en], ed. Jeffrey E. Cohen. Stanford, Calif.: Stanford University Press, 163–82.

Haider-Markel, Donald P., and Kenneth J. Meier. 1996. "The Politics of Gay and Lesbian Rights: Expanding the Scope of the Conflict." [en]. *Journal of Politics* 58 (2): 332–49.

Hannah, A. L., and Daniel J. Mallinson. 2017. "Defiant Innovation: The Adoption of Medical Marijuana Laws in the American States." *Policy Studies Journal* 4 (3): 318.

Hays, Scott P., and Henry R. Glick. 1997. "The Role of Agenda Setting in Policy Innovation." *American Politics Quarterly* 25 (4): 497–516.

Heidt-Forsythe, Erin. 2017. "Morals or markets? Regulating assisted reproductive technologies as morality or economic policies in the states." [eng]. *AJOB empirical bioethics* 8 (1): 58–67.

Heidt-Forsythe, Erin A. 2013. "Reconveiving the State: Morals, Markets and State Regulation of Assisted reproductive Technologies." [en]. PhD Dissertation. State University of New Jersey.

Henderson, Carrie. 2014. "The Community College Baccalaureate Degree in the United States: An Event History Analysis." [en]. PhD thesis. Florida State University.

Hill, Kim Q., and Carl Klarner. 2002. "The Many Faces of Elite Power in the "System of 1896"." *The Journal of Politics* 64 (4): 1115–36.

Holbrook, Thomas M., and Emily van Dunk. 1993. "Electoral competition in the American states." [en]. *American Political Science Review* 87 (4): 955.

Hollander, Robyn, and Haig Patapan. 2016. "Morality Policy and Federalism: Innovation, Diffusion and Limits." *Publius* 47 (1): 1–26.

Hosmer, David W., Stanley Lemeshow, and Susanne May. 2008. *Applied survival analysis: Regression modeling of time-to-event data* [en]. 2nd ed. *Wiley series in probability and statistics*. Hoboken, N.J.: Wiley-Interscience.

Imhof, Sara L. "Promoting a "Good Death": Determinants of Pain Management Policies in the United States." PhD.

Imhof, Sara L., and Brian Kaskie. 2008. "Promoting a "good death": determinants of pain-management policies in the United States." [eng]. *Journal of Health Politics, Policy and Law* 33 (5): 907–41.

Jacoby, William G., and Saundra K. Schneider. 2001. "Variability in State Policy Priorities: An Empirical Analysis." *The Journal of Politics* 63 (2): 544–68.

Jensen, J. L. 2003. "Policy Diffusion through Institutional Legitimation: State Lotteries." *Journal of Public Administration Research and Theory* 13 (4): 521–41.

Jones, B. S., and R. P. Branton. 2005. "Beyond Logit and Probit: Cox Duration Models of Single, Repeating, and Competing Events for State Policy Adoption." [en]. *State Politics & Policy Quarterly* 5 (4): 420–43.

Jones, Dale E., Clifford G. Sherry Doty, James E. Horsch, Mac L. Richard Houseal, John P. Marcum, Kenneth M. Sanchagrin, and Richard H. Taylor. 2002. *Religious congregations & membership in the United States 2000: An enumeration by region, state and county based on data reported for 149 religious bodies* [en]. Nashville, Tenn.: Glenmary Research Center.

Jordana, J., D. Levi-Faur, and i Marin, X. F. 2011. "The Global Diffusion of Regulatory Agencies: Channels of Transfer and Stages of Diffusion." [en]. *Comparative Political Studies* 44 (10): 1343–69.

Kam, Cindy D. 2017. "Obesity." *Public Opinion Quarterly* 81 (4): 973–95.

Karch, A., and M. Cravens. 2014. "Rapid Diffusion and Policy Reform: The Adoption and Modification of Three Strikes Laws." [en]. *State Politics & Policy Quarterly* 14 (4): 461–91.

Karch, Andrew. 2007a. *Democratic laboratories: Policy diffusion among the American states* [en]. Ann Arbor: University of Michigan Press.

———. 2007b. "Emerging Issues and Future Directions in State Policy Diffusion Research." [en]. *State Politics and Policy Quarterly* 7 (1): 54–80.

Kim, Gook J. 2016. "Policy innovation and diffusion through policy typologies: Examining the predictors of medical marijuana legalization in states." The Florida State University.

King, David C., Richard J. Zeckhauser, and Mark T. Kim. 2004. "The Management Performance of the U.S. States." *SSRN Electronic Journal*.

Kingdon, John W. 2003. *Agendas, alternatives, and public policies* [en]. 2nd ed. *Longman classics in political science*. New York: Longman.

Klawitter, Marieka, and Brian Hammer. 1999. "Spatial and Temporal Diffusion ofLocal Antidiscrimination Policies for Sexual Orientation." In *Gays and lesbians in the democratic process: Public policy, public opinion, and political representation / edited by Ellen D.B. Riggle and Barry L. Tadlock. Power, conflict, and democracy*, eds. Ellen D. B. Riggle and Barry L. Tadlock. New York: Columbia University Press, 22–38.

Knill, Christoph. 2013. "The study of morality policy: analytical implications from a public policy perspective." [en]. *Journal of European Public Policy* 20 (3): 309–17.

Kreitzer, Rebecca. 2015a. "Policy making at the margins: the modern politics of abortion." PhD. University of Iowa.

———. 2015b. "Politics and Morality in State Abortion Policy." [en]. *State Politics & Policy Quarterly* 15 (Accessed December 2014).

Lacy, T. A., and David A. Tandberg. 2014. "Rethinking Policy Diffusion: The Interstate Spread of "Finance Innovations"." *Research in Higher Education* 55 (7): 627–49.

Lankford, Tina, Dominique Hardman, Chris Dankmeyer, and Tom Schmid. 2013. "Analysis of state obesity legislation from 2001 to 2010." [eng]. *Journal of public health management and practice : JPHMP* 19 (3 Suppl 1): 8.

Larsen, Lars T. 2010. "Sinners in the Laboratory. Morality Issues from the Politics of Sin to Biomedical Regulation." [eng].

Lee, Mei-Hsien. 1996. "The Politics of Morality Policy: An Event History Analysis of U.S. States Death Penalty Policy Adoption." [en].

Leiser, S. 2015. "The Diffusion of State Tax Incentives for Business." *Public Finance Review*.

Leiser, Stephanie. 2014. "Essays on State Business Tax Incentives and Policy Diffusion." PhD. University of Washington.

Lewis, Daniel C. 2011. "Direct Democracy and Minority Rights: Same-Sex Marriage Bans in the U.S. States*." [en]. *Social Science Quarterly* 92 (2): 364–83.

Lewis, G. B., and S. S. Oh. 2008. "Public Opinion and State Action on Same-Sex Marriage." [en]. *State and Local Government Review* 40 (1): 42–53.

Li, Amy Y. 2017. "Covet Thy Neighbor or "Reverse Policy Diffusion"? State Adoption of Performance Funding 2.0." *Research in Higher Education* 58 (7): 746–71.

Lindaman, K., and D. P. Haider-Markel. 2002. "Issue Evolution, Political Parties, and the Culture Wars." *Political Research Quarterly* 55 (1): 91–110.

Lowery, David, Virginia Gray, John Cluverius, and Jeffrey J. Harden. 2013. "Explaining the Anomalous Growth of Public Sector Lobbying in the American States, 1997–2007." *Publius: The Journal of Federalism* 43 (4): 580–99.

Lowi, T. J. 1988. "Foreword: New dimensions in policy and politics." [en]. In *Social regulatory policy: Moral controversies in American politics* [en], eds. Raymond Tatalovich and Byron W. Daynes. Boulder: Westview Press.

Lowi, Theodore J. 1964. "American Business, Public Policy, Case-Studies, and Political Theory." *World Politics* 16 (04): 677–715.

Lutz, James M. 1987. "Regional Leadership Patterns In The Diffusion Of Public Policies." *American Politics Quarterly* 15 (3): 387–98.

Maggetti, Martino, and Fabrizio Gilardi. 2015. "Problems (and solutions) in the measurement of policy diffusion mechanisms." [en]. *Journal of Public Policy:* 1–21.

Makse, Todd, and Craig Volden. 2011. "The Role of Policy Attributes in the Diffusion of Innovations." *The Journal of Politics* 73 (1): 108–24.

Mallinson, Daniel J. 2016. "Building a Better Speed Trap: Measuring Policy Adoption Speed in the American States." *State Politics & Policy Quarterly* 16 (1): 98–120.

Marijuana Policy Project. 2013. "State-By-State Medical Marijuana Laws: How to Remove the Threat of Arrest 2013." [en]. Marijuana Policy Project. http://www.mpp.org/assets/pdfs/library/State-by-State-Laws-Report-2013.pdf (February 2014).

Marlow, Michael L. 2013. "Determinants of state laws addressing obesity." [en]. *Applied Economics Letters* 21 (2): 84–89.

Martin, Christian W. 2010. "Interdependence and Political Ideology: The Conditional Diffusion of Cigarette Taxation in U.S. States." *World Political Science* 6 (1).

Martin, Christian W., Federica Genovese, and Florian Kern. 2017. "Policy Alteration: Rethinking Diffusion Processes when Policies have Alternatives." *International Studies Quarterly*.

McNeal, R. S., C. J. Tolbert, K. Mossberger, and L. J. Dotterweich. 2003. "Innovating in Digital Government in the American States." [en]. *Social Science Quarterly (Wiley-Blackwell)* 84 (1): 52–70.

Medoff, Marshall H., Christopher Dennis, and Kerri Stephens. 2011. "The Impact of Party Control on the Diffusion of Parental Involvement Laws in the U.S. States." *State Politics & Policy Quarterly* 11 (3): 325–47.

Meier, Kenneth J. 1992. "The Politics of Drug Abuse: Laws, Implementation, and Consequences." [en].

———. 1993. "The Politics of Funding Abortion: State Responses to the Political Environment." [en]. *American Politics Quarterly* 21 (1): 81.

———. 1994. "The Politics of Sin: Drugs, Alcohol, And Public Policy." [en].

———. 1999. "Drugs, Sex, Rock, and Roll: A Theory of Morality Politics." *Policy Studies Journal* 27 (4): 681–95.

Mendes, Elizabeth. 2010. *New High of 46% of Americans Support Legalizing Marijuana* [en].

Meseguer, C. 2006. "Rational Learning and Bounded Learning in the Diffusion of Policy Innovations." [en]. *Rationality and Society* 18 (1): 35–66.

Miller, C. R., and B. Richard. 2010. "The Policy Diffusion of the State R&D Investment Tax Credit." *State and Local Government Review* 42 (1): 22–35.

Mintrom, Michael. 1997. "Policy Entrepreneurs and the Diffusion of Innovation." [en]. *American Journal of Political Science* 41 (3): 738–70.

Mitchell, Joshua L., and Elizabeth Petray. 2016. "The march toward marriage equality: Reexamining the diffusion of same-sex marriage among states." *Public Policy and Administration* 31 (4): 283–302.

Mohr, Lawrence B. 1969. "Determinants of innovation in organizations." [af]. *The American Political Science Review* Vol. 63: 111–26.

Monogan, Jamie. 2012. *The Fifty American States in Space and Time: Applying Conditionally Autoregressive Models to State Politics* [en]. University of Georgia (Accessed February 2014).

Mood, C. 2010. "Logistic Regression: Why We Cannot Do What We Think We Can Do, and What We Can Do About It." *European Sociological Review* 26 (1): 67–82.

Mooney, Christopher Z. 1999. "The Politics of Morality Policy: Symposium Editor's Introduction." *Policy Studies Journal* 27 (4): 675–80.

———. 2001a. "Modeling Regional Effects on State Policy Diffusion." [en]. *Political Research Quarterly* 54 (1): 103–24.

——, ed. 2001b. *The public clash of private values: The politics of morality policy* [en]. New York: Chatham House.

Mooney, Christopher Z., and Mei-Hsien Lee. 1995. "Legislative Morality in the American States: The Case of Pre-Roe Abortion Regulation Reform." [en].

——. 1999a. "Morality Policy Reinvention: State Death Penalties." *The ANNALS of the American Academy of Political and Social Science* 566 (1): 80–92.

——. 1999b. "The temporal diffusion of morality policy: The case of death penalty legislation in the American states." [English]. *Policy Studies Journal* 27 (4): 766–80.

——. 2000. "The Influence of Values on Consensus and Contentious Morality Policy: U.S. Death Penalty Reform, 1956–82." [en]. *The Journal of Politics* 62 (01).

Mooney, Christopher Z., and Richard G. Schuldt. 2008. "Does Morality Policy Exist? Testing a Basic Assumption." [en]. *Policy Studies Journal* 36 (2): 199–218.

Mossberger, Karen. 2000. *The politics of ideas and the spread of enterprise zones* [en]. *American governance and public policy series*. Washington, DC: Georgetown University Press.

Musto, David F. 1987. *The American disease: Origins of narcotic control* [en]. *Oxford paperbacks*. New York: Oxford University Press.

Nelson, Bakeyah S. 2007. "Innovation Diffusion: An Event History Analysis Of States' Adoption Of The 1915(C) Waiver For People Living With HIV/AIDS." [en]. PhD. University of Maryland.

Nice, David C. 1994. *Policy innovation in state government* [en]. 1st ed. Ames: Iowa State University Press.

Nicholson-Crotty, Sean. 2009. "The Politics of Diffusion: Public Policy in the American States." [en]. *The Journal of Politics* 71 (1): 192–205.

Oliver, J. E., and Taeku Lee. 2005. "Public Opinion and the Politics of Obesity in America." *Journal of Health Politics, Policy & Law* 30 (5): 923–54.

Pacheco, Julianna. 2011. "Using National Surveys to Measure Dynamic U.S. State Public Opinion." *State Politics & Policy Quarterly* 11 (4): 415–39.

——. 2012. "The Social Contagion Model: Exploring the Role of Public Opinion on the Diffusion of Antismoking Legislation across the American States." *The Journal of Politics* 74 (1): 187–202.

Pacheco, Julianna, and Graeme Boushey. 2014. "Public health and agenda setting: Determinants of state attention to tobacco and vaccines." [eng]. *Journal of Health Politics, Policy and Law* 39 (3): 565–89.

Paynter, Sharon R. 2008. "Judicial Performance Evaluaion: Policy Diffusion Across the American States." [en]. Doctoral.

Pew Research Center. 2011. "Fewer Are Angry at Government, But Discontent Remains High: Republicans, Tea Party Supporters More Mellow." Washington, D.C. http://www.people-press.org/2011/03/03/fewer-are-angry-at-government-but-discontent-remains-high/# (2016).

Philander, Kahlil S., and B. L. Abarbanel. 2014. "Determinants of internet poker adoption." [eng]. *Journal of gambling studies* 30 (3): 609–23.

Pierce, Patrick A. 2009. *The Comparative Politics of Policy Diffusion Across the States* [en]. Prepared for presentation at the annual meetings of the Western Political Science Association, Vancouver, British Columbia, March 19 – 21, 2009.

Pierce, Patrick A., and Donald E. Miller. 2000. *Variations in the Diffusion of State Lottery Adoptions: How Revenue Dedication Changes Morality Politics* [en]. Vol. 1226 of *ICPSR*. Ann Arbor, Mich: Inter-university Consortium for Political and Social Research [distributor].

Pierce, Patrick A., and Donald E. Miller. 2004. *Gambling politics: State government and the business of betting* [en]. Boulder, Colo.: Lynne Rienner Publishers.

Raftery, A. E. 1996. "Hypothesis testing and model selection." [ca]. In *Markov chain Monte Carlo in practice* [af]. *Interdisciplinary statistics*, eds. W. R. Gilks, S. Richardson and D. J. Spiegelhalter. London: Chapman & Hall, 163–89.

Rodriguez, Gail M. 2010. "Weighted Policymaking: The Federal, State and Individual Politics of Obesity." [en]. PhD.

Rogers, Everett M. 1983. *Diffusion of innovations*. 3rd ed. New York: Free Press; London : Collier Macmillan.

———. 2003. *Diffusion of innovations* [af]. 5th ed. New York: Free Press.

Roh, J., and F. S. Berry. 2008. "Modeling the Outcomes of State Abortion Funding Referenda: Morality or Redistributive Policy, or Both?" [en]. *State Politics & Policy Quarterly* 8 (1): 66–87.

Roh, Jongho, and Donald P. Haider-Markel. 2003. "All Politics is Not Local: National Forces in State Abortion Initiatives." [en]. *Social Science Quarterly* 84 (1): 15–31.

Sabatier, Paul A., ed. 2007. *Theories of the Policy Process* [en]. 2nd ed. Westview Press.

Schlager, Edella. 2007. "A Comparison of Frameworks,Theories, and Models of Policy Processes." [en]. In *Theories of the Policy Process* [en]. 2nd ed., ed. Paul A. Sabatier. Westview Press, 293–319.

Seljan, E. C., and N. Weller. 2011. "Diffusion in Direct Democracy: The Effect of Political Information on Proposals for Tax and Expenditure Limits in the U.S. States." *State Politics & Policy Quarterly* 11 (3): 348–68.

Smith, Kevin B. 2002. "Typologies, Taxonomies, and the Benefits of Policy Classification." *Policy Studies Journal* 30 (3): 379–95.

Smith, Daniel A., and Dustin Fridkin. 2008. "Delegating Direct Democracy: Interparty Legislative Competition and the Adoption of the Initiative in the American States." *American Political Science Review* 102 (03): 333–50.

Sponsler, Brian A. 2010. "Coveting more than thy neighbor: Beyond geographically proximate explanations of postsecondary policy diffusion." [en]. *Higher Education in Review*.

———. 2011. "State Adoption of Undocumented Student Tuition Policy: An Event History Analysis." [en]. PhD. The George Washington University.

Stoutenborough, James W. 2010. "State and Federal Renewable Energy Policy: Understanding Influences and Impacts." [en]. Phd dissertation. University of Kansas.

Stoutenborough, James W., and Matthew Beverlin. 2008. "Encouraging Pollution-Free Energy: The Diffusion of State Net Metering Policies *." *Social Science Quarterly* 89 (5): 1230–51.

Stream, Christopher. 1999. "Health Reform in the States: A Model of State Small Group Health Insurance Market Reforms." *Political Research Quarterly* 52 (3): 499.

Sylvester, Steven M. 2016. "Putting the Public into Public Health: Health Policy Related Opinion and Public Policy." Phd. University of Kansas.

Sylvester, Steven M., and Donald P. Haider-Markel. 2016. "Buzz Kill: State Adoption of DUI Interlock Laws, 2005-11." *Policy Studies Journal* 44 (4): 491–509.

Tatalovich, Raymond, and Byron W. Daynes, eds. 1988. *Social regulatory policy: Moral controversies in American politics* [en]. Boulder: Westview Press.

———. 2011. *Moral controversies in American politics* [en]. 4th ed. Armonk NY: M.E. Sharpe.

Taylor, J. K. 2007. "The Adoption of Gender Identity Inclusive Legislation in the American States." PhD.

Taylor, J. K., D. C. Lewis, M. L. Jacobsmeier, and B. DiSarro. 2012. "Content and Complexity in Policy Reinvention and Diffusion: Gay and Transgender-Inclusive Laws against Discrimination." *State Politics & Policy Quarterly* 12 (1): 75–98.

U.S. Census Bureau. "Census Divisions and Census Regions." https://www.census.gov/geo/reference/gtc/gtc_census_divreg.html (March 6, 2017).

United States Census Bureau. Various years. "Intercensal Estimates of the Resident Population by Race for States and the United States." [en].

———. Various Years. "Statistical Abstract of the United States." [en]. Washington, DC: U.S. Government Printing Office.

Walker, Jack L. 1969. *The diffusion of innovations among the American states* [en]. Ann Arbor, MI: Institute of Public Policy Studies.

Weesie, Jeroen. 1999. "Seemingly unrelated estimation and the cluster-adjusted sandwich estimator." *Stata Technical Bulletin* 52: 34–47.

Welch, Philip J., Joseph A. Dake, James H. Price, Amy J. Thompson, and Sunday E. Ubokudom. 2012. "State legislators' support for evidence-based obesity reduction policies." [eng]. *Preventive medicine* 55 (5): 427–29.

Wellever, Anthony L., Amanda Reichard, and Marc Velasco. 2004. *Obesity and public policy: Legislation passed by states, 1999 to 2003: Interim Report to the Sunflower Foundation on Project 02-103-20 KHI/R 04-2* [en]. Topeka, Kan.

Weyland, Kurt. 2005a. "The Diffusion of Innovations: How Cognitive Heuristics Shaped Bolivia's Pension Reform." [en]. *Comparative Politics* 38 (1): 21–42.

———. 2005b. "Theories of Policy Diffusion: Lessons from Latin American Pension Reform." [en]. *World Politics* 57 (2): 262–95.

———. 2009. "The Diffusion of Revolution: '1848' in Europe and Latin America." [en]. *International Organization* 63 (03): 391.

Weyland, Kurt G. 2006. *Bounded rationality and policy diffusion: Social sector reform in Latin America* [en]. Princeton, N.J.: Princeton University Press.

Williams, R. L. 2000. "A note on robust variance estimation for cluster-correlated data." [en]. *Biometrics.*

Witte, Tracie. 2013. "Battling Moralities: Competing For Medical Marijuana Legislation." [da]. PhD dissertation. State University of New Jersey.

Wong, Kenneth K., and Warren E. Langevin. 2007. "Policy Expansion of School Choice in the American States." [en]. *Peabody Journal of Education* 82 (2-3): 440–72.

Wong, Kenneth K., and Francis X. Shen. 2002. "Politics of State-Led Reform in Education. Market Competition and Electoral Dynamics." [en].

Yackee, Susan W. 2009. "Private Conflict and Policy Passage: Interest-Group Conflict and State Medical Malpractice Reform." *Policy Studies Journal* 37 (2): 213–31.

Zhu, Ling. 2009. "Beyond the Neighbor Effect: Policy Learning in Managing the Risk of Childhood Obesity in Schools." In *104th Annual National Conference of the American Political Science Association*